EXPLORI

"These are adventures that were once common in human history, but not in our time. The author brings a real and useful humility to his encounters with the larger world outside our walls; these are not macho and mindless encounters, but the opposite."

—Bill McKibben, author of *The End of Nature* and *Falter*

"From the boreal forest of northern Minnesota's Boundary Waters, where my home is, to the arctic tundra of the far north and the wilds of Africa, I have spent a lifetime photographing unique moments in nature, including magnificent wolves, lions, and rhinos. John Rust's adventures encountering large predators in primeval nature takes me back into the wild and creates a feeling for place and terrain. While reading John's quite visually descriptive accounts with deep nature, I felt that I would have very much liked to be at his side to photograph what he saw. If you have never been to these places, you will feel the wonder, electricity, and awe of being in the wild and in presence of some of Earth's greatest predators."

—Jim Brandenburg, award-winning photographer with the National Geographic Society for 30 years and author of *Brother Wolf: A Forgotten Promise*

"John Rust's journeys among America's most magnificent predators will leave you breathless. His observations are vivid and his insights penetrating. I'd rather go hiking with him in wild country, myself, but these pages are the next best thing."

—Sy Montgomery, author of *The Soul of an Octopus* and *Spell of the Tiger: The Man-Eaters of Sundarbans*

"Fueled by an unquenchable desire to experience nature as intimately as possible, John Rust has sought out the remotest, wildest corners of North America and the world, often with only pen and paper as his traveling companions. The result is these vignettes: a beautiful articulation of the elation, peace, and trepidation we feel when fully within nature's grasp. Written with honesty, self-awareness, and a careful eye for detail, this was an engaging read."

—JONATHAN C. SLAGHT, WILDLIFE BIOLOGIST AND NORTHEAST ASIA COORDINATOR FOR THE WILDLIFE CONSERVATION SOCIETY, AND AUTHOR OF *OWLS OF THE EASTERN ICE: THE QUEST TO FIND AND SAVE THE WORLD'S LARGEST OWL*

"This is a contemporary remake of the meaning of wilderness in an urbanized world. It portrays life on the landscape with large predators, of time in tranquil nature punctuated by suspense and danger. Woven throughout is a grand story about the ecology and value to humanity of primeval landscapes."

—LEE E. FRELICH, DIRECTOR OF THE UNIVERSITY OF MINNESOTA CENTER FOR FOREST ECOLOGY AND AUTHOR OF *FOREST DYNAMICS AND DISTURBANCE REGIMES: STUDIES FROM TEMPERATE EVERGREEN-DECIDUOUS FORESTS*

"A book highlighting encounters with top predators on wilderness treks might seem like a fix for adrenaline junkies. But these contemplative essays read more like a Buddhist monk's pursuit of enlightenment. Writing with an engaging 'in-the-moment' style, John richly illuminates his day-by-day trail experiences with a feast of reflections, both deep dives into the natural and human history of the regions he visits and the greater Cosmos, putting our life here on Earth into perspective. As though answering William Blake's challenge 'to see a world in a grain of sand,' John finds deep meaning and provocative insights along each step of the trail."

—PAUL SCHURKE, ARCTIC EXPLORER AND COAUTHOR WITH WILL STEGER OF *NORTH TO THE POLE*

"Reading about John's adventures in nature rekindles our desire to stay connected with wild lands and their inhabitants. He writes in an infectious way. John's words remind us of the need to act if we've been captive too long in our urban shackles. The adventures recounted by the author fill the need to find, to feel, to taste, to be exhausted by wild country, and in the process feel fragile and small."

—DAVID ZENTNER, FORMER NATIONAL PRESIDENT OF THE IZAAK WALTON LEAGUE OF AMERICA

"John Rust's account of time spent living in the company of apex predators on magnificent public lands in North America and India is the perfect antidote to a misguided ideology that says economic utility is the sole measure of the value of wild places. Rust is an exemplar of those who understand that spiritual sustenance is the ultimate prize to be gained from the wonder and mystery of life in the wilderness. We can only hope that his view will ultimately prevail. Human survival depends on it."

—Becky Rom, national chair of Campaign to Save the Boundary Waters; former national chair of the Wilderness Society; and governing council member of the Wilderness Society

"Though I spent the best part of my scientific career as a biological chemist, of which over fifty-five years were spent investigating natural products from both prokaryotes and eukaryotes as sources of drugs for use in humans, I recommend this book to anyone who is interested in the larger role of nature as a source of inspiration in many biological and chemical areas, not just as a source of medicaments.

This is a book for non-biologists/chemists as an example of what can be observed by an interested party who asks the question, 'Why does X occur?' and then proceeds to investigate.

The book consists of interesting vignettes and longer chapters describing in detail, the observations of a modern-day explorer in areas of the globe where observation of nature in all its manifold glories lead one to ask the question, 'Why did these organisms occur and evolve/survive?'

Yes, Darwin did this in the Galapagos over 150 years ago, but these are the observations of a self-taught naturalist, asking questions from his observations and then trying to determine the answers. One very interesting story, of a number, is the role of chemical agents from the observation of nature, specifically from wings of butterflies, where compounds building on discoveries in the 1940 to 1950s, led to both antibiotics and antitumor agents (specifically Pemetrexed also known as Alimta).

—David Newman, DPhil., former director of the Natural Products Branch at the National Cancer Institute and coeditor of Chemical Biology of Natural Products

"Portraying a wild and wondrous world, John Rust's essays will inspire readers to take up their own wilderness adventures. His tales of marvelous encounters with wolves and grizzlies convey a deep respect that overcomes the uninformed prejudice that these persecuted predators too often face."

—COLLETTE ADKINS, CARNIVORE CONSERVATION DIRECTOR AT THE CENTER FOR BIOLOGICAL DIVERSITY

"It took me back. Watching a seemingly lifeless, snowy rock start to move. Head raised to assess its surroundings followed by an arched back and then a turbulent shake of the body. Mystery solved—a wolf. Patience paid off for John as readers shivered along with his eloquent discovery. After watching wolves for twenty-five years in Yellowstone National Park, I just magically returned for the twenty-sixth time. Wilderness is an American endowment to use with great care, and John has invested and won with each word. We need new wolf tales for our times to peel back the truth and inspire our future. John succeeded."

—NANCY GIBSON, COFOUNDER OF THE INTERNATIONAL WOLF CENTER IN ELY, MINNESOTA, AND AUTHOR OF *WOLVES*

"John Rust explores the basic properties of wilderness seeking—he is addressing an audience that is facing new social challenges, social media, and games that were not part of the world that I experienced when I first found wilderness. Since my birth, the population has expanded three and a half times. The message is more difficult and thus more necessary. John shows what is still possible, and he creates adventures that are both challenging and obtainable. It is both example and challenge. If there is one great lesson above all others, it is the need to find the adventure that meets your personal goals and do it. In these stories, John shares the experience but also the reward and that is the real promise of wilderness—a reward in the unexpected, the beautiful, the inspiring."

—MIKE LINK, FORMER EXECUTIVE DIRECTOR OF THE AUDUBON CENTER FOR THE NORTHWOODS, AND COAUTHOR OF *GOING FULL CIRCLE: A 1,555 MILE WALK AROUND THE WORLD'S LARGEST LAKE* AND *THE SKY ISLANDS OF SOUTHEAST ARIZONA*

"John Rust has a zest for wild places, wilderness, and wildlife. And not just any wildlife. John has a fascination with predators, like grizzlies, wolves, and wildcats. These kinds of predators put us humans in a unique position in the wild ecosystems in which they live today. In such wild places, we humans are no longer the apex predator but are in a lower, subordinate position to those magnificent wild creatures. This collection of essays takes the reader along with John on his journeys to experience the wild places and wild predators that inhabit them."

—Kevin Proescholdt, conservation director for Wilderness Watch, author of *Glimpses of Wilderness*, and coauthor of *Troubled Waters: The Fight for the Boundary Waters Canoe Area Wilderness*

"*Exploring Wilderness*, John Rust shows how even in the twenty-first century, urban dwellers can have deeply meaningful wilderness experiences in terrains with large predators and survive on a small budget. This book details some of the author's greatest adventures while touching on fascinating accounts of the human history of early exploration and wildlife science."

—Peter Sorensen, Department of Fisheries, Wildlife and Conservation Biology at the University of Minnesota, and founder and former director of the Minnesota Aquatic Invasive Species Research Center

"John's account of his nine-day Seymour Canal kayak paddle on Admiralty Island is a great introduction to learning and exploring in one of the richest ecosystems on Earth. Seymour Canal can test the most experienced paddler with high seas, winds, and twenty-five-foot tides. When the paddler becomes the camper in the dense old-growth rainforest with salmon runs in most every stream, the challenge becomes the brown bears. Many have found this wilderness travel and wilderness education life changing. The true power of wilderness."

—K.J. Metcalf, the first Admiralty Island Wilderness and National Monument Ranger and founding member of Friends of Admiralty—promoting the Island's scientific, educational, and wilderness values

"Thank you so much, John, for this narrated glimpse into wild places I may never personally see—places that are the 'essence of wild, where predators roam the landscape as freely today as they have in the ancient past.' I am envious! And very grateful for your wonderful eyewitness stories. I too love our wild spaces—and know it is crucial to protect our apex predators for these amazing places to remain vibrant and healthy."

—Lois Norrgard, national field organizer at
Alaska Wilderness League

"On wilderness adventures ranging from Yellowstone to Alaska and beyond, John Rust has dealt with drenching rainstorms, frigid glaciers, whitecapped lakes and bays, and thick brush and timber where who knows what awaits. All of this for one central purpose: to experience North America's greatest predators, from wolves and mountain lions to grizzly and brown bears, up close. Sometimes really close. Rust's spare, unassuming prose eschews the heroic narrative to show how an unarmed human remains subordinate to these apex predators. As he ventures into some of the wildest reaches of the continent, we are treated to skin-tingling glimpses of nature at its most sublime and magnificent. It reminds us that our world is not complete without the keystone species at the top of the food chain."

—Frederick H. Swanson, author of Where Roads Will Never
Reach: Wilderness and Its Visionaries in the Northern Rockies
and Wonders of Sand and Stone: A History of Utah's National
Parks and Monuments

"Amy and I have undertaken many extended backcountry adventures over the years, including paddling the lush jungles of Amazon's rainforests, circumnavigating Lake Superior by kayak, and dogsledding across North America. John Rust's descriptions of exploring the wild and encountering predators captures the very essence of wild nature. They bring to mind the feeling of cold water splashing across one's face while paddling in a storm, feeling bitter cold on one's fingertips when starting a fire when the air temperature is -20°F, and the awesomeness of being in nature and appreciating the solitude of wilderness and all that it has to offer. Time spent nourishing one's soul in the Boundary Waters or any wilderness is priceless."

—Dave and Amy Freeman, National Geographic Adventurers of
the Year 2014 and authors of A Year in the Wilderness: Bearing
Witness in the Boundary Waters

EXPLORING
WILDERNESS
From Heart-Racing Adventure to Tranquility

JOHN RUST

BEAVER'S
POND
PRESS

Edited by Judith Brenner
Book design and typesetting by jamesmonroedesign.com
Cover photograph by John Rust
Interior illustrations by Sven Bellanger

The base layer for all maps illustrated in this book are from information available online from the United States Geological Survey (https://www.usgs.gov/) or from the Government of Canada Open Maps (https://www.canada.ca/en.html).

ISBN 13: 978-1-64343-726-2
Library of Congress Catalog Number: 2022920962
Printed in the United States of America
First Edition: 2024
27 26 25 24 23   5 4 3 2 1

Beaver's Pond Press
939 West Seventh Street
Saint Paul, MN 55102
(952) 829-8818
www.BeaversPondPress.com

BEAVER'S
POND
PRESS

To order, visit https://sites.google.com/view/john-rust-wilderness.
Contact the author at imgahn2u@yahoo.com or
see https://sites.google.com/view/john-rust-wilderness
for speaking engagements and interviews.

For all life on Earth: past, present, and future

CONTENTS

FOREWORD

John Rust has a zest for wild places, wilderness, and wildlife. And not just any wildlife. John has a fascination with predators, like grizzlies, wolves, and wildcats. These kinds of predators put us humans in a unique position in the wild ecosystems in which they live today. In such wild places, we are no longer the apex predator but are in a lower, subordinate position to those magnificent wild creatures.

This collection of essays takes the reader along with John on his journeys to experience the wild places and wild predators that inhabit them. From camping amid the Druid Peak pack of wolves in Yellowstone and grizzly bears in Alaska's Katmai National park, to grizzlies and wolves in Denali and the wolves of Minnesota's Boundary Waters Canoe Area Wilderness, John describes his adventures (and some misadventures) in wild places with amazing stories.

John accurately senses that, with the growing worldwide human population and the increasing human reach into formerly wild places, the experiences he shares in this book may no longer be available to future generations. Yes, in the US we have magnificent national parks and great designated wildernesses protected by the 1964 Wilderness Act. But even these protected areas may not be large enough to maintain populations of predators long into the future.

I share John's curiosity with wild places and predators, and his yearning to experience them. I still enjoy my visits to the Boundary Waters with its robust population of wolves; I thrill with the sight of a grizzly on my visits to Yellowstone. I've spent much of my life trying to protect areas like these. John's experiences give us vivid glimpses of some of the reasons why we must continue striving to protect them.

John also delves into some of the deeper meanings with his experiences living among wildlife and in wild places. "In wilderness with predators, humans are but another link in nature's web of life," he writes. "We exist neither at the top nor at the bottom of the food chain."

During one of his trips to Alaska, John relates, "Here, I am alone in a vast wilderness, sharing the immediate area with two Alaskan brown bears and a multitude of bear tracks scattered at my feet. I am a small being surrounded by living, breathing predators, alone in the elements with powerful forces at work."

How fitting that at the end of a Yellowstone adventure, he shares: "As we travel in silence across Yellowstone's extraordinary thawing landscape, the afterglow of our encounter with the wild lingers within our souls."

—KEVIN PROESCHOLDT

Kevin Proescholdt is the conservation director for Wilderness Watch, a national wilderness conservation organization. He has worked for more than forty years to protect wild places, including Minnesota's Boundary Waters Canoe Area Wilderness. His books include *Troubled Waters: The Fight for the Boundary Waters Canoe Area Wilderness* and *Glimpses of Wilderness*.

AUTHOR'S NOTE

This book is dedicated to readers now and in the future.

Readers living at the time of this writing (2022): May you seek, if you so choose, renewal of spirit in nature, and find solitude and peace in the natural world, as well as the thrill of exploration and adventure in a wilderness that contains predators.

Readers in year 2200 and beyond: Despite what unimaginable changes we cannot foresee six generations from now, may you have the opportunity to experience the raw, natural, and primeval world, and be able to experience wilderness on equal terms with predators, as humans have for eons, and thus be humbled while in their presence.

INTRODUCTION

Dear Reader,

A person living in the early 1800s could little imagine the societal and technological changes that have occurred these past two hundred years. Yet today, if we so choose, we can still venture into wilderness with predators and thus reduce the elements of our existence to the basic necessities of survival. While doing so, we elicit the same feelings and emotions of those who lived long in the past, before civilization and technology engulfed the world. We rekindle ancient feelings of connection to the natural world—contentment, serenity, and sublime happiness, but also trepidation, vulnerability, and fear—while experiencing the satisfaction of a physical existence.

One of the goals in putting to print this series of essays is that you will be imparted with a bit of wisdom by reliving another person's experiences seeking solitude in wild nature. I don't mind sharing that some of the decisions I have made may be considered as lacking in good judgment or downright foolhardy. While having gained experience in the wilderness, I have learned lessons, forgot them, and relearned them. Consequently, this author is fortunate to have come out alive and in one piece as of this writing. But there have been some close calls. I'm relieved to not be one of those reported lost, drowned, frozen, killed by a fallen tree, struck by lightning, or mauled or attacked by a bear or cougar. These and a myriad of other mishaps give us pause. When my survival has been determined by pure and simple dumb luck, rather than some sort of wisdom about the outdoors, I am humbled. At the end of the day, maybe you will have some of your own adventures and avoid some of the nerve-racking situations that I have found myself in. If that is the case, then this author will have succeeded in imparting a little bit of wisdom to a kindred spirit whose soul yearns for adventure in wild nature. Here is an opportunity to learn from my mistakes.

The wilderness stories that follow are primarily solo experiences, but some have been with family and friends. Most of these areas I have visited repeatedly. In particular, I have explored Yellowstone National Park, the Boundary Waters Canoe Area Wilderness, and areas of Alaska several dozen times, hiking, paddling, and tent camping. These essays highlight predator encounters over a span of decades. Human memory is frail, imperfect, and morphs with time. Therefore, I have referenced journal notes for some, while other memories are indelibly etched in my mind. After all, isn't that what we want when we venture into the wilderness? We are left with impressions and the relished feeling of solitude within a primeval landscape, of nature untouched and untarnished by artifacts of civilization. I share these memories hoping you, too, will find sustenance to your soul and that these essays bring you some of the joy and wonder that I have experienced and now cherish years later.

EXPLORING
WILDERNESS

EARLY EXPERIENCE

Nothing sparks the imagination of a young child more than monsters coming to get you in the middle of the night. Is there something hiding in the closet? Under the bed? Maybe it is something inbred into our primordial genes, that fear of being eaten by a predator, especially when we are young and defenseless. When I was six or seven years old, our family spent a long weekend on the north shore of Lake Superior, or Gitchi-Gami ("great water") as it is known by Ojibwa people who inhabit lands around it. Along the ragged cliffs and stupendous pines, my father had rented a little rustic cabin. My memory is dim, but I recall a favorite pastime which is considered the quintessential Minnesota thing: skipping smooth rocks which were found aplenty along the shore. We'd compete to see who could achieve the most skips across the icy cold water.

We hiked a trail through green spruce and fir trees along the shoreline. The trail veered to the left, out to a rocky point with dark, jagged cliffs that cascaded down to the lake surface below. Near the edge of the cliff, we spied a boulder the size of a large vehicle that had fallen away from the cliff and now rested in shallow water. On the cliff face one could see the hollowed-out impression from where the boulder had fallen away. This was my first lesson in nature. There are great forces at work here in this rugged landscape. At one point, the boulder had filled the impression and was a part of the cliff face, and my young self wondered if it had fallen yesterday or in the ancient past.

After spending a night in the cabin, we woke to a thick fog that covered the entire coastline, limiting visibility. I couldn't see the oceangoing freighters on Lake Superior—coming and going from around the world to and from the port city of Duluth. That morning, a freighter must have been blasting its foghorn every few minutes, warning other watercraft of

3

its presence. Periodically, a great, deep bellow would sound. To a young boy, it was a mysterious noise in a raw landscape of wooded evergreens, jagged cliffs, and icy cold water, far from the norms of my urban neighborhood. Intuitively, I understood that primeval forces were at work in this ancient landscape. We were not in the familiar circumstances of buildings, schools, cars, and stores. When I heard the deep bellowing, I did what I thought was best. I warned my family that we couldn't go outside of the cabin until it was safe. They asked me why. My response: "Bears!"

IDEAL TRAVEL COMPANION

Some of my best wilderness travel companions have been books. As a travel companion, a book does not complain about hardships or spontaneous course changes. With a book, there is no need to worry about where to camp and whether the camp is good enough. It never second-guesses decisions or complains about being bored. A book is as tough as the person packing it. It has no desire to return to the comforts of civilization before it is time. I've spent hours in the delicious heat of the midday sun reading in the tent while hordes of mosquitoes buzzed at the door screen. I also have spent hours in a tent, snuggled inside a warm sleeping bag, reading by candlelight while the temperature dipped below zero. An engrossing book provides stimulating dialogue and thoughts. It has a good attention span and is interested in the same things as the person carrying it.

Paperbacks save weight when backcountry camping. My preference is to bring enough to last the duration of the trip. There has been a trip or two where I have had to reread a book or read the acknowledgments and glossary in detail to stretch out the time. I choose books about science, nature, and the Universe. These essays, at times, use my reading material as jumping-off points to ponder some of humankind's greatest discoveries. Some offer a deeper understanding of the human condition or put into perspective how *Homo sapiens* fits within the grand scheme of life on Earth. Some essays offer reflections of where Earth fits within the greater Cosmos. After all, there is no better place to contemplate the mysteries of the Universe and our place within it than in the solitude of nature.

WILDERNESS

As a seeker of solitude in the wild, my impulse is to seek nature in its most pure, natural, and wild form. I'm drawn to powerful nature that is raw, primeval, and unaltered by humans. Where Earth's landscape and nature are presented as survival challenges, as humans lived in a rudimentary and primitive manner before the advent of civilization. Wilderness travel is not car camping with marked campsites. Rather, it's hiking and paddling where the landscape is devoid of human landmarks or artifacts and has no cell phone towers. Or as Howard Zahniser so elegantly stated in the Wilderness Act of 1964: "A wilderness, in contrast with those areas where man and his own works dominate the landscape, is hereby recognized as an area where the Earth and its community of life are untrammeled by man, where man himself is a visitor who does not remain."

I prefer to venture into wilderness under minimalist conditions, bringing sleeping and eating gear, hiking boots, a backpack, rain gear, a tent, and if paddling, a canoe or kayak. What I and others with a similar mindset seek is a primitive existence, one of simple day-to-day physical activity: exploring, hiking the landscape, and paddling the waterways. Of encountering and overcoming challenges and obstacles that nature presents in the wild. Of observing wildlife in its natural setting while pausing to slowly inhale the natural beauty of the terrain, whether it is mountains covered in deep green forest or topped by glistening snowfields. Of cyan skies with looming thunderheads in the distance or sparkling turquoise waterways with emerald shorelines.

Another motivation is to satisfy a need to experience and explore the natural world firsthand—to engage in an active endeavor where one knows not what new thing may be beyond the next hill, around the switchback in the trail, or curve on the river. Although humans have mapped in detail Earth's continents and oceans and have catalogued much of its flora and fauna, a person may yearn to behold and experience Earth's untrammeled landscape and nature for themselves. While doing so, the experience transforms an unknown landscape filled with dragons of our imagination into a place that is better understood, knowing it is filled with wildlife and predators not to be feared, but rather respected and preserved for future generations.

Why do some people seek and endure primitive experiences and physical hardship in the wild? Because there is an innate sense of satisfaction and accomplishment in overcoming physical hardship, including intense climatic conditions such as cold, heat, wind, rain, or snow. Like all life on Earth, humans have evolved over time, overcoming hardships in nature. Our genes have been culled and selected to survive nature's challenges. As a result, our minds and bodies have been shaped by the evolutionary forces of nature. Consequently, seeking a return to the original conditions that have created our minds and bodies may very well be natural. This question of why people seek "wild" experiences can be answered just as easily as the analogous question, "Why do people find vistas of craggy mountains, emerald forests, and blazing sunsets aesthetically pleasing?" The answer is fundamentally unknowable but we usually agree that a certain vista is beautiful. Photographs of landscapes on Mars are intriguing, impressive, and have a certain sterile beauty, but their beauty does not compare to vistas of a verdant Earth, puffy clouds in a blue sky, or Earth's blazing sunsets.

With every trip into wilderness, a person learns something about nature, gains wisdom, and sees life from a perspective that differs from everyday existence. When we venture into wilderness, we gain insight into remembering and knowing that our existence is a small part of nature's grand symphony of life. This symphony has been ongoing for billions of years; its crescendos supporting rich biological diversity and nadirs as the Earth and its biosphere experience extinction events.

Some cultures and societies have deep respect and reverence for wildlife. Hindus and Buddhists believe that humans, animals, and birds share the same plane of existence. In India, peacocks, elephants, and tigers hold sacred positions. Ancient people of Egypt deified cats. Indigenous people on the great plains of North America depended on vast herds of buffalo and featured buffalo during ceremonies. Eagles and eagle feathers are revered by multiple American Indian cultures. The Zuni of New Mexico refer to the eagle as the "Hunter God of the Upper Regions." The culture and livelihood of Indigenous peoples of the Pacific Northwest revolve around salmon. They identify themselves as "Salmon People." Plains Indians both feared and revered grizzlies, making necklaces from their claws as an emblem of bravery. Ancient Mayans, Aztecs, and Inca revered the jaguar. Traditional Chinese culture holds the tortoise as sacred.

Western culture, during much of its history, has long held beliefs that predators are creatures to be feared, competed with for game, loathed for depredations on livestock, and that they should be eradicated. During the Euro-American settlement of North America, grizzly bears, mountain lions, wolves, coyotes, bobcats, alligators, wolverines, and rattlesnakes were systematically eliminated. Coyotes and rattlesnakes still are. Wilderness was viewed as something to be subdued, conquered, tamed, and eventually cultivated. As Earth's societies industrialized, vast tracts of land were cleared and plowed, replaced by monocultures—domesticated plants and animals. This continues today.

Moreover, much of Earth's landscape is scarred or polluted by extracting minerals, oil, and natural gas. Anything that becomes increasingly rare is often prized and sought after. As wilderness and predators have diminished and become rare, some attitudes and beliefs have evolved to offer a degree of acceptance of them, or even to placing a high value on them.

As Earth's human population approaches ten billion and the globe is indelibly imprinted with towns and cities, farmland, rangeland, mines, and industry, certainly people could survive in a pragmatic and utilitarian "Brave New World." But Earth's biosphere would be outrageously diminished for having lost its cradle of creation, the natural world that has created every living thing on the planet during the past four and a half billion years.

Here is to hoping that humanity does not turn Earth's biosphere into a pragmatic and utilitarian world, that humanity instead finds a way to preserve wilderness and predators. Predators fill important ecological and evolutionary roles. Many are keystone species whose effects are felt directly and indirectly throughout our planet's many ecosystems, with a prime example being the return of wolves in Yellowstone National Park.

Keep in mind, however, that ecosystems are complex and change over time. Wildfire, windstorms, ecological succession, volcanic eruptions, floods, changing climate, and shifting weather patterns change ecosystems. In some ecosystems, apex-level predators create a dynamic equilibrium by limiting grazers and browsers, thus keeping a biological community balanced. That predators may limit the population of prey species below them on the food chain, however, is not necessarily true in all cases. Trophic cascades also occur from the bottom-up. Whereas a top-down cascade is predator driven, a bottom-up cascade is driven by abundant food at the bottom of the food chain in the form of plants, phytoplankton, or zooplankton, thus enabling small animals and herbivores to proliferate, which in turn supports intermediate and larger predators at the top. Top-down and bottom-up cascades can occur simultaneously and act on the same or different threads within a biological community.

Beyond their impact on trophic cascades, predators have an evolutionary role of culling less-fit individuals, thereby sculpting prey species over long periods of time. Besides ecological and evolutionary roles, predators are fundamental in enabling ecological communities to function naturally and remain wild. Without predators, ecosystems are less wild and only a semblance of their former biological complexity.

Let's hope that humanity finds a way to not only care for itself, but that predators and naturally functioning wild ecosystems are valued by people for esoteric qualities that speak to the human spirit and remain a part of Earth's biosphere far into the future.

When we venture into wilderness, it's important to note that adventures can have consequences that involve matters of life and death. Of survival. Nature and wilderness have nurtured life on Earth. But it has also culled it. The conditions found in wilderness have shaped Earth's life and are bred into our genes. Those who venture into the wilderness with prudence, respect, and caution are likely to survive unscathed. But still, bad things can happen, even with the best of experience and preparation. Bad things can happen whether one is venturing into wilderness or crossing a street at a busy intersection.

CIRCLE OF LIFE

"Perhaps the wilderness we fear is the pause between our own heartbeats, the silent space that says we live only by grace. Wilderness lives by this same grace.
Wild mercy is in our hands."

—TERRY TEMPEST WILLIAMS,
REFUGE: AN UNNATURAL HISTORY OF FAMILY AND PLACE, 1991

Let's take a journey back in time. Imagine a westbound pioneer in the 1800s traveling two thousand miles across the high plains to reach the territories of California, Oregon, or Washington. A typical day meant walking fifteen to twenty miles alongside carts pulled by oxen or mules, filled with supplies to last five months. Hardships entailed deadly cholera, dysentery, exhaustion, drowning, or heat stroke.

Today we see on the high plains of the West their trails, eroded into desert soil and hard rock by thousands of wagons having made the westward journey. Imagine early pioneers' feelings of hope in settling a fertile land. Contemplate the struggle, the day-after-day fatigue and hardship under a hot and unrelenting sun. Then with evening relief and rest, sleeping under a clear, dark desert sky filled with resplendent stars and the shimmering Milky Way slowly rotating overhead in epic silence, occasionally interrupted by the howl of a coyote.

Along the westward trail, at about the halfway mark, pioneers encountered the two-thousand-foot granite monolith called Independence Rock where thousands carved their names and date of passage.

They followed freshwater and grass along the Platte and North Platte Rivers, then along the Sweetwater, then passed Devil's Gate where the Sweetwater cuts a gorge through an arm of the Granite Mountains. After passing a landmark dubbed Split Rock, they approached a gray, gloomy shimmering in the distance. Perhaps a large dark cloud or mirage on the horizon? No! Neither cloud nor mirage, a barrier of rock and ice blocked their path. Stretching as far as the eye could see to the north are one hundred miles of precipitous, gray granite peaks topped with gleaming white snow and glacial ice—the Wind River Mountains. To the south are the Oregon Buttes and the badlands of the Red Desert, where water is scarce, or if found, brackish. South of the Red Desert, the full thrust of the Rockies regain their rugged splendor with the Sierra Madre and Park Ranges.

With no easy pass over the Rockies to the north, scarce water in the Red Desert, and no easy path to cross the Rockies to the south, the westward trail traverses the Continental Divide at a low point, just 7,400 feet above sea level. Here at South Pass, the Sweetwater River emanates from the Wind River Mountains as an essential source of water, and granite spires forming the spine of the Rockies are bypassed. At this place, wagons could be pulled over a saddle of sloping terrain covered with grass and sagebrush. Such are the quirks of geography and history that without South Pass, it may be that the Southwest would still be part of Mexico and the Pacific Northwest still controlled by or part of Britain.

Before the transcontinental railroad connected East with West, the starting point for many pioneers was Independence, Missouri. Before the 1840s, travel routes in the West were rugged and little mapped, used primarily by Native Americans, explorers, mountain men, and fur traders. With time and repeated use, pathways to western territories became better known. By the 1840s, the Oregon, Santa Fe, and California Trails were established. Led by an experienced guide, families with young children could feasibly make the journey. Over 400,000 people used trails to the West, making it one of the largest migrations in history.

Upon leaving departure points, pioneers were not equipped with the skills and temperament to live on the landscape as Indigenous people have for eons. Pioneers passed through the territories of various tribes: Pawnee, Arapaho, Cheyenne, Crow, Ute, Navajo, and Shoshone. Most were friendly and allowed peaceful passage. The Shoshone led by Chief

Washakie traded with migrants as they traveled the trail the Shoshone called "the White-top Wagon Road."

Early explorers and pioneers encountered abundant wildlife, including deer, pronghorn, elk, and initially great herds of bison, at times augmenting their supplies. Coyotes and wolves were widespread, preying on ungulates. Occasionally, pioneers came across tracks of a mountain lion or chanced upon a black bear. Grizzlies were encountered not only in the Rocky Mountains, but also on the high plains, inhabiting western portions of North Dakota, South Dakota, Nebraska, and Kansas. Indeed, Theodore Roosevelt encountered grizzlies in western North Dakota in 1884.

Starting out, explorers and pioneers traveled westward over gently rolling lands carpeted with tall-grass prairie. After a month, they entered rugged terrain with hills, buttes, and ravines. In the rain shadow of the Rockies, the terrain becomes dryer, supporting short-grass prairie and sage.

Far from any urban area, self-sufficiency is paramount. In western Nebraska, when fetching water from North Platte's river bottom, one might happen upon unusual tracks in the mud. They could be quite large, up to twelve inches long. At the head of each track are impressions of five toes. Beyond each toe print, piercing deep into mud, are claw marks. Imagine a pioneer seeing grizzly tracks for the first time and experiencing wonder and dread. She scans the area, looking past nearby brush, and listens. Satisfied there is no immediate danger, she finishes filling the water container, and quickly returns to the group to tell others what she has seen.

Unlike the explorers and pioneers of 150 years ago, my group of intrepid explorers are sitting comfortably on a jet traveling 550 miles per hour. We are being served dinner and drinks by flight attendants with robotic efficiency. Our flight is over the Alaskan panhandle and southern Yukon Territory. Our destination is Katmai National Park on the Alaskan Peninsula. Currently we are flying over the mountain-and-ice kingdom of Kluane (clue-ON-ee) National Park.

Below us, emanating from Earth's largest nonpolar icefield, spectacular, sinuous rivers of ice wind down valleys of the Wrangell and Saint Elias Mountains. Many of the glaciers are more than twenty-five miles long. As a glacier flows down a valley, it erodes and steepens the mountainside. Rocky debris accumulates on, inside of, and especially along the glacier's edges. Looking out a window on the right side of the aircraft, I see the fifty-mile-long Kaskawulsh Glacier and its mile-wide tributaries. Where tributary glaciers meet, the dark stripes of medial moraines follow the Kaskawulsh's length to its three-mile-wide terminus. Plate tectonics and volcanism built up the Wrangell and Saint Elias Mountains, but glaciers and weathering are tearing them down. Robert Frost says that the world may end in fire or ice, but in the Wrangell and Saint Elias Mountains, fire and ice are continually recreating and reshaping it.

The pilot tells us to look out windows on the left side of the plane. The view is astonishing. We are above Mount Logan; at 19,551 feet, it's the highest peak in Canada and the second-highest peak in North America—only Denali is higher. Its north and east faces are shrouded in deep gray-blue shadow. The west face is sparkling and shining white as rays of sunshine ricochet off snow clinging to its crags.

After an overnight in Anchorage, we board a small aircraft for a flight southwest along the Alaskan Peninsula. Our destination is the town of King Salmon, an outpost on the banks of the Naknek River, which supports a year-round population of four hundred hardy souls. Twenty miles west of King Salmon, the Naknek River empties into Bristol Bay, the world's most prolific sockeye salmon fishery, supporting runs of twenty to sixty million fish annually. The source of the Naknek River is Naknek Lake in Katmai National Park, fifteen miles east of King Salmon.

Of the five species of salmon that reproduce in Alaskan lakes and rivers, the most numerous and prolific on the Alaskan Peninsula is the sockeye. Every year, two million sockeye swim up Naknek River and into Katmai's lakes and creeks. After reaching Naknek Lake, some proceed up Brooks River, leaping over iconic Brooks Falls and past a gauntlet of hungry brown bears. Past the falls and the bears, they enter Lake Brooks and tributary creeks to spawn. Others swim through a narrow gap in the terminal moraine that separates Naknek Lake from the Iliuk Arm.

Having entered the Iliuk Arm, many spawn at Margot Creek, where again bears await their arrival. Many bypass Brooks River and Margot Creek, migrating twelve miles up the fast-moving and sediment-filled waters of the Savonoski River to enter the Grosvenor (GROW-ven-or) River. Because the Grosvenor is not glacially fed, its water runs clear. After swimming three miles up the Grosvenor, the sockeye enter Grosvenor Lake to spawn where Hardscrabble Creek empties into Grosvenor Lake. But for some, the journey is not yet complete. If the origin of their hatching is farther upstream, instinct impels them to swim up American Creek, some going to Hammersly Lake. In the shallow waters of lakes, rivers, and streams, hundreds of Alaskan brown bears gorge on the salmon as they spawn.

Katmai National Park supports about two thousand coastal brown bears. Because they feed voraciously on salmon, they grow large, with an adult male weighing up to 1,200 pounds. There are no black bears in Katmai, likely due to competition with the large and numerous brown bears. Because salmon runs on the Alaskan Peninsula are remarkably prolific, as the bears gain weight, they often eat only the highest-calorie and choicest parts of the salmon: eggs, brains, and the fatty layer of skin, leaving the rest for gulls, eagles, subordinate bears, or as nutrients for vegetation.

Arriving in King Salmon, we connect with the owners of a small hotel where we have reserved a room. They help us carry gear and a two-week supply of food for our stay in Katmai. We load our duffel bags into a big old SUV and ride one-quarter mile to the hotel. Little did we know that we had landed on a primeval landscape. This town is encircled by a vast, untamed, uncultivated wilderness. The road in town connects King Salmon with the fishing town of Naknek on Bristol Bay. We walk across

Sockeye salmon
(Oncorhynchus nerka)
by Sven Bellanger

17

the road and eat at a restaurant. Traveling by aircraft allowed us to travel over three thousand miles in six hours. It transported us to a time and place where the unregulated laws of wild nature rule. A place where large, charismatic megafauna dwell: caribou, moose, Canada lynx, wolverines, wolves, and gigantic brown bears.

Being naive, we perceive ourselves to be meandering about a tame and civilized town. We quickly learn this is not true. There are the usual items found in most towns: an airport, a few hotels, a bar, two restaurants, and a general store. The trappings of civilization deceive us into a feeling of familiarity. At King Salmon's periphery, there is a subtle and invisible boundary. At the boundary, the edge between civilization and wilderness is blurred. At one moment a person is standing inside the town's limits, with its established rules of commerce and civilized conduct. In the next moment, and with one more step, one crosses an imperceptible boundary into wilderness, leaving the harmless, docile remnants of civilization behind. At this point one enters another world. Outback Alaska. Wild Alaska. Tooth-and-claw Alaska.

After dinner, daylight lingers. The evening is pleasant as we explore the town and the surrounding vicinity. From the general store, we follow the road a hundred yards northwest to Eskimo Creek. Someone in our group asks if salmon spawn in the creek. Almost certainly they do. Crossing the two-lane bridge over Eskimo Creek, we come to sandy areas on either side of the road. Beyond the sand is thick willow and alder. One member of our party finds tracks in the sand. Large bear tracks. It is surprising to us city dwellers to come across bear tracks so close to town center.

The tracks lead toward brush on the left, then back to the road on the right. Several days old, they were likely made while the bear was sneaking around at night. Perhaps it was looking for an easy meal by tipping over a garbage can. After crossing the road, the tracks continue in sand, then lead into thick brush. So far, we have followed them for thirty feet next to the road, just one hundred yards from town center. In my mind, we are intrepid trackers tramping through rugged wilderness. Seeing bear tracks is confirmation that large coastal brown bears really do inhabit the Alaskan Peninsula.

We stand ten feet off the road as I look back toward town. On the left is the restaurant where we ate dinner. On the right is the general store where we bought fishing licenses. We walk a few more steps to where the tracks disappear into alder brush. We don't walk into brush following bear tracks. After a pause, we decide to return to the hotel for the night.

A member of our party whispers, "Stop." We stand still as alder brush blows in the breeze. Is that a swishing sound? Is it heavy breathing? *Let's not be paranoid. We are within spitting distance of the town center. There is nothing to be worried about.*

Abruptly, my thoughts of comfort are pushed aside as a humongous, gangling bear bursts from the thicket to stand twenty feet away. Its dark brown eyes are fixated on us. Its head is held high. Its jaw is agape. All of us, including the bear, freeze for a moment in time that is forever emblazoned in my memory.

I cannot speak for my companions, but I am seeking to experience the beauty of nature and a oneness with the natural world. My goal is to observe wildlife foraging on a vast and epic landscape. To witness great flocks of birds in flight and innumerable salmon migrating upstream, going about their lives undisturbed by humankind. I hope to observe from a distance the power and mastery of a brown bear fishing for salmon. To shed off the dregs of civilization. To experience life by embracing the natural world and to come to an understanding of what wild nature is about. To connect with wildlife and leave my dreary existence staring at a computer screen five days a week. My intention is to observe nature's grand life cycles and migrations, and to connect with the circle of life on Earth and the greater Cosmos.

Standing in front of us, suddenly and spectacularly, my goal has been achieved. A five-hundred-pound part of the Cosmos in the form of an Alaskan brown bear is twenty feet away looking at us eye to eye. Each of us are intensely feeling part of Earth's grand circle of life. Unfortunately, our circles may soon be coming to an end, and we may indeed become "one with the greater Cosmos" as we are within smelling distance of the maw of nature. If this bear were to attack, kill, and devour us, we would become one with nature. The nutrients in our bodies becoming nourishment for it, keeping the circle of life going not for us, but for the bear and its offspring. This is not the oneness with the Cosmos I had envisioned. This oneness feeling is not comfortable and not what I had come for. The timing is wrong and the situation is not what I had imagined. We are face-to-face with wild nature in its most raw and powerful form. It is obvious the bear may be as distressed as everyone in our group. Staring at us, with us staring at it, we look into its eyes. With no time to react, we are motionless and aghast.

A short while ago, we had exited a technological marvel of air travel. We had a cozy dinner in a restaurant with polite servers. We checked into our hotel. We walked over to the store, bought fishing licenses, and chatted with the friendly cashier.

In an instant, everything has changed. My mind can't fathom the idea that we are now being confronted by a prehistoric predator. There are no signs in town that say, "Caution: Large Carnivorous Brown Bears Roam This Town." The pepper spray is back with our luggage at our hotel room. We have not yet entered Katmai National Park and its wilderness. The reality we are facing, however, is quite compelling.

Just as quickly as it burst into view, the bear bolts across the road. As each paw lands on pavement, we hear its claws: Click-click-click . . . click-click-click . . . click-click-click. Then it is gone—disappeared into thick brush on the far side of the road. No one has so much as twitched a muscle. Not entirely sure what had transpired, we look at each other, bewildered. *Did this really happen?* Looking at the ground at our feet, the big tracks of the bear are visible where they have torn up sand and soil with claws as it fled. Yes, this happened.

Fortunately, there are three people in our group, all standing near one another. If it had been a single person, the consequences may not have turned out as benign.

We return to the security of our hotel for a good night's sleep. We have confirmed that there are indeed coastal brown bears inhabiting the Alaskan Peninsula, and they do not respect the town boundaries of King Salmon. Our bush flight taking us into Katmai National Park is scheduled for tomorrow. As I fall asleep in the safety of the hotel room, in the back of my mind I wonder, *If this happened in town, what might happen while we camp and travel in the wilderness of Katmai?*

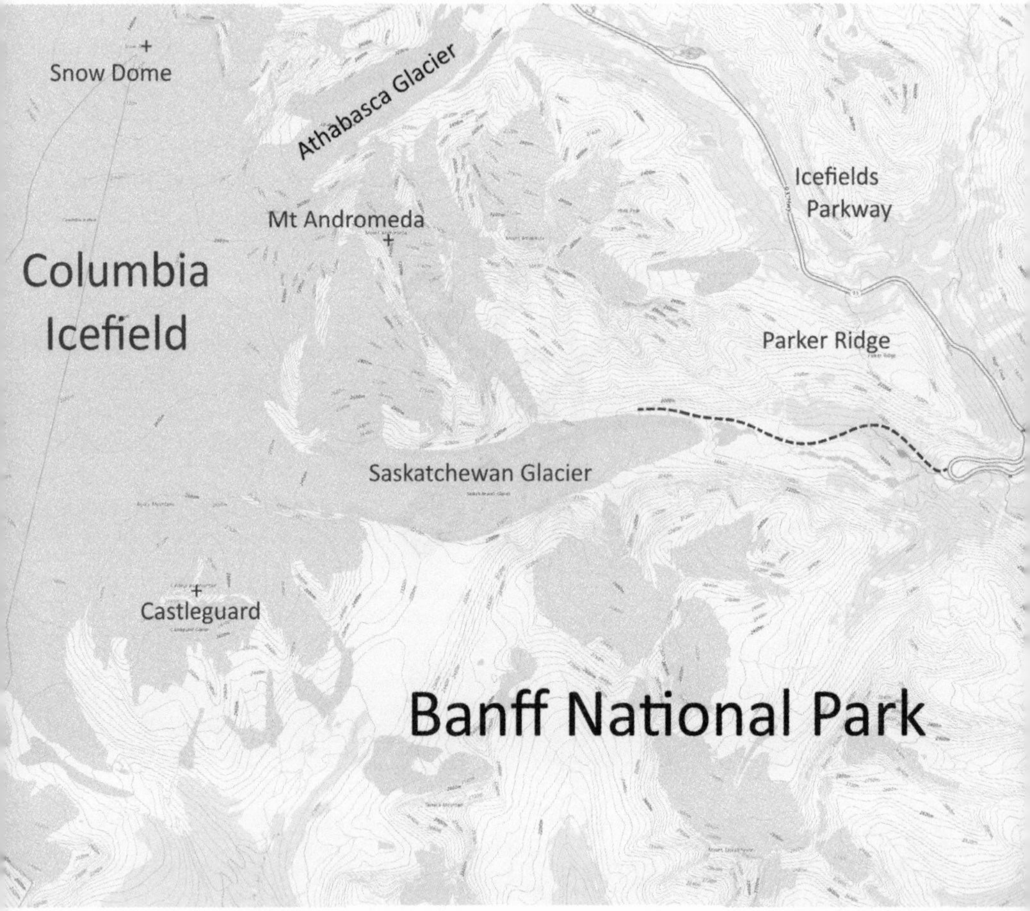
Snow Dome
Athabasca Glacier
Mt Andromeda
Columbia Icefield
Icefields Parkway
Parker Ridge
Saskatchewan Glacier
Castleguard
Banff National Park

PANIC

"The view that lay before us in the evening light was one that does not often fall to the lot of modern mountaineers. A new world was spread at our feet; to the westward stretched a vast icefield probably never before seen by human eye and surrounded by entirely unknown, unnamed and unclimbed peaks. From its vast expanse of snows, the Saskatchewan glacier takes its rise . . ."
—HUGH E. M. STUTFIELD AND J. NORMAN COLLIE, *CLIMBS AND EXPLORATIONS IN THE CANADIAN ROCKIES*, 1903

The Canadian portion of the Rocky Mountains stretches for almost a thousand miles, from the northern reaches of British Columbia south to the border with the United States. Unlike the American Rockies, which have large compositions of metamorphic and igneous rock such as gneiss and granite, the Canadian version of the Rockies are comprised of sedimentary limestones and shales with many layers having been laid down around 500 million years ago as part of an ancient seabed. The fossilized remains of ancient sea-life can be found on many slopes of the Canadian Rockies and especially at a site called the Burgess Shale, which contains the relics of trilobites, brachiopods, and more exotic species such as *opabinia*—which had five eyes and a mouth-like grasping arm—or *hallucigenia*, whose form so perplexed paleontologists that for decades they were not sure which end was the head and which side was up.

23

Ensconced in the high-altitude border region that straddles Banff and Jasper National Parks, the crown of the Canadian Rockies is the Columbia Icefield covering 125 square miles, with peaks Andromeda, Castleguard, Columbia, Snow Dome, and North Twin not only embracing but piercing its icy grasp. There are larger ice fields in North America, however the Columbia Icefield is the largest in the Rocky Mountains. Several major rivers of ice emanate from the ice field, including the Athabasca, Castleguard, Dome, and Stutfield Glaciers. The longest glacier the ice field feeds is the roughly seven-mile-long Saskatchewan. Like most glaciers in recent times, the Saskatchewan has experienced significant melting, and by the time you read this, its length may be substantially less.

For the last 2.6 million years, Earth has been engulfed in the Pleistocene ice age. At present, Earth is experiencing a ten-thousand-year period of interglacial warmth with geologist and paleoclimatologist expectations that the planet will cool again and continental ice sheets will advance. There have been twenty or so periods of interglacial warmth during the Pleistocene ice age. Since the last glacial maximum, the Saskatchewan has partially melted back and re-advanced several times, including at least three times in the last 350 years.

While most people visit the more easily accessible Athabasca, the Saskatchewan Glacier can be reached by following a hiking trail over a hill, which is accessible from Icefields Parkway at a point where the parkway makes a giant hairpin turn near Parker Ridge. During my hike to the Saskatchewan, in a few short hours, several mistakes were made, lessons learned, and some wisdom was gained. Let me take you back to that early spring day.

The sky is blue with puffy white clouds. The hill I'm hiking over divides the outwash plain at the toe of Saskatchewan Glacier from the North Saskatchewan River Valley.

I am following a well-worn trail that traverses the base of Parker Ridge through an emerald forest of Engelmann spruce and subalpine fir. My intention is to hike five miles to the Saskatchewan Glacier and return before evening. The glacier is about one mile wide and rests at the bottom of the mile-wide valley carved out during its many advances and retreats. After traveling through forested area, I hike down to the valley floor, leaving the cover of the forest, and then it is a three-and-a-half-mile hike on the rocky glacial outwash plain to the glacier's tongue. Being that I am a little nervous about hiking solo in an area whose habitat contains grizzlies, it feels more comfortable hiking in sunlit open space. Now on the valley floor, precipitous walls of sedimentary rock are visible towering on either side. Visible in the distance to the west, a large meltwater pond emanates from the toe of Saskatchewan Glacier.

At one time the Saskatchewan Glacier entirely engulfed this valley. The rocky plain is now a stark and desolate place with little vegetation. Over the course of time, vegetation is slowly reclaiming the landscape that the glacier has begrudgingly given up after its latest retreat.

Hiking for a couple hours over uneven, hardscrabble terrain, the glacier's tongue is reached. There are ice-cold glacier meltwater streams emanating from ice caves at the bottom of the glacier tongue. Lacking the equipment, experience, and skills to extricate myself from a glacier crevasse, I have no desire to walk across its surface. I munch on a granola bar from my daypack while watching water gush from caves at the base of the glacier's tongue.

Even the perimeter of the glacier requires a wide berth, where large chunks of ice are covered by rocks and gravel. These piles of detritus and moraines may appear to be solid, but within their depths the ice is weak with melting and likely contains caverns with pools of water and rushing streams. Over the years there have been reports of people or wildlife that have attempted to walk on or cross a glacier and had the unfortunate experience of either falling into a crevasse or collapsing a snow bridge, thus falling into a deep hollow in the glacier. Unable to extricate themselves, the animal or person becomes entombed within the ice. As the glacier advances, the remains held deep within the glacier are slowly transported forward toward the glacier's snout. Many years later the frozen remains melt out of the glacier and are released back into the unfrozen world. Becoming entombed inside a glacier is a fate to be avoided.

Satisfied with the hike to Saskatchewan Glacier, I decide it is time to return to the vehicle. However, I do not follow the well-trodden trail back to Icefields Parkway but instead follow the open valley floor as far as possible and then take a shortcut directly over the small hill where my vehicle is parked on the other side. An off-trail exploration of the forested area on the hill will make an interesting side adventure.

After traversing back and reaching the end of the outwash plain, I reach the craggy, forested hillside that divides this valley from the greater North Saskatchewan River Valley. With heavy breathing, I hike directly up the hillside and then into evergreen brush and forest. Now twisting and turning through brush, I encounter shallow snow, causing boot tread imprints to follow my path. Being early spring, there remains deep snow on slopes which lack long-term sun exposure. In the shadows of the forest, the snow becomes deeper. Having had forethought, I have strapped to my daypack a pair of snowshoes. Pleased with myself for having thought ahead, I put on the snowshoes and continue my shortcut through snow, brush, and forest. Eventually, and unfortunately, I have taken a convoluted path and get turned around. The trees are thick with no clear views of the horizon. My gut feeling is that I should be getting close to the far side of the hill, ready to descend toward my vehicle. By good luck, there is a clearing in the trees where there is a view through the forest. Coming to the clearing, my expectations are high. As I peer over low-lying branches and evergreen shrubs, the view opens to a wonderful vista up the valley toward the Saskatchewan Glacier. No car in sight. This is disorientating and disheartening. I reorientate myself and continue the trek, huffing through deep snow in what I think is the opposite direction of the glacial valley. This shortcut is turning out to not be a shortcut at all. Snow depth becomes deeper and now the hillside slopes downward. Although I have snowshoes strapped to my boots, the bindings are cheap and not secure. With each step, when a snowshoe does not plant squarely and firmly, it twists and slides awkwardly over unseen rocks and branches buried in snow. At times, one snowshoe or the other detaches from a boot, sliding sideways against an ankle. It must then be reset and re-buckled. Although I am making what I think is progress in the proper direction, my body is floundering in the deep snow. My pants are wet from having fallen into snow multiple times. My lower body and legs are cold and wet. I need to gather my wits.

Sitting quietly for several minutes while wallowing in deep snow, I catch my breath, then crawl over to a nearby crater at the base of a large spruce tree. Here the branches of the tree have protected the ground from deep snow, and the tree's dark color has absorbed heat from the sun and partially melted the snow. At least now I can maneuver somewhat without floundering and pause to think things over. Eventually my mind comes to the realization that thoughts of frustration about bindings do not help the situation. I put negative thoughts out of mind, at least for now.

After some thought, my plan is to backtrack. This will be a simple procedure: follow my snowshoe and boot trail back to the glacial outwash plain. Then return to the well-trodden hiking trail on the south-facing snow-free slope that I came in on and back to the vehicle. It is a simple plan and makes sense. I take the snowshoes off and strap them to my backpack. Success is assured.

Attempting to backtrack, I crawl uphill through the snow. My breathing becomes heavy and my heart starts to race. With each attempt at crawling upwards, my body slides downslope, again and again. The problem is that I have traveled in a downward direction on a northeast-facing slope where snow varies between thigh and waist deep. This is indeed frustrating. Pausing, I catch my breath. Again, with large effort I crawl uphill as if on a treadmill as snow slides down and backwards beneath my arms and legs. Traveling upward just a few yards is exhausting and after each attempt, while pausing to catch my breath, I slide back down. With no significant progress being made, envisioning the effort to successfully crawl uphill for any distance is daunting.

Contemplating the time of day, I wonder how much daylight is left. In a couple hours, it will be dark. Being cold, wet, and stuck in deep snow overnight is an uncomfortable thought. Boughs of evergreen branches could be broken off to construct a makeshift bed in a bowl of snow. That would insulate my body for the night. Refusing to give up, I make more attempts, but progress is nil. Exhausted, I am in a predicament. Being that this is a day hike, I have a few snacks but no supplies or map. I am not sure where I am, where the vehicle is, or what direction to travel. There is one thing I know for sure. I know the map is resting on the passenger seat in the vehicle.

My next step is to methodically add to my confusion by retrieving a compass from the daypack. During all previous wilderness trips, I have brought a compass. This hike is no exception. This is the first time, however, that I attempt to use a compass in *a situation that matters*. Certainly, a compass is a simple instrument that points north. That is straightforward and obvious. Being confused and disoriented, however, things are not clear. Holding the compass in my hand, and away from the metallic zipper on my jacket, the red and white ends of the compass shift back and forth before settling down in a steady direction. Yet, I do not know which of the two ends of the needle points north. Is it the red or the white end? I *think* the red end points north but am not certain. My disorientation is sufficient that the compass does not provide any useful insight.

There is another complication to using a compass that, at the time, I was unwittingly ignorant about. The magnetic declination between true north and magnetic north depends upon the location where the compass is used. In my home state of Minnesota, magnetic declination is pretty much zero; true north and magnetic north coincide. In the Canadian Rockies, magnetic declination is approximately fourteen to sixteen degrees. Here, the red end of the compass needle points between fourteen to sixteen degrees east of true north. It should also be noted that Earth's magnetic North Pole can shift by as much as thirty miles in a year. By the time you read this, Earth's magnetic North Pole may have shifted some distance, possibly hundreds of miles. I put the compass back into a zippered pocket of the daypack. Use of a compass should be mastered before a person becomes disoriented.

For several moments I feel panicky and consider shouting for help, but it is unlikely anyone is nearby. If someone is close enough to hear my shouts I would be embarrassed, feeling like a helpless child requiring assistance. After all, I am an adult, experienced and competent in the outdoors, and maybe a bit proud. I envision a search-and-rescue helicopter flying between mountain peaks. Stuck in deep snow, hidden below a thick cover of evergreens, I would never be seen. Even if a search-and-rescue team was sent, several days would pass, perhaps a week before my family would fail to receive an overdue phone call. No, getting out of here is something I must do myself.

With no mountain peaks visible through the forest and the compass not providing helpful information, my sense of direction to travel is arbitrary. A decision must be made. *Do I continue to crawl uphill in deep snow? If not, what else is there to do?* After contemplating the situation and shifting around in the snow, my body has a natural tendency to slide downward. Why fight the tendency? Going with the downhill tendency, I shove my body while seated, then slide down using both hands and arms, going feet-first through deep white powder. As I approach a tree, I angle my feet to one side and scoot around it. Then another and another. I don't know where this will end up. It is not a huge hill, but I am tired, disoriented, and distressed about being lost with darkness looming. The downward path could lead to the outwash plain of the glacier valley, or it could lead in the direction of the Icefields Parkway and the vehicle. As my slide continues, I end up at a small pond about three hundred feet across.

Leaving deep snow and arriving at the edge of the pond, I stand and brush snow and moisture off my pant legs and backside. Hiking through knee-deep snow, I circle clockwise around the pond to the far shore. Here the slope is south facing, and snow has completely melted—a great relief as travel is much easier on solid ground. If I don't find my way out of here before sundown, spending the night on dry ground is at least a tolerable prospect.

Continuing to follow the shoreline clockwise, the pond's outlet is a stream filled with small boulders. The outlet leads to an unknown destination, but at least it is downhill and likely away from the Saskatchewan Glacier valley. Instinctively, I follow the stream. Being that my lower extremities, including boots and feet, are already wet, I hike in the shallows of the stream—following it wherever it may lead, avoiding the overgrown and rocky banks. After following the stream a quarter mile, the forest opens to a clearing where the sky is visible. Upon reaching the clearing, I look downward. There, to great relief, is the Icefields Parkway and my vehicle.

Normally reluctant to be expressive but being that there are no people around, I let out a few whoops that echo back and forth across the valley. I am thankful to have extricated myself from the floundering snow. Rather than sleeping in a snow crater tonight, I will have access to hot food and a warm bed. It was not a certainty. Even a day hike can result in worrisome situations.

Sometimes it is not the big worries like falling into a crevasse or a grizzly attack that arise. Simple things can become magnified, such as not having a map or knowing how to use a compass. When taking shortcuts off-trail or through brush, one can easily become disoriented. Unforeseen difficulties can be encountered while traveling through rough terrain. There is usually a reason the trail takes the path it does. By staying on trail, one is less likely to become lost.

The sky has clouded over and it begins to snow. I hike down the hillside over to my vehicle, start the engine and turn on the heat, then breathe a sigh of relief. Looking over at the passenger seat, I notice the map sitting there, chide myself a bit, and vow to be better prepared from now on.

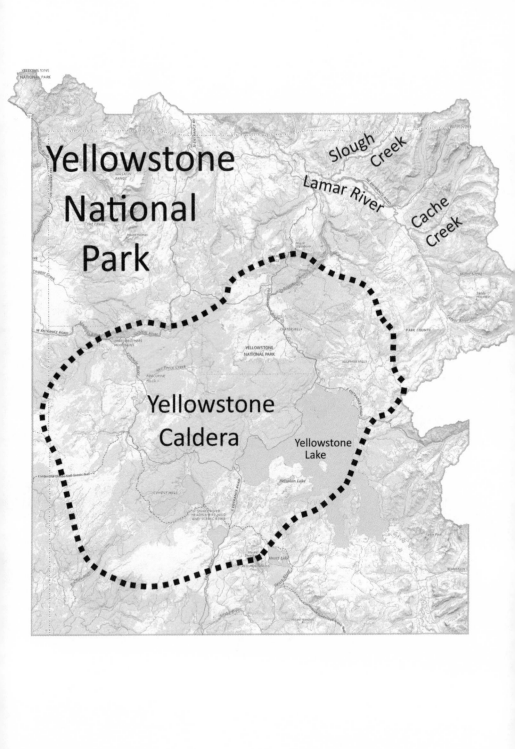

ERRATIC

"We reached the old wolf in time to watch a fierce green fire dying in her eyes. I realized then, and have known ever since, that there was something new to me in those eyes— something known only to her and to the mountain. I was young then, and full of trigger-itch; I thought that because fewer wolves meant more deer, that no wolves would mean hunters' paradise. But after seeing the green fire die, I sensed that neither the wolf nor the mountain agreed with such a view."

—Aldo Leopold, *A Sand County Almanac*, 1949

Yellowstone National Park and the mountainous volcanic plateau it is part of reside over one of Earth's hotspots—a region where magma and heat from the mantle penetrate Earth's outer crust. As water seeps into ground from above, it is heated well past the boiling point, in some places to four hundred degrees. With intense pressure and heat it reverses course, finding pathways through cracks and fissures to the surface, eventually emerging to create enchanting and deadly thermal pools, mesmerizing travertine-terraced hot springs, and spectacular geysers. Over the last two million years, at rough intervals of 600,000 to 800,000 years, Yellowstone's volcanic plume erupts into a super-volcano spewing rock and lava, along with enough volcanic ash to bury much of western North America.

The volcanic plume did not always reside beneath Yellowstone. Sixteen million years ago it was under the border between Oregon and Nevada. As North America's continental plate slowly inches westward, it passes over the plume. Twelve million years ago the plume was under southwestern Idaho. Six million years ago it was under southeastern Idaho. For the past two million years the hotspot has been beneath the Yellowstone plateau. As pressure builds and the outer crust weakens, it ultimately bursts through the crust in a super-eruption, or several eruptions that start and stop over years or decades, eventually relieving pressure and for a time going silent, then starting the cycle all over again. From the surface, it appears eruptions travel across the landscape, starting in southern Oregon, then southern Idaho, and more recently in northwest Wyoming.

The circular West Thumb of Yellowstone Lake is a caldera—formed by the collapse of the mouth of a large volcano that erupted 174,000 years ago. Yellowstone's most recent eruption was smaller and occurred just 70,000 years ago, spewing the lava flows of the Pitchstone Plateau. The hotspot's most recent super-eruption, the Lava Creek eruption, occurred 640,000 years ago. It burst through Earth's surface with a Volcanic Explosivity Index (VEI) of 8—ejecting over one thousand cubic kilometers of rock, magma, and ash, or one to two thousand times the volume of the Mount Saint Helens eruption in 1980. The caldera left after the Lava Creek super-eruption is forty miles wide, whereas the Mount Saint Helens crater is one mile wide. Ash from the Lava Creek super-eruption covered all the Rocky Mountain states as well as southern California, North Dakota, parts of Minnesota, Iowa, Missouri, Oklahoma, Texas, and northern Mexico.

During the two to three hundred thousand years of human existence, few if any humans have experienced or witnessed such a massive continental-wide cataclysm. There is the possibility that another super-eruption will occur in the near future. It may occur tomorrow or maybe not for tens of thousands of years.

It will be an interesting experience, hiking and looking for wildlife in an area that is a super-volcano. I just hope it does not have a major eruption while I am here.

34

This adventure starts with my having walked out the door after Christmas dinner 1996, leaving my wife and young children, then driving cross-country through a blizzard. My wife questioned my plan, accusing that I was about to "abandon our family."

"You are going to spend time tramping alone in subzero temperatures in search of wolves? Crazy!" she had said.

Maybe. But not to me. I am determined to drive cross-country through the blizzard, during which I encounter heavy snow and treacherous ice. Few people are out driving in these conditions. They have more sense. Some stretches of the two-lane road are not even plowed. Snowflakes stream out of darkness toward my windshield. Anxiety pervades, along with guilt. *Am I doing the right thing?* Still, I drive forward. And so, despite considerable angst, the wild urging inside my soul impels me forward.

Traveling south through Paradise Valley, I arrive at the gateway town of Gardiner, Montana, then cross the bridge over the Yellowstone River. My vehicle passes underneath the Roosevelt Arch and I am now inside Yellowstone National Park. The park boundary, however, is invisible to both humans and wildlife. It is a simple demarcation on a map. Depending upon which side of the boundary one puts their feet, the consequences for people and wildlife are real. For wildlife the implications are often deadly.

In my mind this will be the quintessential wilderness experience. It is a quest to see wolves in the wild. During the past two years (1995 and 1996) a total of thirty-one wolves from Canada had been reintroduced back into Yellowstone. This marked the first time in seventy years that Yellowstone's landscape had been trod on by wild wolves. As Doug Smith, Rolf Peterson, and Douglas Houston wrote, "The reintroduction of gray wolves to Yellowstone National Park (YNP) surely ranks, symbolically and ecologically, among the most important acts of wildlife conservation in the 20th century." Starting it all was the Endangered Species Act of 1973 that set into motion the return of wolves to Yellowstone.

At the Mammoth Hot Springs visitor center, I discuss with a park ranger my plans for backcountry travel and camping at Slough Creek. The ranger cautions about several items: Be careful on steep slopes, which pose an avalanche danger. There are cougars in the Slough Creek area, and they do not hibernate. Coyotes may become aggressive while attempting to snatch food if it is left unattended.

"Hang food and keep a clean camp. Bears are in hibernation, but there may be a grizzly that has not fattened up enough. If it becomes hungry midwinter, it may be desperate and go searching for winter kill or other food sources," he said.

I heed his warnings. I am well prepared, having packed plenty of warm clothes and winter gear. In fact, I might be too well prepared, having brought more clothing and gear than necessary.

The only road open to vehicular traffic in Yellowstone during the winter season is from Mammoth Hot Springs to Cooke City. While driving through the park, I see more than a dozen coyotes which are easy to spot against the arctic-looking landscape. Upon reaching the Slough Creek trailhead, I pull into a parking area and unload my gear. There is at least a foot of snow on the ground, and in some places two feet have accumulated. The thought that wolves are living in this white wilderness landscape is foremost in my mind.

Upon arrival at the Slough Creek parking area, I turn off the vehicle, step out of the car, and look over the snow-covered landscape. Slough Creek originates as snowmelt, rainfall, and springs that emanate from the slopes of Yellowstone's Northern Range. The Northern Range along with the Lamar Valley is thought to be the ecological center of Yellowstone National Park because of bountiful deer, elk, pronghorn antelope, bighorn sheep, and bison that live there, as well as the many predators that feed on them, such as coyotes, cougars, black bears, grizzlies, and wolves. Rainfall averages about ten to twenty inches annually; thus the Slough Creek valley floor is semiarid terrain with sagebrush, various species of grasses, and a scattering of glacial erratic boulders. Beyond the valley floor are glacial moraines and rolling hills with upward slopes covered with Douglas fir. At high elevations in the distance are craggy, snow-covered peaks.

After placing duffle bags of gear on a sled, I wrap and secure them with a tarp and bungee cords. It is a weird feeling those first few steps while starting out on such an adventure. It is not that I have never winter camped before. I've done so many times in the Boundary Waters Canoe Area Wilderness of northern Minnesota.

I pull the sled, feeling a brisk wind blowing snow at my back. The elevation is over six thousand feet, and my breath becomes labored as my body hasn't yet adjusted to the elevation as I plow ahead with backpack strapped to my back and snowshoes attached to heavy boots. Across my heavy coat is a rope being pulled taut by the loaded sled. With each step I hear snowshoes crunch through icy surface crust, then sink into soft, fluffy snow beneath. Tangles of ice-coated sagebrush pierce up through the snow, making hiking over and around them strenuous and precarious. When I lift a foot, sometimes the front edge of a snowshoe catches surface crust, almost tripping me, and slowing my pace. Other times the sled rope becomes entangled with sage. It is a clumsy and awkward situation.

To my delight, there are groups of elk and bison nearby, and a couple coyotes, all of which ignore my plodding. What keeps me going is the thought of seeing a wolf, or a pack, knowing how rare they are. They were all killed off in the lower forty-eight states except for northern Minnesota and Michigan's Isle Royale.

I travel north beneath an overcast sky. In the distance are snow-covered boulders strewn in seemingly random locations. These are glacial erratics deposited after the retreat of the last ice age. My goal is to set up camp along the banks of Slough Creek near a confluence of dark trees obscured under the shadows of gray ominous clouds. I have trepidation snowshoeing on my own into the wilderness toward those dark trees and ominous clouds. Not certain of a safe return, fate awaits as I trudge forward. The map shows a gravel road leading from the parking area to Slough Creek, but due to the snow, no trace is visible. My compass guides me north, in the general direction of the dark trees which hide the creek.

Seeing a large snow-covered boulder in the distance, I pull the sled toward it. The terrain slopes from lower left to the upper right. During the exertions of pulling the sled in the flurry of snow and wind, I am not paying close attention to nearby surroundings. It is strenuous work while encumbered with heavy clothing. Lift a foot, bring it forward, step into the snow. Repeat. The wind is pushing icy snowflakes sideways. The inside layer of my clothing beneath my ski bibs wicks away my sweat, but still, it is a cold, clammy feeling.

As I approach the snow-covered boulder, my focus is on physical exertion. My plan is to get to the boulder, shelter from the wind behind it, then rest and take stock. As I approach, I notice something curious. There is a vague shape to its form. It is interesting how the mind plays tricks on itself, identifying patterns and shapes in rocks and clouds. The wind swirls snow around my face mask as my glasses fog over with heavy breathing. I continue to heave the sled forward, step after step. Glancing up again, there are dark splotches on the boulder that are not covered in snow. The front of the boulder is vaguely shaped like an animal's head. Not wanting to waste time, my plodding continues. Now thirty yards away, the boulder appears hunched and, in a sense, facing into the wind and toward me. Maybe it is the exertion and altitude playing with my mind. Gusts of snow fly by. A dark patch on the boulder flutters. Resting, I stare through foggy glasses and blowing snow. Catching my breath I heave the sled forward, scanning the terrain in my immediate path. Then recognition sets in. The "snow-covered boulder" is a bison with thick fur encrusted by a layer of snow. The bison and I face each other, staring at each other in disbelief. I imagine the bison is thinking, *What are you doing out here, human?* My thought process is proceeding along that line as well.

Here we are, two animals in the middle of a snowstorm. The bison is accustomed to the terrain and severe weather. Me? I'm towing a sled loaded with gear, snowshoeing in a snowstorm, and I'm *not* accustomed to these conditions or level of exertion. Clearly, I am the one out of my element.

My expectation is that the bison will concede my presence, move out of the way, and walk off. However, being a newcomer here, my knowledge of bison and their habits is limited. What I am learning firsthand is that rather than fleeing a confrontation, a bison will sometimes stand its ground. I have been following an ill-defined trail, probably a game trail filled in with snow. My body is struggling, sweaty, and tired from pulling gear through snow. I am a bit confused and apprehensive. Apparently, the bison doesn't want to burn precious energy, especially in the brunt of a snowstorm, fleeing from something that poses an insignificant threat. There are few predators that can take down a healthy, full-grown bison. There is no need to retreat when facing an animal that is unlikely to do it harm. On the other hand, I don't want to burn precious energy by pulling my gear around it.

The bison and I face each other, standing perfectly still as snow accumulates on both of us. I contemplate the situation and, after a bit of thought, wave my hands and say, "Hey bison. Hey bison!" I hope it will lumber off. I dare not approach any closer, fearing a charge and goring. We are at a stalemate. One of us must decide to change course, and it is obvious it will be me.

Pulling the sled off-trail, I trek up a slope as I circle around it, feeling it is better to be uphill during a charge. Once past the bison, the slope is now downhill and, with the assist of gravity, much easier. The sled loaded with gear bumps into the back of my legs. Simultaneously, the front edge of my right snowshoe catches on sage covered with crusty ice. The right snowshoe is entangled, but momentum keeps me going forward. With body falling forward and arms outstretched to break the fall, I sink into the snow up to my elbows. Landing face down, I arch my neck and head backwards holding my face an inch from the snow. "This is just great!" I hear myself say. Cold snow has been pushed into the sleeves of the parka and onto my wrists. Now cold, I am thinking, *What else could go wrong?* That question is quickly answered. Having lost a grip of the tow rope, the sled slides past my prone body in slow motion, then picks up speed as it careens down the slope. *There it goes with all my equipment.* At the bottom of the hill, it comes to a stop, thankfully, in an upright position. These are not great distances, steep slopes, or extreme terrain, but with my lack of experience in conditions of snow and wind, this is challenging. My snow-globe fantasy of an epic winter exploration of Yellowstone is upset.

Wallowing in snow, fat with layers of clothing, snowshoes askew, it is a clumsy ordeal to stand again. Had anyone but a bison been watching, I'd be embarrassed. I wonder, *How did mountain man John Colter travel five hundred miles through this area in the brunt of winter?* I am experiencing difficulties attempting to travel just a few miles; thus, my respect for Colter soars to high levels. It would have been easy to lie there and let the falling and drifting snow cover my body. But then a fact sweeps through my mind. A similar circumstance happened to my great-great-grandfather Diedrich in 1891. While walking in blizzard conditions across the open prairies of Minnesota, Diedrich fell and unfortunately never got up. Snow covered him and he went missing. After the snow eventually melted, his remains were exposed and recovered. This prompts me to sit upright.

Out of caution, I look back at the bison and see it has not moved and seems oblivious to the difficulties of a human dealing with the outdoors. Getting myself upright, I adjust my snowshoes, gather my wits, and shake snow out of the parka sleeves. Walking down the slope, I catch up with the sled and check on the gear. Everything is intact. I pick up the tow rope and pull the sled forward toward another snow-covered boulder a few hundred yards ahead. Fortunately, this time it truly is a boulder, one I can use as shelter and rest. Pulling the sled around to its far side, I sit down, now sheltered from the wind. Here I take stock of my abilities, experience, and the conditions.

Having become flustered, doubt enters my mind. Surely there are people that can navigate these conditions. Am I one of them? Not sure. Might I come across a situation that is dangerous, resulting in my demise, thus leaving my wife a widow and my two children fatherless? Quite possibly. Is seeing wolves in the wild worth exposure to cold, wind, strenuous labor, and potential danger? And the fundamental question— why should I be in this winter wilderness among wild wolves? My reckoning comes from a final thought: *Who can put a value on wolves living in wilderness?* After rest and contemplation, I know what the decision is. It comes from a fierce green fire within my gut that defies explanation.

With determination, I stand up, put the tow rope across my chest, and despite the storm, trek deeper into the wilderness.

The sun's position in the overcast sky is nebulous as it slowly inches westward. It will be dark soon. To the right are a group of fir trees on the side of a hill that offer some protection from the wind, so I endeavor toward the trees. Disengaging from the tow rope relieves tension across my chest. Using snowshoes, I stomp down a circular area in a snowdrift and lay out a tarp. The tarp flaps wildly in the wind and tries to blow away, so I take off my snowshoes and set them on the tarp. Attempting to set up the tent, I try to slide freezing aluminum poles into the tent sleeves while the tent undulates. Once I get the tent erected, it wants to fly away. To keep the tent in place, I move duffle bags in, then crouch down and crawl inside to get out of the wind. I roll out two foam sleeping pads, unfurl two sleeping bags, and slide into the sleeping bags to warm up. While lying down snuggled in warmth, I am overcome with a glow of satisfaction, thinking, *I made it. I am here! I am camping in Yellowstone in the wintertime with wild wolves nearby!*

After resting for a while, I again brave the weather, stepping into the evening gloam to organize my gear and make dinner. The bear-proof food container makes a good stool while I heat precooked hamburger which is then added to mac-n-cheese. It is a very satisfying dinner to eat, having struggled through a snowstorm. After cleaning up and stowing the food at least one hundred yards away, I return to the tent in darkness and again burrow into the sleeping bags. Lighting a small candle adds a bit of warmth and ambiance. The candlelight, however, is insufficient for reading, so I use a flashlight as I open a book about explorer and trapper John Colter.

Colter was a member of the Lewis and Clark expedition, as well as a trapper and explorer. He trekked across the Yellowstone Plateau, came across Yellowstone's hot geysers, boiling springs, and bubbling mud pots, and saw the Teton Range and Jackson Lake. Colter traveled hundreds of miles through this area in the dead of winter, endured below-zero temperatures, and often traversed through deep snow.

Putting a bookmark between the pages, I set the book into the mesh tent pocket and turn off the flashlight. While contemplating Colter's story, I sit with the candle flickering in darkness. With each exhalation, a mist of frozen moisture is expelled. The wind howls outside, shaking the tent walls. My short trek is minuscule in comparison. Colter spent day after day for years in the wilderness, often alone. Quite remarkable, and I am humbled.

Day Two

The night was long, and the morning was slow in coming. The air temperature is still very cold. I stay encased inside the sleeping bags until the coldest part of the morning has passed. Daylight and some slight warmth slowly transpire as I begin to stir. Unzipping the tent door, I look outside. There are two elk visible within one hundred yards. They are facing away from my location and are oblivious to my presence. The tent is mostly covered in snow and might appear to the elk as a snow-covered boulder, blending into the snow-encrusted hillside. Stepping out of the tent, the sky is overcast but the wind has calmed. After breakfast, I ready for the day and strap on snowshoes to hike around the immediate vicinity. Nearby are several bison gathered amidst alder brush near Slough Creek. Exploring upstream, winter has encased everything—trees, boulders, and the landscape—with snow. While exploring further along the creek, I discover several large boulders deeper in the forest that would have provided better protection from the wind. Being what the circumstances were yesterday, my camp is where it is; I don't plan to move it. Fearful of venturing far in this foreign winter landscape, I am not sure what might be encountered. I don't want to fall through ice into freezing cold water, get lost, stumble into a boiling thermal feature, or become engulfed in an avalanche.

Journal notes for this day are sparse. My recollections are more emotional than factual. They are recollections of cautiousness. Of seeing a new world, one that I am not accustomed to. Of being filled with wonder. Wonder at being in a winter landscape filled with wildlife roaming and surviving here. Out of this experience, I developed a deep respect for wildlife's ability to endure cold and snow, and to thrive. Food, shelter, and warm clothes are the supplies that I have brought that allow me to live here for a few days. If I were to lose my equipment or supplies, my time surviving would be short. If I did not freeze to death, hunger and starvation would quickly come. Coyotes and foxes, with their acute hearing and sense of smell, can locate small mammals under snow. Leaping into the air, they pounce, diving nose first into soft snow and, astonishingly, emerge with a mouse. My senses are not acute enough to locate a mouse hidden under snow. Perhaps I could eat tree bark, but is it digestible? Could I follow a wolf pack until they kill an elk or bison, then, while carrying a sharpened stick, make myself look large, intimidating the pack into abandoning the carcass?

After exploring the area, I return to camp, make dinner and eat, then retire to the tent. I pull out the book about Colter to read through the evening, while wind with a mixture of drizzle and freezing rain pelt the tent. Putting the book down, I blow out the candle and turn off the flashlight. The storm pummels the tent through the night as I try to sleep. That night marked December 29th. I had not expected rain while camping in Yellowstone this time of year.

Day Three

I pack up gear and pull the sled back through the Slough Creek Valley under mostly overcast skies. The day has a dreary feel to it. It has been a good trip, but alas, I am disappointed. No wolves were sighted, and the weather was challenging. So much so that I ask myself: *Am I ever going to do this again?* Probably not. Arriving at the vehicle, I throw gear into the trunk. Before leaving Yellowstone, it is worthwhile driving through the Lamar Valley for one last chance at seeing a wolf in the wild. Coming across a vehicle parked at a roadside pullout, I see someone looking through a scope on a tripod. I wonder what he is viewing, elk or bison? Stopping to chat, he explains that he has a wolf pack in view. My heart leaps. He graciously lets me view through the scope.

Peering into the scope, I see five wolves resting in snow. This is the Druid Peak pack, captured in British Columbia and released into the park this past April. Not far from the wolves is a partially eaten bull elk carcass with large antlers rising upwards. A quarter mile to the left is a group of fifteen bull elk, again identifiable by large antlers. The elk are alert and tense. The wolves become active, come together, then run through deep snow on the side of the mountain. It is astonishing they have the energy to run through deep snow. They play and rest, then come together again for a group howl. Watching them brings a deep sense of satisfaction, both for having seen them and knowing that they now run wild in Yellowstone. They are active, healthy, full of life, and if I am not mistaken, enjoying themselves. Two are black and three are silver. Using my binoculars, I focus intently on a silver. Its guard hairs can be seen rising from the back of its neck. At times they growl at each other and play-fight. Now they came together again for another group howl. For a while they all lie and rest on the side of the snowy hill. They must not be very hungry, because they leave the carcass behind and run off into the distance. They can go back and eat when they want to. The carcass is aflutter with ravens, but no coyotes are present. It is delightful watching them energetically running through deep snow along the mountainside. I turn to leave and thank the person for letting me view them through his scope.

As I head home, I regard this trip as worth every discomfort, hardship, and struggle. Seeing a wild pack of wolves running through snow in Yellowstone was one of the most meaningful events of my life. The return of wolves restored a piece of Earth's ecosystem, and with my being here to see them, my spirit was lifted to new heights and a major theme of my life clicked into place.

Jasper National Park

Celestine Lake

Snake Indian River

De Smet Range

Celestine Lake Road

CELESTINE

"Take a course in good water and air; and in the eternal youth of Nature you may renew your own. Go quietly, alone; no harm will befall you."

—JOHN MUIR, *Steep Trails*, 1918

Mount Robson is the highest peak in the Canadian Rockies. Its imposing southwest side rises almost two vertical miles from its base. The north and east faces of Mount Robson have impressive cliff-hanging glaciers: Robson, Mist, and Berg. The latter plunges into icy cold Berg Lake where it calves off icebergs. One can reach a campsite on the shore of Berg Lake by hiking thirteen miles along a trail from Mount Robson's base. The trail travels through old-growth forest with massive one-thousand-year-old western red cedar and western hemlock, up through the Valley of a Thousand Waterfalls, then heartbreakingly switchbacks near awe-inspiring Emperor Falls. It skirts a glacial outwash plain and only then arrives at Berg Lake. The views are nothing short of epic. Beyond Berg Lake, trails lead to remote areas, some of which are closed part of the year while woodland caribou calve, feed, and rear their young.

Having hiked the spectacular Berg Lake trail on a previous excursion, I again felt the Canadian Rockies calling my soul. Thus, I am embarked on a fall camping and hiking trip to Jasper National Park, Alberta. Black bears, grizzlies, elk, moose, caribou, wolves, and cougars live where I will be hiking and sleeping. Nonetheless I plan to keep a clean camp and, as wildlife is encountered, will avoid any confrontation. I am looking to experience wilderness and see wildlife in their natural setting. Hiking and living in wilderness involves hazards, but I accept them, just as I accept the possibility of slipping in the shower, being in a car accident, or having a serious health diagnosis. Being of sound mind and body, I accept the risks. Should a bear or cougar attack and maim, or even kill me, I do not want the animal destroyed.

Despite working a desk job in Minneapolis, time in nature is vital to my psyche—whether at a local park or immersed in wilderness with predators. For most people, nature positively impacts their senses and well-being. For me, the very word *west* represents the North American frontier. A rugged, unexplored landscape of adventure that still contains predators. Or as Henry David Thoreau poetically wrote in an 1862 essay, "Eastward I go only by force; but westward I go free."

My flight from Minneapolis to Edmonton covers 1,200 miles in three hours. Two hundred years ago, the Lewis and Clark Expedition journeyed up the Missouri River 1,600 miles, from St. Louis to Fort Mandan, enduring five months of hardship. Despite the scientific and technical progress that has occurred since then, part of the western wilderness still exists and contains viable ecosystems with predators. Could Lewis or Clark, in their time, have conceived of traveling these distances across North America in three hours? Unlikely. Yet still, today, I endeavor to explore the great untamed western wilderness and encounter predators just as they did two centuries ago.

The place of my childhood was small-town Minnesota, north and west of Minneapolis. In my youth, I could walk out the back door to open prairie, the woods, or the tree-lined banks of the Mississippi where we used a rope swing to jump into the river. Back then, very little was developed. Today, however, with the doubling of the area's population, the place of my youth has been overrun by the sprawling Minneapolis-St. Paul metropolitan area.

In 1804, at the time of the Lewis and Clark expedition, Earth's population was about one billion people. In the year 2000, the world's population was a little over six billion. It's startling to think that at the end of 2022, the number is eight billion. Two hundred years from now, no one expects the world population to have increased at a six-fold rate as it did between 1800 and 2000. Current projections estimate that over the course of several decades, it will reach nine or ten billion. Beyond that, it is projected (or hoped) that global population will level and may decline.

Could Lewis and Clark have conceived of eight billion or more people living on Earth? Could they have conceived of 1.4 billion motor vehicles traveling across the planet? What about jet travel, capable of transporting people and goods a distance in three hours that would normally take five months? Could they have conceived of rocket ships, satellites orbiting overhead, humans walking on the moon, nuclear weapons, the internet, or cell phones? From Lewis and Clark's perspective, the future would have been very difficult to predict.

Rising standards of living—generating food, shelter, clothing, and medicine for evermore humans—inescapably puts pressure on nature, ecosystems, and wilderness. In the year 2200, one wonders how much wilderness, if any, there will be. If there are natural areas and wilderness, will there be functioning ecosystems and will there be predators living in them? The future is hard to predict.

Jasper National Park is home to a plethora of species whose ranges interestingly overlap. Here live predators—Canada lynx, wolverine, cougar, bobcat, wolf, coyote, mink, river otter, red fox, and grizzly and black bear. Prey species include elk, caribou, moose, mountain goat, bighorn sheep, marmot, porcupine, pika, mule deer, and whitetail deer. Bird species include golden eagle, bald eagle, great horned owl, boreal chickadee, spruce grouse, boreal owl, white-tailed ptarmigan, and rufous and calliope hummingbirds. Rufous males have an iridescent, rusty-orange throat, while calliope males sport spectacular rays of magenta on their throats. Both hummingbirds migrate here after a winter spent in central and southern Mexico.

This excursion is a backpacking trip to Jasper's Celestine Lake. The drive to the trailhead is sixteen miles along the Snaring River Road. The route eventually degenerates into a rough, one-lane gravel road with hairpin turns. Along the edges of the turns, steep cliffs drop away. There are no guardrails. Vehicle access is restricted to certain hours, based on ingoing (northerly) travel or outgoing (southerly) travel. The restrictions ensure (in theory) that incoming and outgoing traffic does not meet. Meeting another vehicle on the single-lane road at a hairpin turn would require one of the parties to back up around a corner. The views across the Snake Indian River and Athabasca River Valleys are spectacular, but I keep my eyes pretty much focused on the road.

Every few miles, I encounter large piles of bear scat lying in the road. Eventually I come to a parking area for the trailhead. Here there is a road closure as the bridge no longer allows vehicular traffic across the Snake Indian River.

Safely parked, I gather my backpack and begin a one-night back-pack trip. The hike from the trailhead to Celestine Lake is about four miles. As I set out, I recall reading that one should minimize odors when camping in grizzly country. But what about sweat after hiking several miles with a backpack? Should one clean sweat off with a damp towel before retiring to the tent for the night?

After seeing many piles of bear scat in the road, while hiking I begin talking to myself, saying, "Hello there, hey there," to alert any nearby bears. After a few short minutes, I cross a bridge over the aquamarine Snake Indian River, where I view steep cliffs forming the eastern edge of the river. The cliffs are sienna, gray, and dark purple, rising almost per-fectly vertically above the river. The nearly flat rock has deep fractures and crevices. At the top is steeply banked terrain sporadically covered with low-lying vegetation. Above that, where the terrain is less severe, it supports various evergreens. At the base of the cliffs, on a gravel bar in the river, is a dark black shape. Excited to be hiking, I ignore it, as I had just started out on this hike and want to reach Celestine Lake before evening. But pausing for a moment, I take a closer look.

About one hundred yards away is a bear with a glossy black coat. What a beautiful animal. Its head is down with its nose pointed toward its front feet. Claws on its front paws are holding something down. Looking closely, I see it has a white patch on its chest. It puts its nose into something and sniffs, but I can't tell what it is. Whatever it's doing, it is not frightened off by my presence or calling out, "Hey there." The pepper spray is strapped to my belt in a holster, but it is obviously not needed, as the bear is focused on the object at its feet. It almost looks as if it is licking a rock. But no. Maybe eating a fish? No, not that either. Ravens perched in nearby trees are cawing. It is difficult to discern what the bear is examining. The bear appears to be tugging at a furry carcass. It is a beautiful scene: the glossy black coat of the bear, its paws gripping brown, fur-covered carrion on the gravel bar, and sheer cliffs as a backdrop. Unfortunately, I did not bring binoculars, but I think it may be that a bighorn sheep had lost its footing and fell to its death. A rusty-colored butterfly flutters by while I stand still, quietly appreciating the scene. A red squirrel chatters in a nearby tree, and another red squirrel darts past just off the trail. There are four miles to put behind me before it gets dark, so I better get going. Turning, I leave the bear to its meal.

The trail veers to the right and then swings around to the left before going up an incline above the cliffs I admired from the bridge. Hiking along the trail, I come across bear scat every few hundred yards. The dried-out scat contains sedge, grass, and undigested traces of berries. Out of caution, I continue reciting my mantra: "Hey there, hey there."

Golden leaves of aspen, birch, and poplar form a translucent canopy as dappled sunlight sparkles on the forest floor. Periodically, leaves from high branches flutter down, glinting sunlight to-and-fro. It is perfect weather for a fall hike, with blue sky and cool crisp air. Everything is quiet and peaceful. Maybe a little too peaceful. Then I come across another large pile of bear scat and am reminded to repeat "Hey there!" Seeing so many piles of bear scat, I am starting to become concerned. It feels eerie with everything so peaceful. Again, I come across a pile of scat, but this one is different. It is composed of elongated, tubular pieces. It doesn't contain vegetation, but it does contain fur and small pieces of bone. Too large to be from a coyote, it must have been left by a wolf or a mountain lion. If it's from a mountain lion, then we are at the northernmost portion of their range. As deer expand their range northward, mountain lions are likely following. This particular scat, however, I suspect is from a wolf and not a mountain lion.

Moving along the trail, I come to a fork; I take the path to the right toward Celestine Lake, which winds through an open muskeg. Beyond the muskeg, a forested area is on the right. From the shadows of the forest emanates the sound of a large animal's feet rapidly hitting the ground as it runs, the sound fading in the distance. My suspicion is that it was a bear running away.

Beyond the muskeg, the trail winds to the left and then to the right before reaching a camping area on the shore of Celestine Lake. There is no one else here, there is no wind, so everything is calm and quiet. Walking around the area, I come across bear scat. There are picnic tables, camping pads, and a water pump. I fill a water bottle and take a drink of cool water. The tent is set up, and dinner is made. After eating dinner, I find the twelve-foot-high pole for hanging food. Tying a rope to a small branch, I throw the branch over the pole and hoist the food sack up. The glow of an almost-full moon is rising in the east over the tree-lined shore of the lake. After making a small campfire and watching the flames flicker into the evening, I let it die down to glowing embers. The mosquitoes are bothersome, so I get into the tent even though the evening is still young. I pull out a book about the search for and discovery of subatomic particles. One of the particles described is the Higgs boson, which is sometimes referred to as the "God particle." The Higgs boson was theorized by physicists in 1964. Almost fifty years later in 2012, it was confirmed by the CERN particle accelerator near Geneva, Switzerland.

Except for the buzzing of a few mosquitoes at the screen door, there is no sound. The glow of the moon shines on my tent as it rises in epic fashion. Moonbeams quietly shine through the trees, partially illuminating the tent except where tree branches cause variegated shadows to fall.

I have a candle burning for ambiance while reading, but it provides minimal light. So a flashlight is used to illuminate the book. Being that it is so quiet, and after seeing so many piles of bear scat, the darkness makes me a little nervous. To alleviate the silence, I unzip my pack which is just outside the tent, grab the camp stove, light it, and set it a few feet beyond the tent door. The hiss of the stove and the light emitted by its blue flame is reassuring. Perhaps the hissing sound and the open flame will make a bear wary about approaching. If a bear were to come by, I can grab the stove and direct its flames toward its face. While the stove's bright flames are comforting, there is not enough fuel to keep it burning all night.

After reading awhile, I look out the tent door to check the stove. The flames are small and there is no longer a hiss. Zipping open the door, I crawl out and grasp the stove base. Pumping the stove twenty times increases the pressure; the flames brighten and the hiss resumes. I carefully place the stove about three and a half feet away from the tent. My fear is that if it is too close, an awkward movement might cause it to tip, roll toward the tent, and cause the tent to go up in flames. That would be a disaster. The candle inside a holder hanging from the ceiling is pretty much burnt out. Digging through the gear bag, I put a new candle into the holder, light it, and hang it again. There is a slight breeze outside, causing the tops of the trees to gently sway. A nearby owl occasionally hoots. The moon comes and goes behind the clouds. When the moon isn't hidden, tree shadows slowly move back and forth on the tent wall.

It is time to put the book down and sleep. Reaching out the tent door, I turn off the stove. Inside the tent, I leave the candle burning, turn off the flashlight, and snuggle into the sleeping bag. The night is quiet, warm, and calm. Sleep comes fast, but it is fitful. I keep one eye partially open out of nervousness. At times I lie there with both eyes open, thinking and waiting. But nothing overt disturbs the night.

Day Two

Awakening around 5:00 a.m., I hear the pitter-patter of raindrops hitting the tent. Taking a peek outside, the tops of the trees are swaying heavily, but it is not raining except for a few single raindrops. Pinecones and twigs are blowing off tree branches. The horizon over Celestine Lake has the beginnings of daylight eking its way over dark trees across the lake. There are pink and gray clouds in the slowly lightening sky. Due to the proliferation of bear sign, and out of nervousness, sleep has been light and not very restful. The trees in front of the tent form dark silhouettes against the sky. Zipping the tent door back up, I look around inside the tent. The candle left burning last night has burnt down and disappeared.

The only sign of its existence is melted candle wax that dripped onto my sleeping bag and resolidified.

It is starting to rain now. The wind gathers speed and more pine-cones and twigs fall off trees. It is early morning, so I lie back down and fall back to sleep to the sound of rainfall. Finally I wake for good, and the rain has stopped. I get out of the tent and lower the food sack. Break-fast today is oatmeal, hot chocolate, and a chocolate candy bar. The driz-zle resumes, so I get back into the tent to do more reading. The weather continues to be cloudy and blustery, with much rain and drizzle. Not feeling like firing up the stove in this weather, I sneak outside for a quick lunch of pudding and a candy bar.

With a break in the rain, it's time to pack up. After stuffing the sleeping bag into its sack, I take down the wet tent and pack both into the backpack. Walking over to where the food is hung, I untie one end of the rope from a tree, lower the food sack from the bear pole, and pack it into the backpack. Heaving the pack onto my back, I hike away from Celestine Lake. Alongside the trail, near the muskeg, I come across deep-green moss. With the sky overcast and the ground wet, the colors are rich and satisfying. Upon close inspection, the moss and soil have been churned up—in some places to a depth of a foot. Something has been digging here, likely a bear. A portion of a honeycombed hive lies nearby. It appears that a bear dug up and ate yellow-jacket wasps, bees, or their nymphs.

Continuing on, there is wolf scat on the trail. This must be new as I would have noticed it yesterday. Further on, the trail forks. To the right is a pleasant view toward Princess Lake, but I don't take time to explore it. On the main trail beyond the fork, more moss and soil have been churned. Walking farther, I come across piles of pinecones and pine-cone scales. Squirrels have been eating pinecone seeds hidden under the scales, or possibly bears have been digging up and eating the seeds. Continuing forward on the trail, I come across several piles of bear scat. Much of it contains berries from the bearberry plant (also known as *kinnikinnick*). I see that the berries in the scat appear mostly intact. The low-growing plant is ubiquitous. It has thick, waxy, oval-shaped leaves and its berries are bright red. I pick a fresh berry off a nearby plant and open it using a fingernail, revealing a mealy core. Not sure how much nutritional value it has, as those in the scat don't appear to be well digested. There certainly is plenty of bear sign in this area.

I immerse myself in this magnificent landscape, enjoying the hike. After all, there is no better place to free one's mind of mundane concerns than hiking in the mountains, in cool, fresh air, inhaling glorious nature into one's soul. Oxygen is brought into lungs, transferred to the blood, and transported throughout the body. Hiking oxygenates the brain, engages the senses, and stimulates the mind. Not paying particular attention to the surroundings, my mind wanders to the "God particle."

I step off the trail to an area overlooking the aquamarine Snake Indian River. The ground is covered with kinnikinnick and bright-red berries. The view across the valley is spectacular. Dismal dark clouds cascade over the De Smet Range to the west. Rain pours from the clouds into the valley, as if God's giant brushstrokes had created the scene. The storm has not yet reached my location, but it is coming this direction. For no perceptible reason, I look back on the trail. There is a grizzly, perhaps one hundred yards away.

It is off to the side of the trail on a sloping area covered in low green growth. I am puzzled. Where did it come from? While deep in thought, hiking and daydreaming, did I forget to proclaim the "Hey there" mantra? We must have passed each other just a couple minutes ago. The bear is milling around eating kinnikinnick berries. I am tempted to approach for a better view, but that would be unwise. Once a bear takes notice of a person, it may flee, running off into the bush. If it does not flee, it may ignore the person. As the person edges forward, however, an imperceptible boundary is crossed. The bear becomes agitated, clicks its teeth, drools, or makes woofing sounds. These are signs of tension and distress—communicating in bear language, "stay away." Heed the warning—slowly back away. If the person continues to approach, there may be a charge, which may be a bluff. If it is not a bluff and the grizzly makes contact, resistance is futile. Struggling will trigger more agitation and fury until the person is no longer a threat. Playing dead is the recommended course. By playing dead, the bear will likely lose interest. Don't move until the bear has sufficient time to wander away; otherwise if it notices movement, it may return. If the bear does not wander off, the worst-case scenario, however unlikely, is that it attempts to devour its prey.

With these thoughts in mind, I decide there is no reason to cause an unintended confrontation. After watching the bear for ten minutes, it is time to move on. I am pleased with seeing a grizzly in the wild, watching it do what it does naturally from a safe distance, and not disturbing its behavior. Turning back toward the trailhead, I hike away.

It is meaningful being in a wilderness with bears and other predators, even if one does not see one. It is gratifying discovering a rock tipped over, a rotted tree ripped apart, or soil churned up—knowing that a bear has been looking for ants, grubs, termites, moth larvae, a gopher, or a ground squirrel—or coming across predator tracks, scat, or claw marks on trees. Seeing these signs and understanding that predators are doing what they have to do to survive in the wild makes them real.

Thinking about the grizzly behind me, my ears perk up to listen in case it decides to follow. After traveling no more than a few hundred yards, suddenly there is a disturbance—the sound of a large animal crashing through brush and breaking sticks. Looking toward the noise, ahead and to the left, is a dark shape visible through dense brush. It makes deep huffing sounds. I don't have a clear view but see the rear legs and paws of a black bear as it flees through thick brush.

Hmm, there is a black bear in front and a grizzly behind. The black bear is within one hundred yards. The grizzly is, I hope, at least four hundred yards behind. I unhitch the safety strap and take the pepper spray out of its holster. Holding the pepper spray in front of my body, I slowly advance with my thumb on the trigger. The trail makes a turn to the right as it approaches the river. Carefully, I shamble forward, knowing a black bear is in thick brush or around the bend. The loud rumble of the river drowns all sound. With two hundred feet between the trail and the river, I believe it is hidden in the forest. Being that the trail I am on is the only path to the trailhead, I proceed forward. I see the deep rushing rapids and know it would be dangerous for the bear to cross; thus there is little chance it has crossed the river. *It must be nearby, but where?* I don't have an inkling.

Warily, I follow the trail as it curves to the right and around the bend, to a point where it approaches the bridge. Slowly I approach, carefully gazing about, but the bear is nowhere to be seen. Looking upstream and beyond the bridge, there on the gravel bar below the cliffs—a dark object. Yes, the black bear. No, wait. Did it flee, come across the sheep carcass and pause to eat? That seems unlikely. It ignores my presence. That's the same behavior as yesterday. Then I figure it out: this is not the black bear that was running in brush a few minutes earlier. This is the black bear that was here yesterday. There's a grizzly several hundred yards behind. There's a black bear directly in front eating a sheep carcass. Now, there is another black bear in close proximity, but where?

Turning to the right, I look to see if it somehow slipped behind. I look up the hill toward the rear, sure enough—a large black shape! I must have walked past it while looking into the forest toward the rapids. With my back turned, it silently watched from a short distance. It is an adult. Its head is lowered and its eyes are focused—on me. It is nervous and pacing as it moves its head back and forth, maybe trying to get a whiff of my scent. I am fully focused on the here and now as I face this agitated black bear. But it is not stalking me. If anything, it is cornered, frightened, and is avoiding me. Maybe it thinks I am stalking it.

Here we are together, thirty yards apart, it watching me as I watch it. It has teeth and claws. I have pepper spray.

Keeping my body facing its direction, I slowly back away, avoiding sudden movements. Eventually I back onto the bridge and cross to the other side. Once across, I hike the last few hundred yards to the trailhead and recover a sense of security. That was a peculiar situation, encountering three bears in close proximity within an hour. Getting into the car, I take note of the weather. It is a cool, blustery day—overcast, intermittent rain, and drizzle. Not a great day for people to be out hiking, but maybe if one were a bear, it is good weather to be out foraging.

Arriving at the vehicle, I throw the backpack into the back seat, change out of my hiking boots and put on a fresh set of clothes. It is a relief being in the safety and comfort of a vehicle. I pull away from the trailhead and back towards civilization. There are few people out today, so I am not concerned about meeting another vehicle on the twisty, one-lane road. My thoughts are focused on returning to the comforts of a hot shower, a soft warm bed, and a hot meal.

Within a few short miles, I come across a bear in the road. This is a grizzly. I am not in a hurry, so give it plenty of distance. It ambles slowly down on the road, rounds a corner, and is out of sight. As I round the corner, I see it again—still on the road. It looks back at my vehicle, pauses a moment, then trundles off the road, walking up the open hillside. As I approach where it left the road, I stop the vehicle and watch it slowly amble up until it is out of sight—lost in thick brush.

A solid rain comes down as I navigate the winding road in solitude, deep in thought. The windshield wipers rhythmically swish back and forth, almost putting me into a trance. My mind mulls over the events of the last couple days as I drive back to civilization. The Earth and our Universe are truly fascinating and intriguing places.

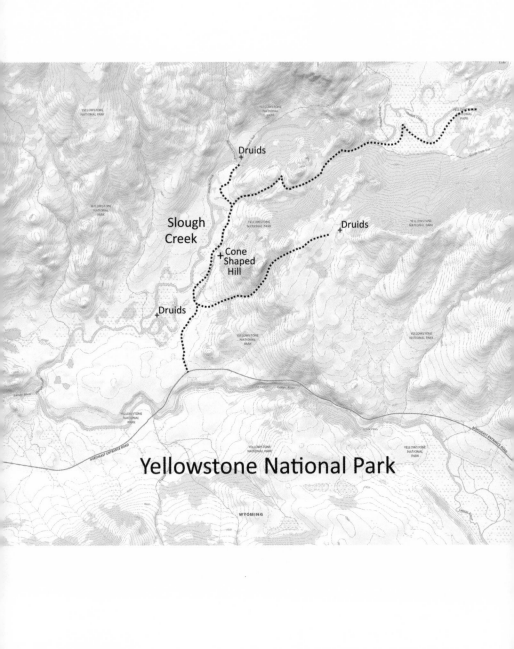

Druids

Slough
Creek

Druids

Cone
Shaped
Hill

Druids

Yellowstone National Park

WYOMING

DRꙌIDS

"The wolf is neither a saint nor a sinner
except to those who want to make it so."

—David Mech, *Journal of Biological Conservation,* 2012

There are several wolf packs with territories up and down Yellowstone's
Lamar Valley as well as where Slough Creek empties into the Lamar
River. One of the packs I am again venturing to see is the Druid Peak
pack. They are my old "friends," as we have seen each other a few times
over the years.

The oldest members of the pack, its founding members, were part
of the reintroduction program which translocated wolves from northern
Alberta. Minnesota has two to three thousand wolves spread throughout the northern forested part of the state. But wolves in Minnesota are
not easy to spot and watch. Wolves in Yellowstone, however, are visible
across broad valleys and open vistas. Thus my motivation for traveling a
thousand miles by car across the frozen landscape of North Dakota and
Montana is to improve my odds of seeing them.

On this trip, I start at the trailhead, pulling a sled loaded with gear
toward Slough Creek. There is four inches of snow on the ground with
four bison lying nearby. As I trudge onward, the bison stand and face
me. After circling the bison, I pause to take off outer layers of clothing
when I notice large wolf tracks, but they do not appear to be crisp and
fresh. Upon approaching Slough Creek, I leave the sled and gear, circling
around to look at various areas for camp. There is an excellent site just

ten feet from the rushing waters of Slough Creek. The spot is under a large fir, whose outstretched branches have shielded a sandy area from snow. The bare spot is where I set up the tent. The site gets good sunlight in the afternoon and early evening and is below the upper creek bank which protects it from wind. It is a bright sunny day. Nearby a huge tree has recently fallen into Slough Creek with its roots carving out a chunk of the creek bank.

After organizing camp, I explore upstream and into the shadows of trees where I come across a huge snow-covered boulder on the creek-bank. Further upstream, the creek is frozen over, forming an ice shelf to the far bank. Snow has accumulated in deep drifts supported by the ice. Beneath the snow and ice, the creek rumbles. It is tempting to cross to explore the far side, but I don't chance it. On the other side of the creek, a hawk spirals near a sunlit cliff. Continuing further, I step over a log which has snagged a tangle of black fur. The six-inch-long morass is probably from a bison or a bear. A bear could nimbly get over the log, but could a bison lift its legs or jump over the log? The air is perfectly still and quiet. I return to camp for dinner.

After dinner, I explore downstream. Coming across wolf tracks, I follow them for a few hundred yards along the creek edge. There in the snow, mingled with the wolf tracks, is a patch of yellow snow. Back-tracking, I follow my tracks back toward camp. Peering through trees, I see my tent in the distance, which now has several bison milling around it. By the time I arrive back at camp, the bison have moved on. The tent is not disturbed. A beautiful streak of pink clouds float in blue sky to the west. Above the clouds, Venus shines brightly as I listen to the heavy breathing and grunting of bison.

Sitting in the tent, the evening is quiet as I turn on a small radio to listen to news of the world. It crackles and hisses until it picks up a station from Fresno. Traffic is snarled as commuters are at a standstill. There is no place I would rather be right now than here, content in a warm sleeping bag. Turning the dial, the radio picks up a station from Nebraska, and next, a Salt Lake station airing the Utah Jazz home game. It is dark in the tent, but with a small flashlight there is a dim light. With each exhalation I see my breath as I tune to a talk radio program. They are discussing presidential election results for Al Gore vs. George W. Bush. It has been two weeks since the election, but it is not decided.

Moving on, the speaker crackles and hisses but generates no further intelligible sounds. As for politics, I am glad to be able to forget it, at least for a while. There are few concerns here: physical activity, exploring the landscape and watching wildlife in cool weather, good hot food, and a warm sleeping bag at night. Feeling content with the day's activities, I turn the radio and flashlight off and set my glasses aside. It is exhilarating knowing I am in wilderness with wolves, grizzlies, bison, elk, cougars, and coyotes on a primordial landscape covered in ice and snow. Curled up in my two sleeping bags, I drift off to sleep, just as content as a grizzly in hibernation.

Approximately 3:00 a.m.

Huffing and grunting sounds are outside the tent. Heavy footsteps are plodding through snow. Sitting up, I unzip a door flap and put my face to the door's mesh, peering into darkness. Just a foot away is shaggy fur. The form moves on, toward the creek, but soon another shaggy form appears and trudges by. Bison are on the move—walking by the tent. A large bison pauses, putting its hoof just inches from the tent base. Its breathing is heavy. Its smell earthy. Now I am nervous. A swift kick could bash me in the head. I pull my face away from the screen. Ice creaks and groans as the bison traverse the creek. Then the sound of tremendous cracking, next crashing through ice into shallow water. After the crash, more huffing and grunting as they wade to the far side.

Day Two

The temperature this morning is -5°F while I eat oatmeal and sip hot chocolate. My toes sting from the cold as I begin my hike up Slough Creek, but with further activity and as the morning cold dissipates, they warm up. There is an unseen bird in the heights of a tree making cawing sounds, likely a raven. Further on, I am pleased to come across wolf tracks. Beyond the wolf tracks are cute little tracks made by a chipmunk or squirrel. Following the wolf tracks, I come across large, fresh, dark wolf scat. Continuing on, the tracks lead to a meadow where sixteen bison are grazing in the distance. Red squirrels are chattering and chasing each other in nearby trees. Despite the cold and snow, the red squirrels are quite active.

I follow the wolf tracks into the meadow where the snowscape is crisscrossed by bison tracks and now another set of tracks made by elk. To the left are craggy cliffs dusted with snow.

Here at the meadow, I pause to behold. At the meadow's edge are conifers covered in frost and snow. The wind picks up, glittering branches sway; flakes of snow and large crystals fall, making tinkling sounds. It feels like a miracle created solely for my pleasure in solitude. But I am not alone. I am surrounded by life that endures, survives, and thrives in this harsh but dazzling winter landscape. Yellow grasses covered in sparkling frost emerge from the snow. Hiking onward, I come across a bowl of snow that has melted, then refrozen into the concave shape of a moose's body. Scattered about are piles of brown ovoid pellets: fresh moose scat. Possibly my arrival has disturbed a moose, and it left shortly before I was able to get a glimpse. There are birds ahead, cawing, as I follow the wolf tracks. Then a crashing sound comes from the woods, interrupting the cawing. Looking in the direction of the sound, a Canada jay sits on the tip of a small fir. Red squirrels continue their chatter. The crashing sound was likely the moose. The wolf tracks approach a large tree, then circle it. Looking at the tree's base, I expect to find a yellow patch of snow, but there isn't one.

Rising out of the middle of the meadow is a snow-covered, rocky hill. It would allow a good view of the meadow and nearby hillsides, so I hike toward the top. Scattered in multiple locations are piles of old, dried moose droppings. Nearby brush emerging between rock outcrops has been snipped off by a moose. At the top of the hill is a blackened dead snag with bright lime-green lichen growing on it. It was probably struck by lightning. Scanning the vicinity, there are four massive bull elk, each with impressive antlers, at a distance of eighty yards to the northeast and on the other side of the creek. One of them sees me and we stare at each other for a few moments. The others, with their heads down, paw at the snow and pay no attention to my presence. I stand at the top of the hill taking in the wild grandeur.

After spending two hours on the hilltop, reading and silently observing the Slough Creek meadow and wildlife, I am famished and hike back to camp.

After lunch, the afternoon hike is downstream toward the Lamar River. After an hour, I climb to the top of a small, cone-shaped hill that has large boulders and fir trees. The overlook offers a broad vista of Slough Creek toward the west and south. Despite the chill in the air, the scene invites me to sit. I spend the afternoon reading and napping behind a large granite boulder. Periodically I stand to stretch and use binoculars to scan hills and gullies in the valley as well as the mountainsides. I lean my chest against the boulder with elbows resting on its surface to steady the binoculars. From this hidden position, I scan for movement or dark shapes. There are plenty of dark objects to inspect against the white snow. Despite my hope, nothing moves, and the dark objects turn out to be bushes, stumps, rocks, and tree snags.

The main part of the afternoon slowly burns off as the sun moves in an arc toward the mountains on the western horizon. I begin to wonder whether it is worth spending hours becoming chilled to the bone. There are many black dots in the distance, which appear to be bison. Using binoculars, I can see they are indeed bison but are partially hidden by willow and alder, standing in small groups sprinkled along meandering oxbows of the creek. I think about heading back to the tent, making a hot meal for dinner, and warming up in the sleeping bag. What is the point of sitting in snow behind a boulder, chilled for hours, periodically standing to stare at bison grazing and lumbering around? They continue their existence perfectly adapted to cold weather, foraging, competing, mating—whether I am watching or not. Bison mating season ended three months ago. If this were the fall rut, bulls would be fighting for females, headbutting, and challenging each other's strength and endurance. If a bull is gored, suffers serious injury, or is exhausted, it becomes vulnerable to a grizzly or wolf pack.

The cold wears on my body after sitting silently for the afternoon, so I pull a jacket, hat, and gloves out of my daypack and put them on. If I were up and about stomping around, exploring this area, I would be warm. Negative thoughts swirl: *Should I go back to the tent? Is this worth it?* Though the orb of the sun is below the western horizon, the sky glows with wisps of salmon-colored clouds hanging in violet twilight.

I am about to get up and return to the tent. Abruptly, there is a spine-tingling low-pitched moan that draws out for twenty seconds, raising the hairs on the back of my neck. The mournful wailing comes from the southwest, the direction of Slough Creek oxbows and meadows. That was not a single howl but a chorus. Slowly rising to my feet and carefully peeking over the boulder, I raise the binoculars to scan the valley floor. Nothing . . . nothing that I can see anyway. But I know what I heard. It was the unmistakable howling of wolves. After a several-minute pause, the twilight deepens; then again, the pack howls. I look vainly in the direction of the sound but again see nothing. They are hidden in a gully or behind a low rise. They have been resting and napping all afternoon, while I have been reading and, like the wolves, occasionally napping. From their howls I can tell their location is not far off. Again, the group howls, and I listen for several minutes. Now a long, dead silence of perhaps twenty minutes. I patiently scan the hills, but wherever they are, they are not visible.

Waiting on my little cone-shaped hill, I wonder if anything more is going to happen. The pack does not make an appearance. This is exciting, but as I am cold and hungry, it is time to return to camp. Twilight is fading, and if the pack stirs, they will not be visible. Attempts at photography will be fruitless. It occurs to me that if I linger too long, I will be walking in the dark back to camp and could stumble across a pack of hungry wolves on the prowl for prey. Nevertheless, with binoculars, I focus on a small hilltop that has glowing sky just above. Darn, this is disappointing, bone-chilling, and futile. Time to return to the tent.

With a last glance toward the top of the ridgeline, the shape of a black wolf silhouettes against the luminous western sky. Standing still, it inspects its domain with calm, quiet confidence. My breathing ceases. For what seems like an eternity, with its head held high, the wolf gazes over its realm.

Then, just as soon as it was there, the black wolf trots down the hillside into a gully and disappears. But for a moment or two, it was a spectacular sight. Starting to breathe again, I scan low elevations and into the gully's murkiness, but it is nowhere in sight. Then in an instant, at the top of the hill, another wolf appears. It too pauses, then descends and disappears into the gully. Now a third wolf appears on the hilltop, pauses, and descends into the gully. Staring through the binoculars at the ridgeline I am fixated. A fourth and a fifth appear and disappear. At this point I start counting, almost subconsciously. That has been five so far. *Wow, this is why I am here!* Again, I scan the gully, hoping to peer into its shadows, but wherever they are, they are hidden. Cunning creatures, following the bottom of the gully, getting closer to prey before being noticed.

Focusing on the top of the hill, another wolf appears and disappears. Then another and another. Ten, eleven, twelve, thirteen—where they are going, I cannot say. The gully angles toward my location. Nineteen, twenty, twenty-one, twenty-two . . . and counting. Standing behind the boulder, I am out of view except for my shoulders and head. With luck, they will rise out of the gully and appear directly in front of me. That would be awesome. But the gully veers to the left. As I search for the leaders, the rolling terrain makes their location uncertain. The pack is hidden, traveling single file along the gully bottom. I focus on the top of the hill, where more wolves appear and disappear. So far, I estimate to have seen twenty-four to twenty-eight wolves. There is only one pack in Yellowstone that is this large: the Druid Peak pack. Twenty-seven strong, the Druids are dominant, and here I am, standing within their territory, within their domain, within their kingdom, inside their empire.

Fortunately or unfortunately—depending upon one's frame of mind—the entire pack is now traveling in my general direction. They don't know that I am hidden here, behind a boulder. I don't know where they are, except that they are nearby and getting closer. A wolf pack this size has a lot of mouths to feed. If they approach, what if they become curious or aggressive? I picture myself standing on the boulder in darkness with twenty-seven wolves snapping at my feet. That would make for a long night.

Looking into gray dusk, the terrain is fuzzy and vague. Finally, I spot the leader rise out of a gully. It pauses, then trots into foothills to the left. One by one, the rest appear and follow the leader. I blink a few times, then clean off my eyeglasses. As the last of the wolves climb out of the gully and disappear into the foothills, I know what they are doing. They are searching for prey.

I wait to see if anything further develops. Venus shines crisply and brightly. The pack has traveled east and up toward Bison Peak. After waiting for twenty minutes to see if anything further develops, it is time to return to camp.

While walking back, the sound of Slough Creek gurgles to the left as I tramp in darkness. But now there is heavy breathing as large black shapes block the path. I approach slowly. The bison grunt and snort, then scatter, melding into the night's blackness. Beyond this group, there is another, but this group doesn't scatter, so I circle around, walking through a grove of trees and over deadfall.

Back at the tent, I put on a headlamp and gather a dry bag of food and cooking gear. Walking a few steps to the creek edge, I dip a pot into the creek, filling it with icy water. Next, I set up the stove and flick the lighter. The lighter sparks but there is no flame. To warm the lighter, I put it under my clothing against my bare skin. Once warmed, I flick the lighter and transfer the flame to the stove, igniting a blue circular flame. Carefully, I set the pot of water on the stove. Not wanting to waste battery life, I turn off the headlamp. While sitting in the darkness, staring at the stove, I hear the clunking sounds of bison. It takes several minutes for the water to boil. I add a packet of powdered cream of chicken soup, dehydrated corn, peas, carrots, and onions. A packet of chicken-flavored noodles is put into the mix, then topped with a sprinkle of pepper. The hot soup warms me under the crisp starlit sky. I reflect back on a satisfying day knowing that I will fall asleep in a cozy little tent next to Slough Creek surrounded by wolves, elk, and bison.

Inside the tent, I change out of damp socks and turn on the transistor radio. Turning the dial to news talk, the Florida Supreme Court has ruled that a recount of the Al Gore vs. George W. Bush election can continue. I click off the radio and lie down—eventually falling asleep. After deep sleep, I am awakened by freezing and cracking noises from the creek. Then a booming and crashing sound. A bison or moose has broken through the ice. Not bothering to sit up to see what it was, I turn over and fall back to sleep.

4:00 a.m.

In the middle of the cold black night, I am awakened by howling. Opening my eyes, I see nothing but darkness. The mournful cries come from the other side of the creek. This is not the tremendous sound of the entire Druid pack but perhaps six to eight wolves. Warmly ensconced in the sleeping bag, I shut my eyes and listen to their sorrowful bass harmony. They are aware of my camp. Otherwise, why would they be nearby howling? I try to fall back asleep but my feet are cold. Sitting up, I rub them and look out the tent door. There are six bison about twenty-five yards away plodding through snow. In the dim starlight, they approach the creek, then crash through the ice as they cross. The wolves are gone, and I fall back asleep.

Day Three

After breakfast, I hike north along Slough Creek. After a cold night, being on my feet and hiking warms me up. There is a large pile of wolf scat on the trail. Now I come across the disarticulated remains of an elk—skull, leg bones, vertebrae, and scattered fur. Further on, I pause to listen. Up the valley to the north, far off in the distance and hidden in the foothills, the Druids howl in unison.

Cold and hungry, I return to camp for lunch, then trek downstream toward the Lamar. Here are the tracks of a single wolf. Its prints are on top of my sled tracks and travel in the same direction. *Was it tracking me? Maybe I should look to the rear more often.* After heating ham and bagels for dinner, I rapidly wolf down the meal and start water to boil for hot chocolate. Holding the cup of hot chocolate with both hands, I slowly sip it, warming up while savoring the sun slowly dipping to the west. Turning in for the night, I read by flashlight before falling asleep.

3:30 a.m.

Noises outside the tent rouse me from my slumber. Unzipping the tent door, I peer out to see the dark shape of a bison trudging nearby. Watching it for a few moments, I zip the door closed but now hear rhythmic purring. Peeking outside again, there is nothing but murky darkness. Perhaps a bobcat or Canada lynx? Maybe a cougar? Cougars are rarely seen, but there is a healthy population in Yellowstone's Northern Range, including the Slough Creek area. But then again, raccoons, skunks, and badgers make purring-like sounds. Tilting my head, I try to locate the purring. Breaking the moment, the Druids start howling. After the howling, I listen more, but now everything is quiet. Zipping closed the tent door, I recline, shut my eyes, and resume my slumber.

Day Four

Today is Thanksgiving. I slept warm and am content. As I get out of the tent, freezing cold stings my exposed skin. I put on a hat, gloves, and face mask. There are millions of butterfly ice crystals adhering to the tent, the sled, and every object. Walking out of the shade and into sunshine, the snow-covered landscape shines with a multitude of sparkling crystals reflecting sunlight. Bending down, I ponder the intricate, whirling, feather patterns. Up through the cold-crisp air is vivid blue sky. If I were not here to appreciate the crystals, would they be here? *Did God create this grandiose snowscape just for me?* Jarring me, there is pain; my left leg is hurting. Maybe I strained a tendon or ligament navigating snow-covered rocks yesterday.

After filling my daypack with supplies, I hike south and west. Traveling a couple miles, I trudge up a rise overlooking Slough Creek and set up a campstool. In the quietness there is a woodpecker tapping. Magpies chatter as they fly by. There is a long lateral moraine that parallels the north side of the valley. Terminal moraines and glacial erratic boulders are deposited where Slough Creek joins the Lamar River.

Coyotes are yipping, their sound echoing through the valley. Wolves have deep, drawn-out howls and will kill coyotes. When wolves were reintroduced into Yellowstone in the mid-1990s, coyotes had to contend with a large, fast, more powerful competitor. Despite this, coyotes learned to scavenge off wolf kills by grabbing a chunk of meat or bone and running off. This is a dangerous game of survival. If wolves are nearby and see the coyote, they will chase it, and, if caught, kill it. In the aftermath of wolf reintroduction, Yellowstone's coyote population dropped. Several generations later, however, coyotes have rebounded.

Bundled up in warm clothes while sitting on my campstool at seven thousand feet of elevation, I slowly scan the snow-covered mountainous landscape, taking in wondrous views. At this moment I feel at peace, contentment, and gratitude. But it is time to move on.

Folding up the campstool, I attach it to the daypack and head east toward foothills that abut lower flanks of Bison Peak. Following a worn game trail, slowly hiking upwards, I stumble on a robust leg bone. It must be the femur of a bison, moose, or bear. Pausing, I set up the stool and sit. Picking up the bleached white bone, I rotate it in my hands. It is quite hefty. Whatever the species, it very naturally could be used as a club. Using the binoculars, I patiently scan the landscape, looking for the Druids. Peering down into the valley, the silver-and-black Lamar threads across the snowscape toward its confluence with the Yellowstone.

Proceeding onward, I see more bones scattered about and protruding through snow. Stepping over them, I continue to higher elevations. At a plateau, I come across several beds made by bison or elk where snow has melted and refrozen. Beyond the beds, there is a large elk antler whose tines rise through the snow. The antler could be one that was shed or may be associated with the bones. Unhurriedly, I continue my progress, occasionally pausing to look past nearby brush and into the shade of evergreens where large boulders are strewn about. Upon reaching the shade of a large Douglas fir, I sit and rest. There are fir cones and cone fragments scattered about—left by squirrels.

It is satisfying hiking in a craggy landscape among large lichen-covered boulders and twisted evergreens. Leaving the fir tree behind, my slow pace continues up the hillside. Looking forward, just ahead in the shadows of a thicket of evergreens, there is a subtle movement. It may be the swaying shadow of a tree branch. Or maybe something more.

Stopping in my tracks, my breathing slows while my vision zooms to the movement. Among tall yellow grass and in the shade of trees is a dark shape, likely a rock. No . . . wait, that is not a rock! A black wolf raises its head above the grass. It is focused to the left and is unaware of my presence. Everything below its neck and shoulders is concealed by grass and brush. Behind and to its rear is another wolf. This one is gray; its head is down and eyes are shut. Immediately, I drop to my stomach, hiding behind grass and sage.

How fortuitous is this? To slowly hike up a hillside and encounter resting wolves without them detecting me. I lie quiet and still for ten minutes. Now I take a quick peek. Propping up on my arms and raising my upper body above the grass, I see the original black wolf, the gray wolf just behind it, and three more black wolves back in shadows near a huge boulder. After the glimpse, I lie back down. There could be unseen wolves behind the boulder or farther in the darkness in the thick of the trees. Resting in snow behind cover, I wait. It is a privilege being here, in their company, and in a place where wild predators live freely. *How rare is that?*

After an hour, I take a chance, prop myself up again, and take another peek. The wolves are still there. The air is calm, but my scent may have wafted over to them. One stands, sniffs the ground, sniffs the air, then walks deeper into the grove. The remaining wolves stand and follow its lead, slowly fading into shadows. Now using binoculars, I watch for several moments as they are visible between trees, until finally, they are fully obscured in darkness. From their unhurried demeanor, I know they have not gone far—and are just beyond the grove of trees.

There is no need to leave, so I wait. Maybe something more will occur. Briefly, I consider following, but I don't want to modify their behavior. Like deer hunting, wolf watching requires patience, stealth, and observation. Rather than savoring venison after a hunt, I will be savoring memories for the rest of my life. It would have been nice to have gotten a photo, but doing so would have alerted them to my presence and altered their behavior. My satisfaction is being in their presence and sharing a bit of space and time. It is hard to say, but two hundred years from now, experiences such as this may be very rare.

Now there is a strange droning sound. I hold my head up to listen. Looking to the sky, it is crystal clear and blue, no clouds, and the sun is shining brightly. There is no wind. It is late afternoon. Wolves are howling. From the tremendous cacophony, more than five are howling. Many more. The entire pack, twenty-seven strong, is howling. It is a rare thing to hear, and one I will never forget—a vibrant and vigorous reverberation emanating from the other side of the grove. Words can't describe it, but this is an attempt: it sounds like a very large truck with horn blaring, screaming down a highway at high speed.

Lying in the snow I continue to listen, but now there is silence. Sitting in sunshine and bundled in layers of clothes, I am warm and comfortable. My eyes close to reduce the harsh glare of sunlight reflecting off snow. My head droops. After several minutes, across the hillside, howling again resonates, with a blend of deep and high-pitch sounds—adults and young raging in chorus. Now things are quiet, and I wait. After several minutes, there is growling, snarling, and guttural noises. Several wolves are agitated and fighting. The growling is deep and throaty, so these are not wolf pups. I imagine the pack fighting a grizzly as the growling and snarling are intense. Maybe there is a carcass and they are fighting over leftovers. Or it may be a dispute about hierarchy or mating.

Sitting amid gnarled branches of large sagebrush with silver-green leaves, I listen to the Druids, sometimes howling, sometimes fighting. Sagebrush can survive in semiarid conditions and can live up to one hundred years. Unusual for a non-coniferous plant, sagebrush retains some leaves even through winter. Most animals don't eat the bitter leaves, but two thrive on them—sage grouse and the Western Hemisphere's fastest land animal, pronghorn antelope. Before European conquest, it is estimated that more than 30 million pronghorns thrived in sagebrush and prairie biomes. By the 1920s, pronghorn were reduced to 13,000. Today there are between 500,000 and 1 million. Being North America's fastest land animal, what predator can chase down an adult pronghorn? There are none in North America, but cheetah of Africa and Southwest Asia could. It has been proposed that extinct species of cheetah-like cats were the evolutionary sculptors for pronghorn, with skeletons of the North American cheetah found in Natural Trap Cave in northern Wyoming and the La Brea Tar Pits in southern California.

The sweet, aromatic fragrance of sage brings back memories of my first trip to the West decades ago. Nothing represents the wide-open space of the American West more than gazing at a mountain vista while smelling sagebrush. The sun continues its progress to the western horizon as it is now early evening. In the western sky, a brilliant motionless point of light catches my eye. It does not have a contrail, so it can't be a jet plane. A balloon? No. That is Venus, one of the few celestial objects that can be seen in daylight.

With darkness approaching, it is time to get off the hillside and return to camp. I descend slowly, stopping every few hundred feet to sit and observe. The sun sets and darkness comes. A shortcut through snow and trees forces me to slide on my butt. Now on the valley floor, I walk around dark shapes to a symphony of heavy breathing and snorting. Dinner is cooked in the dark. Rice and noodles, a toasted bagel with margarine, and hot chocolate. Then to the tent for sleep.

1:45 a.m.

A loud, deep howl awakens me. From the low, throaty pitch of the howl, this is an adult. It doesn't fear the tent or my presence. I lift my head to hear better. There is a long pause and then it howls again. This lone wolf is away from its packmates, just on the other side of Slough Creek. I peek outside the tent and shine a flashlight across the creek into the black night. Nothing is visible except the white bank of snow on the far side. Turning the flashlight off, I zip the tent door shut and lie down.

2:00 a.m.

The wolf howls again, then all is quiet. Moments later, several wolves howl from the north, up the Slough Creek Valley. For several moments, I listen in darkness to silence. Then the nearest wolf howls, and in response, distant wolves howl. They are calling to each other. Being that my campsite is within their territory, this must be a subgroup of the Druids. Feeling around in the dark, I find my pepper spray. I place it next to my sleeping bag and lie back down, hoping to fall asleep again. Now all is quiet.

2:15 a.m.

The nearby wolf howls strong and loud. A progression of wolves up and down the valley howl in response. Now, silence. Then, the sharp sound of ice cracking on the creek. Moments later, the shattering sound of a branch splintering. More ice cracking. Again, the sound of a branch cracking. Thoughts swirl: *Wolves are masters at preying on elk. I am not an elk. I smell nothing like an elk.* That is my mantra as I fumble around in darkness for the pepper spray. Sleep finally comes while the wolves continue howling back and forth. My dreams are fantastical.

Day Five

Upon waking, I peek my head out the tent door. The sky is overcast—the sun an obscured, subdued halo. There is glorious peaceful snow falling across the landscape. Today is going to be a marvelous day. Was the howling I heard last night real? Was it part of a wild dream? Checking my journal, it indicates the exact times I heard howling. It was not a dream. I am gratified to have had the experience.

In the early 1900s, wolves were routinely killed by Yellowstone rangers and by 1930 were eliminated from the park. The elk population grew, thus exerting browsing and grazing pressure. Drought in the 1930s worsened conditions. With less vegetation holding topsoil in place, hillsides eroded. To reduce grazing, browsing, and erosion, rangers killed elk and relocated them outside the park. For thirty years, park rangers replaced one predator—wolves—with another—humans. When rangers stopped culling elk in the 1960s, the northern-range elk herd numbered 4,000. With no wolves, and with cougar and grizzlies greatly diminished, the herd grew to 18,000 in the 1990s.

At the time of my first winter trip to Yellowstone in December of 1996, I saw dozens of elk resting lazily on the Lamar Valley floor in the frigid cold where Soda Butte Creek enters the Lamar River. Wolves had recently been reintroduced into the park but were still few. One could walk to the top of hills and scan snow-covered plateaus to see large groups of elk pawing at snow for grasses and other plants. Now with wolves well established, in many areas elk are not as visible, preferring to graze and browse near cover where they are less vulnerable. One study shows that during summer, elk avoid wolves by moving to higher elevations, less open habitat, burned forest areas, and steeper slopes. Another study indicates that Yellowstone's "Landscape of Fear" is enhanced by wolves, with elk—especially female elk with calves—more vigilant where wolf packs roam.

With wolves present, and cougars and grizzlies having increased, elk numbers have decreased from their high, and their behavior is modified. Growth of willow, aspen, and alder in open areas and along stream banks is enhanced. Increased growth provides additional shelter and habitat for smaller mammals and birds.

When wolves were returned in 1995, none of the prey species, including elk, had experience with wolves. Coyotes, cougars, grizzly and black bears, yes. But wolves, no. For healthy adult elk, besides cougars and wolves, predators are not a severe threat. Without wolves, coyotes partly filled the niche typically held by wolves—sometimes hunting in packs. Now with wolves present, coyotes hunt alone, in pairs, or infrequently triples. During spring, summer, and fall, coyotes eat voles, pocket gophers, ground squirrels, and snowshoe hares. In the spring, they may prey on elk calves and pronghorn fawns. During winter, elk carrion supplies a good portion of coyote food intake. Coyotes prey on vulnerable elk yearlings—and adult elk if weakened by harsh winter conditions—in late winter, and they occasionally take down an adult elk if it is caught in deep snow. Grizzlies and black bears are generally not fast enough or have enough stamina to chase down healthy, mature elk. But they do prey upon yearlings, especially in the springtime, and grizzlies occasionally prey on adult elk if the elk is injured or disabled. Cougars are solitary ambush hunters, commonly hiding among rock outcrops and cliffs near creeks and rivers. When prey comes within striking distance, a cougar makes a powerful burst toward it. In Yellowstone, cougars prey on elk and mule deer, and sometimes bighorn sheep, pronghorn, and even moose.

Wolves hunt alone, in pairs, or in packs. A single, full-grown, experienced wolf can take down many types of powerful prey, including elk, bighorn sheep, moose, and occasionally bison—especially if they are injured or old. Unlike cougars, wolves often hunt in open terrain and at times will relentlessly follow a weakened or vulnerable animal for hours, and sometimes for days.

In January of 1995, fourteen wolves from three separate wolf packs were captured east of Canada's Jasper National Park and brought to Yellowstone. Each pack lived in chain link enclosures for ten weeks—one near Crystal Creek, one near Rose Creek, and one near Soda Butte Creek. While in the enclosures, they were fed road-killed deer and elk. After the acclimation period, they were released in March. For the first time in seventy years, wild wolves roamed the wilderness of Yellowstone. What would they do? Would they passively wait for delivery of roadkill as they had become accustomed to in the pens? Or would they revert to wild predatory ways—hunting deer, elk, bighorn sheep, moose, and bison? Now, with hungry wild wolves roaming the Lamar Valley, thousands of elk and other prey species had no experience with cunning, powerful, fast, pack-hunting predators. The genes of prey species, however, are sculpted by predators. Would instincts for avoiding predators kick into gear? In 1996, seventeen more wolves from four families were captured in Canada and released into the park.

With the restoration of wolves to the Yellowstone ecosystem, the realization of Aldo Leopold's land ethic was achieved: "A thing is right when it tends to preserve the integrity, stability and beauty of the biotic community. It is wrong when it tends otherwise."

How and why did the Druids grow from five to twenty-seven wolves just five years after reintroduction? With no wolves in Yellowstone for seventy years, were elk and other prey naïve? Did Yellowstone's prey species need to relearn survival skills and competencies? In 1995, the northern range elk herd was near a high point at 18,000 and near ecological carrying capacity. Being plentiful and unsophisticated with regard to wolves, maybe the newly introduced members of Druids had an easy time hunting?

Elk being unfamiliar with wolves did not necessarily make them easier prey, as David Mech's study indicates. During the severe winter of 1997, hunting success was 26 percent, compared to 15 percent during the mild winter of 1998. The severity of the winter and not prey naiveite was the larger factor.

With elk abundant, perhaps competition among wolf pack members was reduced. Typically, a single pair within a pack breed and have pups. During the spring of 2000, however, three Druid females bred and gave birth. Twenty-one pups were born with all but one surviving. By 2001, Druid's numbers had risen to thirty-seven—one of the largest packs recorded. From their inception in the park in 1996, the Druids fiercely defended their territory from other packs—from Slough Creek through the Lamar Valley up to Yellowstone's northeast entrance near Cooke City. In 2002, the Druids broke apart into several splinter packs, and by the end of 2010, they no longer existed as a pack. Their legacy, however, in the form of offspring and genes, are carried forward to today, and hopefully far into the future.

After disassembling the tent, I pack up the sled and prepare to leave my creek-side home. I have gotten to know the ebb and flow, the day-to-day pace, of this area. Life here is peaceful and unhurried, even tranquil. Except of course, when a predator chases and takes down prey. In the wilderness, there is no urgency to do anything except to be alive and enjoy life. Now, if only one could encapsulate these feelings of peacefulness and tranquility and permanently embed them into one's soul. When not in nature, one of the few circumstances where I enjoy a peaceful and slow pace is when spending time with my children's grandmother—who is never in a hurry, thus forcing me to slow down and not rush.

As the sun rises, the clouds burn off and morning chill dissipates. After I drag the sled for a mile or so, to my left are gullies that go into foothills toward Bison Peak. Struggling onward, I overheat. Pausing, I take off layers of clothing and strap them under a bungee cord on the sled. The air is still. All is silent except for the cawing of a raven. As I am about to resume, the Druids start howling. They are hidden in the foothills—fairly close. Sitting on the sled, I appreciate their presence. It would have been easy to have struggled past them, unaware they were there. *They know I am here, so why are they howling?* I believe they are signaling their location and strength. I am humbled and grateful for this experience. I don't know if they consider me friend or foe, but I consider myself an ally in their struggle for survival in the modern world.

After several minutes sitting on the sled listening to the Druids, it is time to move. Continuing on, I hear a buzzing sound coming out of the sky. Looking upward, there is a small aircraft circling at low altitude. I suspect the plane contains park biologists conducting a wildlife survey.

Upon arriving at the trailhead, I unpack gear bags from the sled and throw them into the back of the vehicle. Considering that I have spent the last several days in the presence of the Druids, my spirit feels a glow of contentment. The drive through the Lamar Valley and over the Blacktail Plateau gives me time to relish the last few days. My deep-seated yearning for fresh air, physical exertion in glorious terrain, while being in the presence of wolves is sated. At least for now.

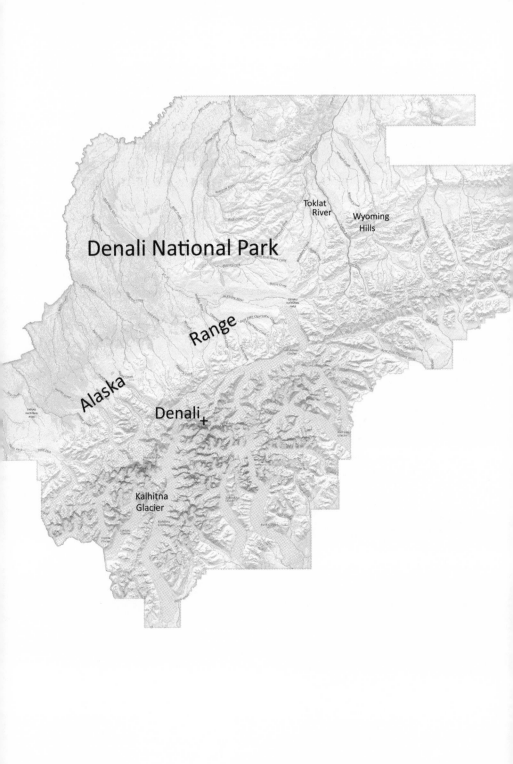

Toklat
River

Wyoming
Hills

Denali National Park

Range

Alaska

Denali+

Kalhitna
Glacier

TOKLAT

"Those who contemplate the beauty of the Earth find reserves of strength that will endure as long as life lasts. There is something infinitely healing in the repeated refrains of nature—the assurance that dawn comes after night, and spring after winter."

—Rachel Carson, *Silent Spring*, 1962

The Alaska Range is a five-hundred-mile arc of mountains in south central Alaska, extending from the Alaskan Peninsula in the southwest to the border of the Yukon Territory in the east. The dominant mountain is North America's highest, Denali, which means "the High One" in the language of the local Koyukon Athabaskan people. Denali was renamed from its former name, Mount McKinley, in 2015.

Two archeological sites in Denali National Park, one east and one west of the Teklanika River, have uncovered stone tools used by prehistoric hunters and gatherers as well as the remains of caribou, sheep, and bison that date to 13,000 years ago. Other archeological sites within the park are the Bull River II and the Costello Creek sites, with stone tools that date to 12,500 years ago.

Denali's summit is 20,320 feet above sea level. When measured from its base, Denali rises three and a half miles, making it one of Earth's highest elevation gains from nearby land, surpassing even Mount Everest, which rises from the Tibetan Plateau. At a latitude of sixty-three degrees north, it is three degrees from the Arctic Circle; thus, much of the land in Denali National Park is permafrost, with just topsoil thawing in summer.

Denali's high latitude and elevation, frigid cold, storms, glaciers, and avalanches make climbing difficult and dangerous. Of the forty or so glaciers in Denali National Park, the Kahiltna emanates from Denali's southwest slope, flowing for forty miles. A landing strip for bush planes on Kahiltna serves as base camp for those attempting to summit. The classic west buttress route requires trekking thirteen miles while gaining two and a half miles in elevation to reach the summit. About one thousand people attempt summiting annually, with 50 percent succeeding. My interest in this area is not in the physical exhilaration of climbing an ice-clad mountain. My preference is hiking and enjoying lower elevations where plant life flourishes, rivers flow, and wildlife thrives.

Because of the park's cold climate, tree line occurs at 2,800 feet. Below this elevation, glacially carved valleys and tundra foothills support both white and black spruce with white spruce in dryer upland areas and black spruce in wetter lowlands. Melting permafrost causes some spruce trees to tilt, creating a "drunken forest." Other trees are larch (tamarack), quaking aspen, paper and dwarf birch, and balsam poplar. Woody bushes and plants include willows, alder, fireweed, cotton grass, sedge, mosses, blueberry, and tussock grass. There are no pine trees in Denali.

No reptiles live in the park, but a single amphibian—the little brown wood frog—does. It is the only amphibian that can survive north of the Arctic Circle. The frog enters a semifrozen state in winter, during which it stops breathing and its heart stops beating.

During Denali's short summer season, arctic terns breed and build nests on sand, gravel, or on short grasses and moss near the thousands of lakes and ponds found in the park. Come wintertime, they migrate over 12,000 miles to coastal waters around Antarctica. One wonders what evolutionary forces have compelled this graceful, grayish-white bird with black cap, forked tail, and bright-red bill to migrate between polar regions, with some individuals travelling almost 50,000 miles annually, utilizing nondirect flight paths.

While the Alaska Range presents challenges to climbers attempting to summit Denali, Mount Foraker, or Moose's Tooth, which abuts the eastern edge of Denali's Great Gorge, the most hazardous activities for those exploring the park's backcountry are crossing streams, being ill-prepared for rainy or cold weather, or hiking a precarious route and taking a fall.

It is a splendid mid-September day as I ride fifty miles in the "camper bus" from the park entrance to the Toklat River. The Toklat is a silt-laden braided river originating as glacial and precipitation runoff from upper valleys and peaks in the Alaska Range. Traveling east to west, the washboard gravel road is dusty, narrow, and at times single lane as it switchbacks around Polychrome Pass. Looking out the bus window, I see spectacular views—glaciated valleys with serpentine braided rivers reflecting sunlight. Coming to an overlook, the bus stops. Looking down into the valley, I see there is a dark, hulking shape crossing the outwash plain—a grizzly. I have some trepidation about roaming the Toklat River Valley and sharing the terrain with grizzlies.

Upon arrival at the Toklat, the bus stops again. There are three other passengers on the bus, but I am the only one to exit. I am relieved they are not getting off the bus, as I am seeking solitude. With backpack full of food and gear on the ground beside me, the camper bus rumbles off in a cloud of dust, traveling up and over the hill to the west. As the noise and dust settle, it is now quiet, and I am alone in the Denali Wilderness.

The afternoon is cool and overcast. Heaving on the backpack, I travel north along the bottom of the river valley on rock and gravel next to the cloudy rushing water of the Toklat. Hugging the right-hand side of the riverbank, I travel through scattered groups of willow, alder brush, and scrub plant life. As I meander around brush, much of the river bottom is dry, but occasionally a long step is needed to cross side streams and rivulets. Hiking on the valley floor provides a good travel corridor, much less strenuous than hillsides where tussocks make footing treacherous and walking through alder-willow thickets is exhausting.

Along the edge of the eroded riverbank is a large porcupine ambling along. It is not concerned with my presence, having hundreds of large yellow quills bristling on its back. Each quill has microscopic barbs that can hook into a predator that gets too close. When threatened, a porcupine can swing its tail, impaling the predator with quills. I keep a safe distance. Leaving the porcupine behind, I continue traversing the rocky bottom of the river channel. In the mud are wolf tracks made by a lone wolf. Above the river channel, up on the tundra are small holes dug by arctic ground squirrels in the open spaces between willow and alder.

A dreary sky drizzles off and on. I take the pack off my shoulders, dig out a rain jacket and put it on. While hiking alone in this immense landscape of tundra, snowcapped mountains, and broad river valleys, this rugged wilderness brings to mind rounding a bend in the river and stumbling upon a group of woolly mammoths. Regrettably, most mammoths died out 10,000 years ago, but remnant groups lived on. One group inhabited Alaska's St. Paul Island until 5,500 years ago and another group lived on Russia's Wrangel Island until 4,000 years ago, as civilizations flourished in Mesopotamia and Egypt. Occasionally found frozen in arctic permafrost are mammoths, cave lions, wolves, steppe bison, horses and other species. Maybe with luck, I will come across a freshly exposed corrugated mammoth tooth or a long curving tusk.

After having hiked about three miles north, I come across large bear tracks in a sandy area. After pausing to look at the tracks, I hike another two miles but am wet and chilled. Evening is coming, so I decide to set up the tent on a gravel bar where it is protected from wind by willow and alder bush. Instead of using tent stakes on the rocky river bottom, I tie the tent to willow branches. With the overcast sky and the sun low on the horizon, darkness looms. I'm eager to change into warm, dry clothes, then settle down in the sleeping bag.

Nearby, hidden in brush, are clacking sounds intermixed with chattering and purring. I can't identify the sound or the animal making it. A raccoon? But there are no raccoons here. Perhaps a bear cub? Ground squirrel or hoary marmot? Maybe a Canada lynx? As the sounds dissipate, my focus continues to be on setting up camp. As I am cold, wet, and hungry, a hot meal will be satisfying.

Walking one hundred yards from the tent, I set cooking gear on a gravel area. While lighting the stove, I see a five-hundred-pound grizzly about fifty yards away. Standing up, I watch it. Grizzlies in Denali are inland bears; they work hard for food on the tundra. In Denali, it is prohibited to approach closer than three hundred yards.

For fifteen minutes, I observe the bear digging in the gravel river bottom. I have been noisy while setting up the tent and calling out "Hey there," so it knows I am here, but it ignores my presence as it wanders about digging roots. In the coolness of the evening, my wet body shivers. Dinner has been missed.

I could tear down the tent, pack up gear, and hike to another area to set up camp in darkness and drizzle. But there is the possibility of stumbling into another bear in the brush. Another option is to retreat and hike back to the park road. But there won't be a camper bus until tomorrow. *Why am I even here?* Certainly, I enjoy physical exertion in the outdoors. That, along with having a thirst for exploration, adventure, seeing wildlife, and discovering evidence of Earth's natural history are reasons to stay. Fortunately, or unfortunately, I am getting exactly what I came for.

With the darkness and rain, the decision is made by default. The wisdom may be questionable. Walking back to the tent, I untie it from the willow branches, then drag the tarp, tent, and gear out to an open area of the gravel bar. With the tent out here, the bear won't stumble across it in thick brush during the night.

Having moved camp, I wait in the drizzle, listening, wondering what the bear will do next. After thirty minutes, nothing happens. Is this grizzly going to approach? I know it is moving around not far away, hidden by brush and darkness. I shiver, regretting that I didn't pack rain pants since mine are soaking wet. This is a miserable situation. Finally, I take my cooking gear and food and walk two hundred yards away from the tent. Instead of cooking a hot meal which would release food smells, I quickly eat cereal with dry milk, then repack all food into a bear-resistant container. Now, walking in the dark through the low-lying brush along the gravel bars, I make my way back to the tent. Again, I stand guard, keeping a watchful eye. Despite not seeing or hearing anything, I speak in a loud voice every few minutes. I want my presence known to avoid an encounter in the dark. The bear spray is on my belt in a holster, ready if needed. The bear *knows* I am here but is ignoring me. Am I an irrelevant object? Something to be neither frightened of nor curious about? Not a threat nor a source of food?

Comforted that there is no immediate threat, I enter the tent, change out of wet clothes, and scoot into the sleeping bag. It has been a good day of physical exertion backpacking along the Toklat and feeling the elements on my skin. My feet, ankles, and legs are sore from hiking across rocky terrain. The fresh, cool air has been invigorating. The vistas have been breathtaking, and my senses are heightened. I turn on a transistor radio to see if it can pick up a signal, maybe from Russia? There is nothing but static as I turn the dial back and forth. With no signal, I turn to a book. Being warm and dry in the sleeping bag while protected from rain pelting the tent is comforting. Putting the book down, sleep comes to my exhausted body.

I wake in the middle of the night. The rain has stopped. Peeking outside, the sky has cleared. Exiting the tent, I stand and peer into the darkness, vaguely seeing silhouettes of foothills and mountains. The partial moon illuminates nearby snowfields. A sprinkle of stars forming the edge of the Milky Way galaxy shine in an arc across the night sky. I assume the grizzly is bedded down not too far away as I contemplate our shared existence on this third planet from a star named Sol. I look up at the multitude of stars seen and unseen while contemplating life on other planets.

The grizzly and I share a common ancestral bond in Earth's tree of life. Our DNA translates base pairs into the same set of amino acids and proteins, a result of our common heritage. How likely is it that life on other planets will use DNA, RNA, the same four nucleobases, or the same genetic code as life on Earth? Life that has arisen on another planet will be different, making it incompatible with Earth life. Maybe it's a good thing that stars are far apart.

The grizzly and I are both products of wild nature on planet Earth, and maybe we are not so different after all. We are a kind of brethren—kindred spirits. Both of us are out here in the wild, trying to survive in our own ways. With those thoughts in mind, the grizzly could come into my tent and rip me to shreds. It could consume my flesh to further its existence, and that of its offspring, thus continuing its genetic heritage in the tree of life. My branch on the tree of life would be cut short. I crawl back into the tent and go back to sleep.

Day Two

The light of dawn comes not soon enough. Upon waking, I feel relief for having survived the night. Peeking out the tent door into the morning light, there is no sign of the bear, and my sense of security is enhanced. It is a beautiful but cloudy day. Low-lying clouds with deep colors obscure nearby mountains. Breakfast is macaroni and cheese and hot chocolate. It's comforting having a hot meal after the cold dinner last night. Fumbling with the stove, I stupidly burn my thumb. In the uncertainty of last evening, I am not sure where the tent ended up. Exploring the vicinity, my camp is on a little island formed by two small side streams that merge with the Toklat.

It is early fall in Denali with vegetation turning color. The hillsides are painted with deep, earthy colors—burnt oranges, browns, and dark maroons evocative of the autumn cycle. Life doing what it has to do to survive a long, cold winter. The colors suggest life's tragedies and triumphs. For the moment, there is no tragedy or triumph. Just peace, contentment, serenity, calmness, and existence.

With the morning overcast, a cold mist hangs in the air, so I spend time reading in the tent. Setting the book aside, I explore nearby. Here and there the sun pokes through clouds, revealing a hint of blue which lasts a few moments and then is gone. Wind coming from the north brings a cold rain, so I retreat to the tent and the book. Being holed up in the tent in one of the greatest wildernesses of North America is a privilege. After the shower, the sun peeks through briefly but again is engulfed in clouds.

Another cloudburst comes, this time with strong winds shaking the tent, which I brace with my body for thirty minutes. The wind relents, but the downpour continues. With time, the storm moves down the valley to the south. Peeking out the tent door, the landscape is drenched, and the sky to the north is twilight blue. Evening light illuminates hillsides with deep yellows, rusty reds, and greens. After the storm, a fresh dusting of snow covers the dark silhouette of a mountain to the southeast. Part of the sky has a smear of translucent pink. With the astounding beauty of the landscape revealed after the storm, birds chirp with happiness. Drizzle picks up again and I pull back into the tent. Evening is here and I return to the book.

Day Three

I survived another night in the wilderness. There was no rain last night. Around 6:00 a.m., I unzip the tent door and peek outside, then get out and move the tent twenty feet to lessen the impact on meager vegetation. After breakfast, I go for a day hike north along the Toklat River. I come upon a small tributary creek, which requires leaping across to avoid getting my boots wet. Further on, there are two heaping piles of bear scat. A hard, cold rain comes and the wind picks up, so I retreat to the tent.

All is quiet as I read and nap. After a couple hours, I peek outside to check on the weather. In view is a large grizzly not more than fifty yards away. It is not facing this direction and may not be aware of my presence in the tent. I wonder how long it has been wandering around nearby. It has a big brown hump on its shoulders and grizzled fur. Fascinated, I silently watch through the tent door, staring at its immense body as it digs up roots. Its head is massive and its snout is pointed toward the ground. It glances in my direction for a moment, then walks across a small side stream. It is digging up and eating the roots of alpine sweet-vetch (or peavine), which grows along river bottoms and floodplains in the north. This is likely the same bear that I encountered two nights ago. This morning, it could have come right up to the tent while I was reading or napping. *But it didn't. Or if it did, I was asleep and did not wake up.*

Being concerned, I exit the tent, revealing my presence. Standing just outside the tent door, I speak in a calm and steady voice that catches its attention. The bear looks in my direction. Slowly and deliberately, it turns and walks toward me. Holding my ground in front of the tent, I continue to utter random words using a normal voice. It approaches to thirty-five yards. There is nowhere to retreat. Running would induce an impulse to chase. Hiding in the tent would be futile. There are no trees of sufficient size nearby to climb. I am at the humble mercy of wild nature.

The bear ambles forward, closing the gap to twenty-five yards. Standing perfectly still, I hold the pepper spray with thumb on trigger. Ever so slightly, the bear angles to my right, slows, and looks directly at me. It's not only looking at me, it is looking at my face. We make eye contact. This is the essence of wilderness: two creatures on equal terms in the wild—standing face-to-face. At this moment, the only thing that

88

exists in my world is a humungous grizzly standing a few feet away. This is a well-fed bear, and in full daylight its large bulk is apparent. Looking eye to eye, its nostrils flare as it sucks in my scent. "Hey there, hey there," I mutter. Having inhaled my scent, it considers my presence. *Is this animal a friend, a foe, or something inconsequential?* In a regular voice, I continue to let it know I pose no threat. After pausing, the grizzly continues to my right, before ambling off into the brush.

Perhaps it categorized my presence as inconsequential. *The humanoid is nothing to worry about, and from its bad scent, not something to consume.* We have arrived at an implied mutual agreement: "I will not bother you if you do not bother me." I will not break the agreement. The grizzly is too busy foraging for food to bother with me. Sometimes in life, it makes sense to stay calm and do nothing.

With the bear having wandered off, I return to reading on a sleeping pad outside the tent door. There is a cool breeze. The sky is partly cloudy and there is no rain, at least for the moment. After reading, contemplating, and quietly observing, it is time for dinner. Walking over to my gear and food, I unwrap the tarp which protects them from rain. Inside the backpack are a stove and cooking pots. The bear had traveled in this direction after our encounter and could have investigated the gear or ripped it open. Certainly, there are unusual smells emanating from the gear and bear-proof canister full of food, but nothing has been disturbed. Opening the canister, I pull out a meal. The bear-proof container doubles as camp stool. On thinking back, I realize there was no clicking of teeth, no pulling back of the ears, no raising of the hackles, no woofing sounds, no pawing of the ground or charges. Yet still, when I exited the tent, the bear walked in my direction, and at the last second veered off after a close approach. This is a dominant male that is confident and fears nothing. I posed no threat and it knew it.

Now I realize the tent is acting as a wildlife blind. I am sitting quietly within it for hours, reading a book and peeking out periodically to check on the weather. Although the bear had shown no aggressive body language, I nevertheless gather a few good-size rocks from the riverbed and set them by the tent door. Doing this, however, increases my apprehension rather than decreasing it. My mind is focused on a defensive situation, thus the ordinary pen in my hand could be used as a weapon during a future encounter. I could poke the bear in the eye if it came into my tent at night. Exposing oneself to wild nature sharpens a person's defensive thinking—especially after encountering a grizzly. Beyond that, a person can do only so much. There are things that are out of our control. Tragic incidents and deadly accidents happen all the time in the "civilized" world. Are we to withdraw into our homes and never venture out? No.

Dinner is hot and spicy Cajun rice. The sky is partly cloudy, the air is cool, the evening is calm and peaceful. While eating dinner, I notice turf dug up. Bears have been busy searching for tubers and roots. A chirping Canada jay flits by. There are large ungulate tracks nearby, likely moose or caribou. Dall sheep live here but are unlikely to be in the river valley. Off in the distance, the sun's rays diverge as they shine on a nearby peak with a dusting of snow, slowly changing hues as they filter through the clouds.

Returning to the tent, I watch the mountainside as the sun's rays shine on its slopes. Its rays are near horizontal as they stream toward my campsite, bathing my tent and hills in golden sunlight. For a few moments, everything is glowing with warm, yellow light. It feels like the sun is in the sky just for me, at this place and this evening, filling my spirit with euphoria and contentment. After experiencing the monotonous rain and drizzle the past couple days, this is a welcome relief. Now the sun is descending below the horizon and it is gone.

3:00 a.m.

When I step outside for a moment, the mystery and wonder of the Milky Way again touches my consciousness. The moon glows behind clouds near the horizon. A nearby stream makes gurgling sounds. Stars shine brightly in the gloom. My suspicion is that the grizzly is nearby, bedded down for the night. The fog of my breath rises in the chill. This place is pristine, primitive, magical, and raw. Reentering the tent, the radio again blares static. Here, I am the only person alive on a primitive and ancient Earth. There are no roads, buildings, or people to come to the rescue. My shelter is a makeshift enclosure, set in a natural land-scape populated with wildlife that has inhabited this area for thousands of years.

Day Four

Sunrise—it is warm and bright against a blue sky. After breakfast, I hike northeast into the Wyoming Hills. Traveling to the top of a hill, I come to a bog and pond. Along the edge of the pond is an eight-foot-tall mound of cut branches and mud constructed by beavers. With few trees nearby in the spongy tundra, the beavers must have pulled the branches quite a distance. With every step my boots sink deeply into soft moss. Looking down into the Toklat River Valley, I see my little tent on the gravel bar at the edge of a rivulet. The scene is framed by an immense landscape of mountains that straddle both sides of the valley. Hiking the irregular terrain is treacherous as it contains clumps of moss, tussocks, and water seepage. There is a sweet scent in the air, from fresh cuts of balsam poplar made by beavers. There are no hiking trails, thus travel is occasionally through red-and-yellow thickets of alder and willow—hin-dering progress. Bushwhacking through thickets creates plenty of noise, but visibility is limited. I don't want to stumble upon a snoozing grizzly, so I call out with, "Hey there, hey there." Once through the thickets, I achieve the crest of another hill. I sit and rest while drawing a sketch of the epic landscape in my journal.

After napping in soft moss and grass, warmed by sunshine, I head down to the Toklat River, which again requires bushwhacking thickets and reciting, "Hey there, hey there." Back down in the river basin, I hike back toward camp. While walking across a sandy area, I notice bear tracks large and small—a mother and cub. It is good that I have been talking, so as to not surprise them.

Back at camp, I find the tent in good shape and dried out by the sun. While I was away from camp, I worried that a grizzly may ransack the tent looking for food. I walk over to the food and gear and make dinner. After cleaning up, I move the food and gear to a new location so that cooking spills and smells do not build up. It has been a strenuous day—hiking over hummocks, rocks on the riverbed, and through alder thickets. Taking off my hiking boots, I sit on the sleeping pad just outside the tent to relax for the evening.

Yesterday when I exited the tent, there was a grizzly at fifty yards. This was a reminder of the wildness of this place. Without predators, this area certainly contains spectacular scenery. But then again, if Denali lacked predators, another word comes to my mind to describe this area: tame.

Alone in the wild, I feel good. I have food, water, shelter, and good health. I think about millions, or billions, of people living in crowded conditions or in poverty. My thoughts circulate to making a positive difference, giving back to the world in return for the good fortune that I have been bestowed. My attitude is refreshed. With positive thoughts swirling, first dusk, then darkness comes. The fresh air and physical activity are invigorating. My biological rhythms are in sync with Earth's cycles of day and night. The gurgling stream near my camp is soothing. Tonight, I will sleep well.

Day Five

My sleep was sound through the night. About 6:00 a.m., I hear strange sounds in the distance. I'm not sure if I am dreaming or not. Someone is crying, a small child or an old woman is wailing in pain.

Groggily, I sit up and clear blurriness out of my eyes. There it is again! This time, I know it is real. *What is bawling? What is that eerie sound?* Putting on my boots, I step outside to look around. Nothing unusual catches my eye. The mournful wailing occurs again—coming from behind the tent and across the creek. There it is, I see it! A Canada lynx with tufted ears, sitting on the other side of the creek staring back at me, not more than forty feet away. It again wails. I stand motionless, watching for several moments while it glares back. Suddenly, it trots off, steadily and with purpose, following the far side of the creek as it meanders to the right then veers away. I watch it trot off with an easy bounce in its step. It is confident and knows where it is going. After a minute it is gone, having disappeared into brush. Absorbing this, I peer in the direction it went, hoping to see it in the distance. A few moments later, it unexpectedly reappears, trotting back toward my camp. Again, with purpose and steady manner, it returns to its original position across the creek. It pays no attention to me as it trots past my tent. Now it follows the creek to the left and up the valley to the north. It is gone, having disappeared into underbrush.

Canada lynx prey primarily on snowshoe hare but supplement their diet with other small animals. Snowshoe hares eat grasses, leafy plants, and young shoots of spruce, birch, willow, and alder. Hare populations fluctuate between high and low points over ten-year cycles. When snowshoe hares are abundant, Canada lynx focus on them and become abundant. Over time, snowshoe hare overeat vegetation, and with lynx and other predators focusing on them, the hare population declines. When snowshoe hare numbers drop, lynx numbers decline as well. Vegetation then regrows, restarting the cycle. After "my" lynx disappears into the brush, I crawl back into my sleeping bag. The patter of rain lulls me to sleep.

After waking up for good, I have a breakfast of oatmeal and hot chocolate topped with mini marshmallows. After breakfast, I hike back to the tent. There is a dull lime-green caterpillar crawling across the tent. I am not sure what this species is without seeing the moth or butterfly. Do moths or butterflies serve any useful purpose? Chemist Edward Taylor found one. He studied compounds in the wings of the white cabbage butterfly and the brimstone butterfly. After decades of work, the drug Pemetrexed was isolated and approved as a treatment for cancer patients.

There is a strong wind blowing from the south, and the tent suddenly shakes. I ignore it and gather gear for today's hike north along the Toklat River.

After hiking an hour, I come to a steep ravine on the right that cuts into the hillside. This begs exploration. Climbing up and into the ravine, after five minutes of hiking, there are layers of black shale. Further upward is a gnarled tree. Beyond the tree, the ravine narrows. Here the close confines give me an uneasy feeling. After rounding a tight bend, I consider the prospect of encountering a bear. The narrow space allows little room to avoid each other. Thinking better, I retreat back down to the riverbed. There is a warm breeze coming from the south with a massive wave of clouds pouring over peaks of the Alaska Range, then spilling down their slopes. In fascination, I watch the phenomena for several minutes. It is time to head back to camp.

Before reaching camp, I make a side trip to the top of a rocky knoll which overlooks the tent. Here I contemplate life and personal matters surrounded by spectacular pristine beauty. Life occasionally has difficulties, imperfections, chaos, and emotional angst. Solitude in nature is an ideal setting for self-reflection and to gain perspective. After some thought, what comes to mind is the bristlecone pine. It is a tree that survives in the harsh, high elevations of mountains in California, Nevada, and Utah. Although it may end up twisted, scarred, and gnarled, it is one of Earth's longest-lived organisms, with some surviving for five thousand years. Today in the high mountains of the American West are bristlecone pines that germinated five centuries before Khufu and the construction of the Great Pyramid of Giza. And they are still growing. In old age, having survived the ravages of untold calamities, an ancient, twisted, and deformed bristlecone pine is quite beautiful and displays deep character. Is it possible that something analogous occurs in the human psyche as we overcome life's harshest challenges? Maybe as we age, we come to accept life's difficulties and imperfections, work around them, and put them into perspective, thus allowing us to mature, grow, thrive, and develop character.

Back at camp, I find the tent flipped on its side. No animal had ransacked it; it had been blown over by the wind. Turning it upright, I inspect it and find it in one piece with no damage. After five days and nights on the Toklat River, I am starting to feel comfortable and confident here. Certainly, having a grizzly nearby is nervous making, but in this instance the bear is not

Bristlecone pine (Pinus longaeva)
by Sven Bellanger

interested in me, the tent, or the cache of food and gear two hundred yards away. My psyche has turned a corner. Upon first arriving, this place was strange and full of unknowns. Now, I am feeling confident. I no longer feel like a foreign visitor with little understanding, nor am I filled with dread and fear. Getting to know this area has helped me understand a small part of what it is like to live and function in the wild.

Evening has arrived and I retire to the tent. A storm passes through in the middle of the night. Winds and rain come. The tent shakes and wants to blow away. I lean against the tent wall, holding it in place for an hour.

Day Six

After breakfast, I pack up camp and hike out of the valley to the park road. After waiting for a while, a camper bus comes by and stops. Getting on the bus, I travel back to the park entrance, where civilization awaits. I check into a hotel and return to civilized ways of life: doing laundry, taking a hot shower, and eating food that is more substantial than oatmeal, hot chocolate, powdered mashed potatoes, or mac and cheese. Within my inner self there is peace, calmness, and satisfaction as I go about mundane activities. I am grateful for what I have experienced and thankful that there are wild places like Denali.

Day Seven

At the hotel, I bump into a friend from work. He and his wife are on a package tour. It started in Seattle with a sumptuous cruise along the inside passage and culminates with a tour of Denali. Excitedly, they tell me about their bus tour on the Denali Park road. When a bear is sighted, the bus stops and passengers poke cameras through open windows. "Sounds wonderful," I reply, adding, "So nice bumping into you guys—and in Alaska of all places!" That is not the type of outing that interests me: being shepherded around, every arrangement taken care of, viewing wildlife from a window, not feeling the elements against my skin. I do not attempt describing my experiences in Denali. Can words convey the wondrous feeling of being alone in the wild as a wave of clouds pours over the Alaska Range? Can words convey the emotions of having a large grizzly walk past at twenty-five yards, look you in the eye, and flare its nostrils? No, I do not think so. A person must experience these things firsthand to enjoy the mystery and pleasure of spending time in the wild.

Back in the hotel room, I catch up on news. George W. Bush and Colin Powell are talking about invading Iraq and destroying Iraq's weapons of mass destruction. *Wow, what is going on?* After digesting the day's news, I decide to return to the wild.

Day Eight

Fleeing civilization, I take a camper bus back to the Toklat. After being dropped off at river's edge, I hike upriver along the west branch of the Upper Toklat, leading toward the spine of the Alaska Range. Tramping through low brush, I am startled by a flurry of sound and flutter bursting from my feet. After the initial surprise, I pause a moment to watch a willow ptarmigan fly away. Ahead is a spectacular view between two rocky peaks, their snowy slopes framing the headwaters of the west fork. After hiking along the riverbed, I veer to the left up the hillside where I find a level area and set up the tent. Nearby, a silty stream with willows at its edges trickles down the hillside. Exploring the terrain uphill from camp, I come to a tundra bench. Here are several large holes in the tundra where grizzlies have dug for arctic ground squirrels. Some excavations are six feet wide and three feet deep. When a grizzly catches a squirrel, it eats the entire animal, including fur and bones. Beyond the bench in the distance are dark, precipitous cliffs. Near the cliff base, two white Dall sheep with curling horns are precariously perched.

Scanning with binoculars from left to right, I spot eight magpies near a rocky point. Their heads, necks, and backs are black, while their wings and tails are iridescent blue. The shoulders, bellies and wingtips are white. These intelligent, omnivorous birds were encountered by

Lewis and Clark during their trek up the Missouri River. Magpies live in open areas of western North America eating berries, seeds, insects, and rodents, as well as scavenging on carrion.

Day Nine

The day is cool, fresh, and overcast, making for comfortable hiking. There is a valley to explore as I hike further upslope toward the Toklat headwaters. Travel is slow, and I have no objective in mind as I wander among undulating tundra foothills. My path follows a human and game trail on the eastern bank of the river. A waterfall cascades off dark cliffs to the left. Magpies dart about, likely the same flock spotted yesterday. To the right, a ground squirrel stands on hind legs near the entrance to its underground burrow. Sprinkled about are mosses and low-lying plants. A golden eagle flies overhead. Further along the trail is a large pile of wolf scat. Looking forward, up valley where the river originates from glaciers, are more Dall sheep. I head toward the sheep to get a better view. Using binoculars, I count thirty-five on a delta-shaped talus slope. At the base of the slope is a large bull caribou with huge antlers. Sitting, I watch the scene unfold and let time slip by.

The golden eagle soars back and forth high among cliffs. Its regal head is gold, offset by a dark-brown body. Its wingspan is tremendous, almost seven feet. The valleys and open tundra of the Alaska Range support high densities of nesting golden eagles. Patiently, I scope the area with binoculars to see what I may be missing. Now the eagle returns at low altitude, flying just above foothills. Its dark form blends into the landscape as its silhouette is below the skyline. The eagle's stealth flying is similar to tactics used by long-range bombers flying beneath radar. I wonder what it is looking for? Ptarmigan? Ground squirrels? Snowshoe hares?

Walking further, I find terrain churned up. Grizzlies have been busy pursuing ground squirrels. No wonder ground squirrels dig deep burrows, have multiple entrances and exits, and only carefully show themselves to the outside world.

Steep terrain makes me wary of going further. Not wanting to risk a fall, I head back to camp for dinner. Clouds are moving in, shrouding the mountains; the temperature is plummeting. I put on all my clothes. Even so, the thin sleeping bag is insufficient to keep me warm. The night is chilly, causing restlessness and shivers.

Day Ten

Peeking my head outside the tent, there are low-lying clouds moving slowly along the valley. Drizzle welcomes me to a damp, cold, clammy day. I spend time in the tent, quietly reading and cherishing memories of relatives long gone. There is a mouse scurrying nearby, out on the tundra. I call it a mouse, but my ability to identify furry little animals is limited. It could be anyone of these: vole, lemming, mouse, or shrew. The first three are rodents that have sharp incisors. Shrews, on the other hand, have an elongated nose and sharp, spiked teeth. Shrews have a very high metabolic rate, with a heartbeat of seven hundred times per minute, and if excited, up to one thousand times per minute. Whatever this little mouse-like animal is, it is amazing that such a small creature can survive winter despite temperatures reaching -40 or -50°F. None hibernate as they scurry among vegetation and detritus in tunnels beneath insulating snow. Voles are omnivores. Mice and lemmings are mostly plant eaters. Shrews, with their sharp teeth and elongated snouts, are the smallest mammalian predator on the tundra, eating almost anything, including insects, worms, centipedes, spiders, voles, mice, other shrews, and carrion. If it is a shrew, I hope it stays away, as I don't want to get bitten.

Moving up the food chain, weasels, red foxes, coyotes, wolverines, golden eagles, hawks, falcons, and owls keep little mammal populations from exploding in Denali. Small weasels here are the ermine and the least weasel. Both have long bodies, short legs, and are high-energy, voracious predators whose coats turn white in the wintertime (although the slightly larger ermine has a black-tipped tail). Before the 1900s, coyote range did not include Alaska, but by the 1930s they reached Central Alaska and Denali.

The wolverine is a predator-scavenger whose powerful jaws can crack through bone and tear meat from a frozen carcass. They search far and wide for carrion but also hunt arctic ground squirrels, snowshoe hares, hoary marmots, and beaver. Wolverines may prey upon young caribou, young Dall sheep, and young moose. They even take adults if they are weakened or caught in deep snow.

Hearing honking sounds, I unzip the tent door to look. From up here on the tundra bench, I peer downslope. Just above the valley floor are dark specks of Canada geese in V-formation flying through sleet. With the onslaught of snow and freezing rain, it signals them to head south. Feeling somewhat energetic despite the dreary weather, I hike near camp in the midst of cold mist, freezing rain, and snowfall. The golden eagle flies by.

Returning to the tent, I take off my damp socks and put on warm, dry socks. Across the valley is a ridgeline with steep cliff faces that terminate in talus slopes. As the snowstorm gathers strength, frozen pellets hit the tent, making ticking sounds. There are squeaking sounds coming from beneath the tent floor. That must be the "mouse," now crawling under the floor. The burn on my thumb is starting to heal. I hear chirping and look outside to see a robin siting on ice-encrusted tundra. The valley floor accumulates snow and frozen rain. As the storm thickens, the view across the valley is obscured. Dropping temperature and dankness exacerbates a cold, clammy feeling. Wind shakes the tent. My feet are cold, so I take off my socks and massage them to warm them up.

Day Eleven

The night was cold, and I shivered for hours in the sleeping bag. A layer of snow and frozen drizzle has coated the ground and vegetation, turning the Upper Toklat Valley white and gray. Attempting to use the water filter, I find it clogged with frozen water, so instead I boil water for Spanish rice and hot chocolate. After taking down the tent, I pack up gear and hike toward the park road. As the day warms up, the frozen rain and snow melt at lower elevations. In order to make better time, I take a shortcut through thick alder and willow, but it slows me down, and I regret the decision. It is difficult to discern which direction to go, but eventually I make my way beyond the thicket and am relieved. Out in the open again, there are expansive views. Deep in thought, warmed up, and hiking in a grand landscape, I inhale the autumn colors where snow has melted. Dark maroon, burnt orange, and yellow ochre—the colors of vegetation going dormant, preparing for a brutal winter. The evergreens are crusted with snow and ice. Hiking forward, I experience a sense of serenity and happiness, of being alive in the grand scheme of life on Earth. I feel lucky to be alive despite life's imperfections, tragedies, and periods of melancholy.

Here in Denali, I have gained experience and knowledge. Next time, I must bring a warmer sleeping bag. Before this adventure, I had trepidation about taking a backpacking trip in the Denali Wilderness. If a person had asked years ago if I would undertake such a trip, my reaction would have been "certainly not." There is an evolution of experience, maturity, and confidence needed to backpack here. Now that this adventure is nearing completion, I feel satisfaction and contentment, both for having navigated the adventure and in reflecting on and accepting life's imperfections. Continuing the hike, my path returns to the park road, where I wait. It's not long before a camper bus comes by and slows to a stop. The door opens, I climb the steps, say hello to the driver, and walk down the aisle past a few other people who are haggard campers like myself. I pick a seat near the back of the bus. It lurches forward and we rumble down the gravel road toward the park entrance and civilization.

As we bounce down the washboard road, I ponder humanity's existence. Our time on Earth will not last forever. Humans will go extinct or we will evolve into something beyond what we are. But Denali—Denali will transcend us. It was here long before us and will continue to be the Monarch of the North for millions of years, long after we are gone.

VIGIL

"It seems to me that the natural world is the greatest source of excitement; the greatest source of visual beauty; the greatest source of intellectual interest. It is the greatest source of so much in life that makes life worth living."

—David Attenborough

For this early spring trip to Yellowstone National Park, my trekking partner and I look forward to seeing bison, elk, moose, and wolves. With snow still on the ground, we haul our gear by pulling sleds for two-and-a-half miles to Slough Creek. Along the way are mountain bluebirds with cerulean-blue bodies and light-blue breasts. They are effortlessly flitting about the valley as we trudge along. The valley floor and nearby foothills are covered in sage and grasses which protrude up through patches of snow. The mountain bluebirds are collecting nesting material and searching for mates. Their vibrant blue colors put a smile on my face. Along our path we come across large wolf tracks in the snow and two large tubular sections of scat composed of fur and bone bits. To our right is a coyote at the base of a hill. It is not concerned with our presence. It notices our weary struggles and knows it can easily lope away if we approach. There are deeper snow patches under the shadows of nearby trees. We set up the tent near the icy, gurgling waters of the creek and share mac and cheese for dinner. Not far from camp, in the shadows of trees, are snowdrifts that have been disturbed as a bear waded through. The bear's paw prints are not particularly large so are likely made by a black bear or a young grizzly. We turn in for the night.

2:30 a.m.

I have trouble sleeping tonight. Every little noise is exaggerated, running wild in my mind. The sounds are "crack, crack, crack." *It must be a predator approaching and ready to pounce!* My tentmate is sound asleep, breathing deeply. I, however, cannot sleep while repeatedly hearing these cracking noises. *No worries,* I think. *Remain calm.* It must be a mouse or other small animal scurrying around twigs and leaves. But the cracking sounds continue, and curiosity gets the better of me. I peek outside the tent door. To my surprise, thirty-five feet away is a full-grown, antlerless moose silhouetted in moonlight, browsing twigs on a bush. The glint of moonlight sparkles a silver outline off the top of its back. My prediction that it was a mouse or squirrel was wildly wrong.

Day Two

After breakfast, I walk over to the creek, watching its frigid waters rush by. There are a couple of little gray birds perched on rocks on the far bank—American dippers. They bob up and down in a peculiar motion. Occasionally they flit from rock to rock. One dives into the creek and disappears. It is "flying" in the water and at times walking along the bottom against the rushing water. It surfaces moments later, then flies to the creek side and lands on a rock. It is searching for aquatic insects. The bobbing motion is curious. It may be done to blend into the rushing turbulence of creeks, to spot insects in water, or as a signal to other dippers. Their ability to fly under rushing water and locate insects is remarkable. Besides the dipper, cutthroat trout and non-native rainbow trout feed on aquatic insects in Slough Creek.

After returning to the tent, my hiking partner and I head downstream along the creekbank, exploring gullies and hills. There are several bison grazing nearby. The head of each bison, along with its front legs, is covered with long, black, shaggy fur. The fur on their backs and sides is deep, rusty brown. Their horns are set behind and above their eyes, curving out and upward when a bison has its head raised. One bison has large scars on its haunch. Either it was recently attacked by a wolf, cougar, or bear, or another bison had gored it. There are several elk on the lateral moraine across Slough Creek. In the sky are two raptors circling overhead.

Exploring the area further, we stumble across the remains of a carcass. There is not much left of what was once a bison—stocky bones, femur, hooves, and lots of fur scattered about. As we return to camp, several bluebirds fly by as they continue their quest for grasses and twigs.

We share spaghetti for dinner.

Day Three

For breakfast we cook up powdered eggs and fry slices of canned ham. After stuffing our daypacks with lunch, cameras, and binoculars, we leave camp and hike north following a snow-covered trail that rises through semiforested terrain with scattered boulders. Huffing uphill, we pass the ragged remains of a large fir tree that was destroyed by lightning. Bark at the tree's base is a furrowed mixture of dark brown and burnt orange—covered by green moss. Its top is broken off, frayed and charred black.

Further along the trail, we encounter fresh tracks in the snow: ursine, canine, and feline. This is the first time I have come across such a variety of tracks on a single hike and so close to each other. Bear tracks are obvious by their large heel pad, toes, and claw marks. These are probably made by the same black bear or young grizzly that made tracks near our tent. Compared to black bear, grizzly tracks are quite large and have pronounced claw marks. The canid tracks are about the size of my fist and show claws at the front. Due to their size, this must be a wolf. We examine the feline tracks. They are rounder and do not show claws. These were made by a cougar, lynx, or bobcat, with my guess being bobcat. As we examine the feline tracks, the air is calm and all is quiet.

The sound of a woodpecker rapidly tapping against a tree breaks the silence. Moving on, we hike over the top of a rise, then descend through a grove of quaking aspen, which opens to a snow-dusted meadow where the creek oxbows. There is a large rocky hill in the middle of the meadow that Slough Creek winds around. We don't know it yet, but we are about to encounter nature in its most primeval form.

Leaving the trail, we tramp across the meadow and are greeted by staccato rasping sounds. To the north, past marsh vegetation, are three pairs of sandhill cranes—each pair separated from the others. They call back and forth using rough, staccato vocalizations. Either they are migrating through and stopping for a rest, or are nesting in marsh at the meadow's north end. The top of their heads and brows are bright red, their bodies gray and sandy brown. At a height of three and a half to four feet, the top of their bodies, necks, and heads rise above yellow-brown grasses, reeds, and brush.

We circle around the base of the hill and approach the creek on the northwest side as we listen to guttural cackles of cranes echo across the valley. The creek curves back and forth through the meadow. The air is cool and fresh, the sky blue and clear. Further on, we happen upon an elk carcass on the other side of the creek. A portion of the rotting carcass hangs into the creek. Little meat is left on the bones. The elk's skull is connected to neck vertebrae and a few ribs are strewn about. There is probably marrow in the bones. The elk may have succumbed to the harsh winter, wolves, or a combination of both. We sit in soft grass that has emerged from snow across from the carcass—hidden by grass, sage, and alders. We eat lunch and wait. Our reverent contemplations are broken by an occasional whisper. It is a plausible thing to do—stake out a carcass to see if anything develops. During our vigil, we patiently watch the world unfold, inhaling the meadow's springtime essence: yellow grass, red alder, dark-green firs on hillsides. Looking up at the crystal-blue sky, I consider it unlikely that anything will develop, especially in broad daylight and with our being here. Yet, in our quietude something develops.

Out of the sky, a pair of Canada geese come gliding in, stretch their feet forward and land on the creek in front of us. The nearest pair of cranes are standing at a bend in the creek on mudflats. The geese fold in their wings and placidly float on the water's surface. Then, for no discernible reason, the geese paddle toward the cranes. Tranquility is broken as the geese and cranes call back and forth, causing a ruckus. Still the geese approach, exacerbating the interspecies territorial dispute.

Captivated by the avian commotion, we don't notice, at first, a silver-gray wolf trotting in from the foothills of Buffalo Plateau. It must be coming to scavenge off the carcass. As it trots forward, its gait is deliberate and confident. It *knows* the carcass is here. At about fifty yards, it slows, hesitates, and comes to a stop.

This is nature at its most grand and epic. Life's giant mural is being painted right in front of our eyes—the death of an elk, its remains resting on the far edge of the creek, the mated pairs of cranes and geese engaged in a territorial dispute, a wolf trotting in looking for food. Which show should we watch? It doesn't get richer than this. Here we are, lying on the ground, peering through grass, watching nature reveal itself in a sublime landscape. Civilization is a million miles away as we have been transported back to a time when the fundamental and principal elements of nature rule. Mating. Searching for food. Claiming territory. Creatures being cautious, aware of their surroundings, and sensitive to danger. There is no sound of vehicular traffic. There are no buildings. Just us lying in the grass, watching nature unfold as it has for eons. If we had not been present, nothing would have unfolded differently. The cranes, geese, and wolf are acting naturally and are oblivious to our presence, hidden in sage and grass.

Lying on our stomachs, we aim our cameras at the elk carcass and the wolf. The wolf slowly moves forward, but at forty yards it again hesitates and stops. Standing still and alert, it may be wary about a grizzly claiming the carcass. After gorging, a grizzly will rest near a carcass, and if challenged, will fiercely protect it from competitors. The wolf is at attention with head raised observing, listening, smelling. A group of wolves howl mournfully in the hills from where the silver-gray wolf had come. That must be its packmates, but it does not respond. Again, it advances slowly. Now, it hesitates and stands erect. Howls from the hidden pack carry eerily across the meadow. Still, the silver-gray does not respond. We wait and watch for ten minutes. The wolf is suspicious; something is not right. Maybe it is picking up our scent. Maybe it hears the clicks of our cameras. It turns and slowly walks back to its packmates hidden in the foothills. We watch with binoculars for several minutes as it lopes further into the distance. It ascends distant hills in a zigzag pattern. At times, it is hidden by brush or descends into a gully, only to reappear at higher elevations. Now it is out of sight, hidden by the obscurity of distance and undulating terrain covered with brush and trees.

The geese and cranes are quiet, having resolved their dispute. The air is still, and the sky is translucent blue with a sprinkling of wispy horse-tail clouds as the sun warms our faces. It is time to return to camp. Hiking back to camp, we don't speak, as we are immersed in thought.

Yesterday we discovered bear tracks in the snow, and today we find bear prints hiking into the Slough Creek meadow. This time of year, bears are coming out of hibernation, especially males. They are looking for winter-kill carcasses. If a grizzly had claimed the carcass, we might have stumbled upon a situation where it viewed us as competitors for food. We were naive. If a grizzly had been resting nearby, we might have become casualties of nature's wildness. My preference is to remain a quiet observer and not a participant interacting with nature's teeth and claws.

Today was a successful and satisfying day of hiking and wildlife watching. It is one that will forever be emblazoned in my memory. After dinner, we sit and watch the darkness unfold in the sky. There is little conversation. What we saw, experienced, and shared requires no words, only reflection. Pulling out the binoculars, I look to the sky. As we sit in silence by the fire, the stars slowly rotate through the heavens. The bright, shining point of light visible to the southwest is Jupiter.

As I focus, the image transitions from fuzzy to crisp. Jupiter's four largest moons are points of light next to its bright central disk. First seen using a telescope and described by Galileo Galilei, Jupiter's largest moons are Io, Europa, Ganymede, and Callisto. After repeated observations, Galileo knew they never strayed far from Jupiter and, in fact, orbited the planet. Galileo supported Copernicus's idea that the sun and not the Earth was the center of the solar system and recorded his observations of Jupiter's moons in his 1610 Treatise *Sidereus Nuncius*—The Starry Messenger.

From our perspective here on Earth, everything in the sky, including the sun, moon, and stars, have the *appearance* of revolving around us. By extension, it was thought the entire universe revolved around Earth and surely humankind. In contrast, a grizzly bear could have been guarding the elk carcass. Yes, a grizzly could have attacked and severely injured or killed us. Like the moons of Jupiter, which offered proof to Galileo that the heavens do not revolve around Earth or mankind's existence, the natural world relentlessly follows its laws and processes and does not revolve around our continued existence. The natural world supports us and sustains us, but it offers no guarantee of safety or survival. When we are in wilderness, we instinctively know that. That is why we are on edge and observant when hiking in areas with predators. Our senses—sight, sound, smell, touch—are fully engaged. Ask anyone who hikes or camps in grizzly country. One of their foremost thoughts is the prospect of stumbling upon a grizzly. At night while we sleep in a tent, a grizzly could approach and attack. Does a person feel a sense of preordained existence and safety in wilderness with predators? No. Do instincts and senses become heightened and engaged? Yes. As evening approaches, do we become sensitized to movements in shadows or at the edges of peripheral vision? In a tent at night, at the crack of a twig, do we wonder what caused it? We know the answers. It is hardwired into our genes to be wary in the wilderness with predators.

Like a trek into the wilderness where predators and natural hazards exist, we as individuals or humankind can bumble along and, if we are not careful, make a fatal or injurious mistake. Such a mistake may affect an individual or may affect humanity. While we go about our modern lives, we are sheltered from and sometimes lose sight of nature's harsh realities. Like the elk remains on the banks of Slough Creek, an individual, as well as humanity, is not preordained to survive. The unpredictability and value of having predators in wilderness focuses the mind and heightens senses. It makes our existence real, explicit, and brought to the forefront. Predators in wilderness reinforce the knowledge that with each choice we make, whether foolish or prudent, we can detract from or enhance the probability of our survival. If there is any lesson to be learned from predators in wilderness, maybe this is it.

Day Four

Our goal is to explore the Crystal Creek drainage and the higher elevations of the foothills that buttress Specimen Ridge. Loading our daypacks, we hike to the base of Specimen Ridge, where several dozen bison are grazing. Giving wide berth to the herd, we ascend partway up a lower foothill. We stop and rest in the shadow of a large Douglas fir. Using binoculars, I slowly pan back and forth across the bottom of the Lamar River Valley.

My hiking colleague decides to continue to the hilltop. We agree I will catch up in a few minutes and we will rendezvous at the top. He is wearing a red shirt and blue jeans. After carefully scanning the valley, I shoulder my daypack and head up. At the top are craggy slabs of rock and glacial erratic boulders on subalpine meadows. I approach a large boulder the size of a recreational vehicle, then hike to an elevated rocky ledge for a better view. Pausing for a few moments, I scan the vicinity, then circle around, zigzagging back and forth. *Where is he?* After climbing the highest rise in the area, he is not visible anywhere. Maybe there was a miscommunication. Circling around for twenty minutes, I feel my concern heighten. Did he get lost, fall, or become injured? Did a bear or cougar drag him into the forest? Worried, I call his name repeatedly. Listening intently, I hear the wind. *What happened to him?*

Continuing to zigzag, I come to an overlook for the Lamar Valley. Pausing in silence there is a weak human voice. Not sure where the faint cry is coming from—he must be helpless and injured! Again, I yell his name. There are faint sounds on the wind, "Aaaaayeee . . . Aaaaayeee!" *Aaaaayeee?* Then I hear, "Valley . . . valley!" The sound is coming from the valley. *What is he doing down there?* Finally, I see him: a tiny figure wearing blue jeans and a red shirt. Thank goodness he is alive! Quickly scrambling down, I catch up to him. He hiked to the top, waited a minute, then hiked down. While I ascended the hill, he descended. Why we didn't see each other is a mystery.

Perhaps, being alone on the hilltop he became distressed. When I didn't show up quickly, he descended. Having spent a lifetime hiking and camping, I am rarely concerned in the wild. Some people are comfortable in wilderness, with what might be termed "nature confidence." On the other hand, some people are comfortable in a group, having "social confidence." But, for either setting, experience and knowledge increases comfort and confidence.

Day Five

Today we hike to a low rise that overlooks Slough Creek where it empties into the Lamar River. We have packed cameras, binoculars, tripods, scopes, and camp stools. Sitting on camp stools, we focus optics on a group of fifteen elk. They seem tense and are tightly grouped. While watching the elk, we aren't paying attention to our surroundings. Something approaches us from behind.

Catching a glimpse of a looming shadow, I quietly alert my partner. A large bull bison walks within thirty feet of us, veers left, then stops in a sandy depression. It shows no fear, as we are two lightweight creatures with a tenth of its bulk. I wonder if it knows that it is safe from humans within Yellowstone.

Native peoples on North America's prairies hunted bison for food and used the hide for clothing and bedding. Bones and horns were shaped into tools and implements. One method for hunting bison drove them over cliffs or steep embankments, with hundreds of "buffalo jumps" used across the great plains—some dating back twelve thousand years. Head-Smashed-In Buffalo Jump, in southern Alberta, was used for 5,500 years. Its usage was discontinued as late as 1850. With the arrival of Europeans and the completion of the intercontinental railroad, bison, which once numbered thirty million, were so thoroughly slaughtered that they were reduced to a few hundred in private herds and just two dozen living wild and free in Yellowstone.

Our shaggy bison rolls in the sand, shaking itself on one side, then flips onto its other side. Rolling in sand and mud removes long hair from its winter coat for the summer. It shoos away insects and leaves a layer of sand and mud, making it difficult for insects to bite. After rolling in the dust, it lies there with head held high and appears satisfied, as though it were an oversized housecat waiting to be petted. We look at it. It looks at us. We don't pet it.

We return to viewing elk. A black-and-silver wolf slowly approaches. Magnifying our view from a half mile, we quietly watch with scopes. The wolf roams among alder and sage. Moving forward, it disappears behind brush, then into a gully. With patience, we re-sight it, but again it disappears. Now it reappears closer to the herd. The elk are grazing with heads lowered. One elk notices the wolf and raises its head. The wolf carefully advances. Now each elk in turn raises its head. The elk face the wolf and become stiff and upright. A several-minute standoff occurs. We watch and observe, letting nature's drama unfold.

The wolf retreats and disappears behind sage. Minutes later, it reappears and again approaches the group, only to veer away. The elk return to grazing. Using the scope and looking closely, we see an elk sitting on its belly with legs folded and head raised. The black-silver wolf retreats until it is out of sight. Fifteen minutes later, it reappears and again approaches the elk. Once more, the elk stop grazing, raise their heads and stiffly face it. As the wolf approaches ever closer, they gather in a semicircle around the sitting elk. We do not know why one elk is sitting. It may be injured, ill, very old, or malnourished after a long and harsh winter. Using scope and binoculars, even magnified views do not provide enough detail. The semicircle of 500-pound elk is an intimidating barrier. The wolf observes the group, staring from a distance. In its wolf-calculating mind, it evaluates, looking for any weakness. After several minutes, it backs off. It wanders out of view and is gone for now, but as hunger impels its existence, it will be back.

Maybe this is an inexperienced wolf that doesn't know how to panic the group to get them running. On the other hand, perhaps it is an older, experienced wolf that knows better than to tangle with a group determined to protect one of its own. For now, the confrontation is over. I look over to where the bison was wallowing. It has wandered off.

We hike back to camp for lunch. After some downtime, we explore the Lamar Valley. Far off and across the Lamar River are four wolves taking naps near an elk carcass. Not much is happening, as they rest in the shadows of trees. At times, a wolf shifts position, lifts its head, looks around, then lowers its head. Their bellies are full. The pack killed this elk a few days ago. A rib cage rises from the carcass. Two bald eagles are pecking at it. Staying away from the eagles, fluttering and hopping around are a dozen magpies and ravens scavenging from scattered bits.

VIGIL

The relationship between ravens and wolves is well known. Being quite intelligent, ravens follow wolves or packs. Once a kill has been made and the wolves have eaten, ravens move in and scavenge leftovers. After watching the eagles, magpies, and ravens peck at the carcass—and with the wolves bedded down—we head back to camp.

After some rest, we hike to the low rise we had visited this morning. It is early evening. There is a congregation of fifty elk. We set up scopes and camp stools to watch. Dusk is slowly enveloping the terrain; shadows of trees stretch across the landscape. The elk slowly move about, grazing. After several minutes, the elk appear agitated. There may be a wolf approaching. We don't see it, but the elk may sense it. They trot into a gully, splash across Slough Creek, then go up the far bank and onto a hillside. Perhaps an elder decided to find a better place to graze and the rest followed.

As shadows slowly creep up our hill, we continue to watch into darkness. Brilliant points of starlight appear over dark silhouettes of mountains to the west. The crisp air is still, the early evening is quiet. The temperature drops and we become chilled. In the dim light, it is difficult to see. We detach scopes, take down tripods, and silently trek back to camp in darkness as unseen bison grunt in murky shadows of nearby trees.

During our walk to camp, I think about the elk travelling across the creek and up the hillside. To escape Yellowstone's deep snow, elk, deer, pronghorn, and bison undertake seasonal migrations. Many will travel twenty miles with some travelling over one hundred miles to valleys outside the park. At low elevations with less snow, access to grasses and vegetation is easier. While traversing mountain passes and valley bottoms, they are preyed upon by wolves, cougars, and the occasional grizzly. After spending winter at lower elevation, as winter wanes, they migrate back to Yellowstone in search of new growth that springs forth through melting snow. Biannual migrations are natural to the Yellowstone ecosystem. If they did not occur, a piece of Yellowstone's wild nature, one that has been occurring for thousands of years, would be lost.

Back at camp, we recap our adventures. We are famished after hiking ten miles on a grandiose landscape filled with predator and prey. Using a pot, I gather water from the creek and put it on the stove, bringing it to a boil. Dinner is dehydrated potatoes and vegetable soup. After

113

cleaning dishes, I gather more water to boil. At this time of year, water filters freeze up, especially at night. After filling two bottles with hot water, I tuck them into my sleeping bag. They provide sumptuous heat against my feet. My thoughts are filled with the wolf encounter at the elk carcass two days ago. Parts of the carcass were submerged into the creek. *Yes, it is best to boil all creek water before consuming it.*

Turning on a little radio, I rotate the dial, searching for news of the outside world. The civilized world is where humans rule the landscape and go about their lives with impunity. Not true here. On this wild landscape, a grizzly could destroy a hiker that surprises it. Or a grizzly could predate on a human sleeping in a tent. In wilderness with predators, humans are but another link in nature's web of life. We exist neither at the top nor the bottom of the food chain. Tonight, it is a comfort having a hiking partner sleeping next to me.

Another human sleeping nearby, while comforting, does not stop the mind from recalling horrifying man-eater tales. The true story told by Lt. Colonel John Henry Patterson in his book, *The Man-Eaters of Tsavo*, describes two man-eating eating lions in central East Africa (today's Kenya), that terrorized laborers and villagers constructing a railway bridge in 1898. The man-eaters, working cooperatively, would sneak into camp at night, grab a resting laborer from a tent filled with people, and drag the person off into darkness. Once the lions were off into the bush with their prey, the construction crew was forced to listen to the far-off cries of the person being consumed. Of course, the crew took measures to safeguard camp and themselves. They posted guards, built thorny brush barriers, and created bonfires at night. But to no avail. Over the course of nine months, the two cunning man-eaters evaded all attempts at holding them off.

One study analyzed the composition of bone and hair from the Tsavo man-eaters and compared them to the composition found in modern Tsavo lions, which prey upon zebra, impala, lesser kudu, common eland, giraffe, East African oryx, and African buffalo. Along with their natural diet, it is estimated that during their reign of terror, one man-eater consumed the equivalent of ten humans and the other consumed twenty-four. Anecdotal estimates from 1898 put the number of victims at over one hundred. Considering the study is an extrapolation with confidence levels, there being one hundred victims is plausible.

Indeed, while it is comforting having another person sleeping nearby, it does not guarantee safety. Listening to the radio for a few minutes distracts us both. It helps me to think about something besides man-eaters.

Day Six

My hiking partner awoke before me and tells me he saw a black wolf across the creek. Darn, I am sorely disappointed I missed it. I walk a few steps over to the creek. The two American dippers are at the creek side again, bobbing on rocks. I scan back and forth, looking past trees and into the sunlit meadow beyond the creek, but there is no wolf. After breakfast, we hike on our own. My pathway finds me exploring banks downstream along the creek.

Veering away from the water's edge, I take slow, careful steps up the sand and gravel creekbank, leaving footprints in the sand. Upon reaching the top, I make my way through crusty patches of snow, then around large growths of sagebrush. For no reason except that it is there, my travel is toward a large boulder. Sitting down beside the boulder, I tilt my head skyward to examine fluffy white clouds with gray under-bellies. The clouds slowly float east against a translucent blue sky. With my back leaning against boulder, I watch ten bison grazing about sixty yards away. At intervals, the small patch of earth the bison and I share is bathed in warm sunshine. Then just as quickly, we are engulfed in shadow. After thirty minutes, the bison are on the move.

They walk this direction. As they approach, I get nervous and consider options. I could get up and quickly retreat, or I could climb onto the boulder. After thinking it over, it is too late. I don't dare move as they are just ten feet away and getting nearer. *Would a bison walk up and hoof or gore me while I sit here motionless? Do they want to scratch their hides against the boulder?* If so, then I am in a "situation." Not wanting to provoke a reaction, I sit perfectly still. They pass by on either side, within a few feet of me. I see their massive, dark, hairy bodies as they tramp by, breathing heavily and grunting. There is no incident, but they must know I am a living thing, and not a part of the boulder. Apparently, they felt no threat and I am ignored.

After the bison travel a safe distance away, I stand up and hike to camp where I reconnect with my hiking colleague. We follow Slough Creek upstream, coming to a series of cascades. Here are large cliffs and jumbles of boulders ensconced within a wooded area. Along the trail in the snow are wolf tracks. Across the creek at the top of a cliff, the silhouette of a hawk soars against the sky. Perhaps it has a nest near the top of the cliff.

After returning from our hike, we make dinner, compare notes on our activities, then turn in for the night.

Day Seven

The morning is cold and windy with snowfall. Hot drinks ease the chill—coffee for my hiking partner, hot chocolate for me. We dismantle the tent and pack gear. Pulling sleds into wind and flurries, we trudge toward the trailhead. Strong gusts of wind bite at exposed extremities. I put on gloves and a hat and zip my jacket to the neck. Now sweat builds, creating a hot-and-cold, clammy feeling. Lowering the zipper, wind again bites into sweat, causing my neck and chest to chill. Ignoring discomforts, we trek forward. After struggling over a low hill, it's a relief to see the vehicle. Reaching the trailhead, we load gear into the vehicle and pull away from our excursion into the primeval. With heater on, we luxuriate in serene comfort while terrain passes by the vehicle's windows. Traveling in silence across Yellowstone's extraordinary thawing landscape, the afterglow of our encounter with the wild lingers within our souls.

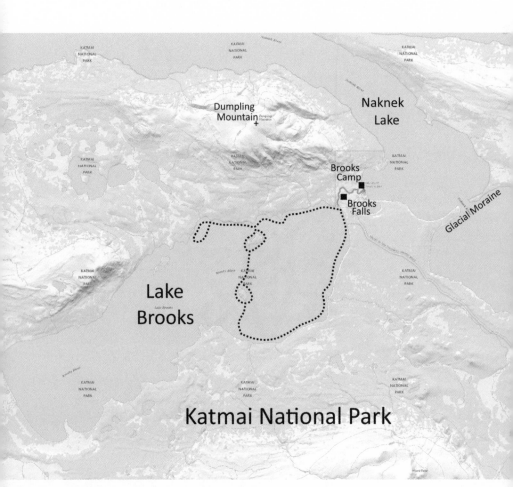

Dumpling
Mountain
+

Naknek
Lake

Brooks
Camp

Brooks
Falls

Glacial Moraine

Lake
Brooks

Katmai National Park

NIGHTMARE

"I believe that life should be lived so vividly and so intensely
that thoughts of another life, or of a longer life, are not
necessary."

—Marjory Stoneman Douglas, *Voice of the River*, 1987

Brooks Camp is a fishing and wildlife viewing area in Katmai National
Park. People fly in by floatplane to spend a few days in rustic cabins or at
the National Park Service campground. Anglers enjoy fly fishing Brooks
River for salmon, arctic char, or rainbow trout. Watching brown bears
from the walking bridge spanning Brooks River is popular, as the brown
bears are plentiful and, depending upon the month, can number over
two dozen. Another option is to hike the mile-long trail to the Brooks
Falls viewing platform. From the safety of the platform, visitors watch
brown bears capture some of the thousands of salmon leaping over the
falls. With patience, it is possible to capture a photo of a salmon jump-
ing into the gaping jaws of a bear. After spending a day or two at Brooks
Camp, most people fly out.

The small NPS campground is enclosed by an electric fence which
protects sleeping campers from the comings and goings of bears, especially at night. Upon arrival, visitors are required by the National Park
Service to undergo orientation on bear etiquette. The three main rules
are yield, back away, and stay at least fifty yards away.

Up to this point, my experience with kayaking has been limited to
two short warm-water excursions off the coast of Florida. My cold-water

paddling experience is nil, but a pretty blue kayak—available for rental—is calling to me. With two minutes of instruction, I am set to paddle Lake Brooks for a few days, exploring the lake and its environs. Lake Brooks and its tributary streams are a spawning area for up to a half million sockeye salmon. During the salmon run, Lake Brooks and Brooks River turn into an all-you-can eat buffet for Alaskan brown bears.

Being that the put-in is a mile from Brooks Camp, two staff from the lodge use a vehicle to transport the kayak and my gear to Lake Brooks. From the naiveté of my questions, it is obvious I am inexperienced. They take turns explaining some of the basics of paddling a kayak: how to hold the paddle, rudimentary paddle strokes, and getting into and out of the cockpit. After dropping me off at Lake Brooks, I am alone with my kayak and gear as water quietly laps the shore. It is obvious that bears inhabit this area, as large-clawed paw prints stretch up and down the beach. After storing food and gear in forward and aft compartments, I contort my body into the tight cockpit opening. Along with lack of experience, another concern is inclement weather while paddling. For those engaged in outdoor activities in Alaska, endeavors that involve cold water are risky.

Using the paddle, I shove the kayak away from the sand-and-gravel shoreline. Now, with the kayak freely floating, my mind relaxes. A sense of calm sets in. It feels good to be on the water. Being cautious, I stay within fifty yards of shore. With each paddle stroke, the kayak gently glides forward, up and over small rolling waves. The green shoreline reflects in the curve of each wave, with the kayak rising then dipping as it passes. I paddle north toward the base of Dumpling Mountain. Pausing for a moment, I dip my hand into the cold water. To the right is a bald eagle perched on a branch emerging from a submerged log. The sky is brilliant blue. The shoreline arcs to the west. Paddling is slow and sporadic as I approach a small stream tumbling down the slopes of Dumpling Mountain, its water crystal clear as it snakes through a sandy delta into Lake Brooks. Pointing the kayak toward the delta, I give a couple of strong strokes to surge the kayak forward until it comes to rest on gravel.

Exiting the kayak, I stand on the gravel bar but am cautious. There could be spawning salmon here. Silently, I survey the area. Bears may be in dense brush resting nearby in day beds. The stream comes down a slope that is heavily vegetated. Due to the steepness of the terrain, it is unlikely salmon swim far up the cascade. No salmon are visible, but my presence may have spooked them. Salmon retreat from dark shapes, and if panicked, they flee with vigor, causing the water to boil.

Warily stepping forward, I follow the stream as it carves an S-shaped path through sand and gravel. I am satisfied for the moment that it appears safe. Crouching down, I stare into the water. Sunlight glints off silver-green salmon minnows. Looking uphill, the stream comes cascading down through dense vegetation. I consider following the stream, but that seems unwise.

It is peaceful listening to the babbling stream. The sun is out, the air is warm, there is no wind. A perfect day to mill around streamside, but I should be on my way. There is more exploring to do and a place to camp must be found before evening arrives. Standing, I am about to walk back to the kayak when a motion to the right catches my eye. A large shadowy figure moves slowly in thick woodland not more than thirty paces away. Gradually, calmly, I turn to see a hulking brown bear. It is slowly walking through the trees toward the stream—and me.

Standing motionless and quiet, I wonder what it will do. *What should I do?* One option—scramble over to the kayak, squeeze into the cockpit, and shove off. That would take twenty seconds. This hefty bear is less than a moment away. Retreating abruptly may entice it to follow. But clearly it already knows I am here. While I crouched down to watch minnows, the bear was silently lumbering in brush, getting closer. Perhaps I stood up at just the right instant. It doesn't appear agitated. It continues to advance, emerging from tall grasses, willow brush, and balsam poplar; now fifteen paces away. Facing me, it walks forward without hesitation. Standing still, I hold my ground, watching with undivided attention. Its head is down, its face expressionless. It knows I am here but doesn't look directly at me. Instead, turning its massive body, it veers toward the creek. Stepping forward, it crosses the creek, then steps into the brush and is out of sight. It unfolds in nothing more than a few heartbeats. I stand in place looking at the green brush where the bear disappeared. It is gone. The sky is blue. The air is calm. I am still here.

Entering the kayak and shoving off, I continue my journey westward—following the north shore. The distance travelled is not great or fast, but I am in no hurry. The kayak zigs for a while and then it zags. While I pause to eat snacks and drink water, the kayak calmly bobs up and down. An experience like this is rare and must be slowly and deeply inhaled. I pause to absorb these wild surroundings until they become a part of my being. Melded into my soul, they form a part of me and who I am. Floating in the kayak, I embrace the quietness, the solitude, the grand Alaskan wilderness that surrounds me, and am grateful.

Using binoculars, I focus on the shoreline, looking for activity. Nothing catches my eye, so I set the binoculars aside and paddle forward, looking for a place to camp. The site should not be too buggy, and it would be nice to have good exposure to sunlight. My preference is that it not be surrounded by thick vegetation where a bear could emerge from the brush and stumble into my camp.

I choose a point on a small peninsula where it will be breezy and receive plenty of sunlight. Another factor: a bear traveling nearby would likely bypass my camp and instead cut across the peninsula. Unless, of course, it was curious about odors, but those will be kept to a minimum and food will be stored away from camp.

After making and eating dinner, I repack unused food into a dry bag. Everything has been sealed twice, first inside plastic bags, then inside the dry bag. Despite this, I am sure a bear's keen sense of smell could detect even minute odors emanating from the dry bag. Carrying the dry bag along moss-covered shoreline for about one hundred yards, I find there are no suitable trees to hang it in. So, I secure it at a height of about five feet in dense brush. Maybe tomorrow I will find the dry bag ripped open and the food missing. Returning to camp, I sit on shore and open a book. As dusk falls, the air becomes still and the lake placid. Now the sun dips below the horizon and the sky turns dark and murky. I enter the tent and continue reading.

Putting the book aside, sleep comes slowly and when it does, is fitful. My mind is in rumination mode. The hulking bear I saw at the stream earlier today is probably no more than a mile or two away. It could easily follow its nose to my campsite. At every crack of a twig, my body cringes. My eyes open, only to stare into darkness. Then, after a few moments of silence, I shut them again and struggle to convince myself there is nothing to fear. Do bears sneak up on prey? I can't imagine a bear cautiously and silently approaching prey. A bear lumbers right up to whatever it wants to eat and eats it—*correct?* Willfully suppressing thoughts, I drift off to sleep.

Suddenly I wake with a start in the darkness. From what I can hear, a hefty bear is outside the tent. Clear as a bell, its feet are splashing in shallow water no more than fifteen feet away. Tilting my head at an angle, I attempt to get a fix on the splashes. The bear is wading through water, moving from left to right. It must be circling the tent. Sitting up, I listen in silence. After several moments, I slowly, almost imperceptibly, breathe in, breathe out. What a miserable situation to be in, and what a dumb and regrettable choice I have made. This is a situation I would give anything to undo. But it is too late. With beads of sweat forming on my brow, I wonder if the arc of my life will continue into the future.

The splashing continues as the bear walks back and forth. I can't just sit here like a mouse. "Go away!" I yell. Sitting silently, breathing and listening, I wonder what is going to happen. Darn it. It is still out there. The splashing sounds now come from the left. It must have circled back. *What is it doing out there? Why doesn't it go away?* Frustrated I yell, "Go away!" Waiting a minute, I barely breathe and listen for what feels like an eternity. The bear is persistent and unfazed. This is intolerable. Again, I yell in a loud voice, "Go away!" Still, there is no change. It is in the water, not always at the same location but slowly moving around.

I decide to make it clear that I am a human and will stand my ground. I will not retreat, because I cannot. Certainly, I am not going to run into the dead of night with a bear chasing me. That would be disaster. One must be brave. Or at least put on a brave façade. Standing my ground means I will use pepper spray and hope it works. On the other hand, I do have a medium-sized knife. Whatever is out there, I am going to confront it.

Unzipping the tent door, I stand up and peer into darkness. In the gloom of night, I see the gravel shoreline along the beach, a few scattered logs, and nearby brush. Waves are gently lapping at the beach. Looking left and right I don't see the bear. *Had I been imagining this? What about the sounds of a bear splashing as it waded through water?* Pausing for a moment, I listen. The splashing occurs again. It is not the sound of waves hitting shore. The lake is too quiet for that. Walking out to the shoreline, I focus on the next series of splashes. With each splash, there appears a dorsal and tail fin breaking the surface. These are the splashes of salmon. Females undulating in shallow water, creating gravel nests. Males fertilizing eggs. Salmon spawning in the gravel shallows of a wilderness lake under the light of the moon. Nature at its most primordial. Life, recreating precious new life. I feel fortunate to be an observer of this ancient process. With a sigh of relief, I return to the tent and sleep.

Day Two

Upon waking, I am groggy, but the day is sunny and warm, the sky azure. Walking one hundred yards to where the food bag is stashed, I search for but cannot find it. I wonder if a bear has dragged it off, but in a few moments, I see it exactly where it had been stashed. Pulling the bag out of the brush, I examine it for claw or bite marks. There are none. After breakfast and reading under the warmth of the sun, my grogginess has worn off. Taking down the tent and packing gear into the kayak, I am ready to embark. Using the paddle, I push off from shore, then paddle backwards as I check the campsite for anything forgotten. The vegetation where the tent had been is matted down, but it will recover.

Paddling over and through small waves and into a breeze, my spirit is lifted. Following the shoreline to the west, I use sweeping strokes to rotate the kayak toward a nearby island to the south. Crossing a small channel, each stroke of the paddle brings the island closer. The island's northern point is a gravel beach. Beyond the beach is thick vegetation. Continuing past the gravel point, I hug the island's northwest side, paddling past rocky volcanic cliffs, and enter a small protected bay. Circling out of the bay and around the island's western perimeter, I paddle south and am surprised to encounter a small, rugged, tree-covered island. The day is calm, so paddling is pleasant. There are no worries about the rest of the world. Everything that matters for the moment exists here and now, spread before my eyes as glorious natural beauty. Deep greens. Bright blues. Shades of brown. Soft breeze. Gentle water. Air going in and out of lungs. Heart pumping. Tranquility.

Having circled the island, I arrive back at the gravel beach. My objective is not putting in long days paddling mile after mile. Rather, the objective is to explore, observe, and learn. To get to know this area and experience it in an unhurried manner. So, I decide the gravel beach will make a nice camp. This island will be my wilderness paradise for the night. Here, I will have a peaceful night with no worries—or so I think.

Turning toward the beach, I paddle until the kayak bottom hits submerged gravel. Getting out, I haul gear up shore. Next, I carry the empty kayak away from the water's edge, bringing it twenty yards inland, ensuring it doesn't get tossed into the lake during a storm. After setting up the tent and rolling out a sleeping pad, I open my book. This is not a tropical beach destination but still very pleasant and enjoyable. After reading awhile, I gaze at the blue sky. What an incredible place this is. Salmon spawning, bald eagles flying, large bears roaming the landscape. Whatever word used to describe it—pristine, primordial, primeval, primal—the word is insufficient. One must experience this wildness to have an understanding or appreciation.

Evening arrives while I make and eat dinner. After washing utensils and pans, I perform the nightly ritual of stowing the food dry bag in a bear-resistant location. Finding a high bush well away from camp, I hang it in the bush where the terrain is steep and rugged, but is likely not high enough to keep it out of reach of a large bear. Returning to camp, I enter the tent for the night and read. Having slept fitfully last night, I feel drowsy; thus setting the book down, I fall into a deep slumber. The night is peaceful, up to a point.

Suddenly, I am awakened. The tent is bowing in, almost to the point of collapse. A howling wind is whooshing from the northwest. Quickly I exit the tent, grab the kayak paddle, dismantle it, then use the rounded blade to brace the tent from the inside. That supports the tent for the moment, but the wind is relentless. For twenty-five minutes, I support the paddle. There is no way I can fall asleep while sitting and bracing the paddle. Exiting the tent, I grab two corners of the tarp, then drag gear and tent across the gravel beach, around to the east side of the island. High vegetation now takes the brunt of the wind, and the tent is protected from the storm's full force. Finally, I reenter the tent and sleep peacefully through the remainder of the night.

Day Three

This morning, the stiff wind persists as whitecaps stream across the lake. After breakfast of rehydrated milk and cereal, I decide not be on the water. Resigned to staying on the island, I pull the sleeping pad out of the tent and set it on gravel in sunlight. White puffy clouds float swiftly across the blue sky as waves crash on the beach. I grab my book to read, periodically peeking up to look around. Seagulls fly overhead. A bald eagle, perhaps the one I saw two days ago, soars through the sky and perches in a spruce tree on shore. A brown log is floating on the water— pushed by waves.

I read for ten minutes, then again look up to observe. The wind is blowing clouds. Gulls are flying about. The bald eagle is still perched in the tree. Waves have pushed the log closer. Grabbing binoculars, I zoom in on the eagle. It is stoic as it contemplates its domain. The gulls fly fast and are difficult to follow. I focus on the log being swept along. *Goodness gracious, that is not a log bobbing in waves.* That is a bear swimming in whitecaps. Yes, a bear is swimming in this direction. Its massive paws rise above the water, reach forward, then plunge into the water, making powerful strokes. It is a strong and proficient swimmer. The bear has my undivided attention. Perhaps it will bypass the island? After a few moments, the realization comes—no, it is swimming toward this island. My island.

Setting the binoculars down, the bear is close enough that I see the wild of its eyes as it thrashes through waves. Now I stand up, alert. We make eye contact. Urgently, I grab the kayak and set it near the water in case a quick shove-off is needed. Leaving the tent, I grab bags of gear and set them next to the kayak. At least I will have gear. At about forty yards, the bear veers to the left, swims to the beach, and exits the water near dark cliffs. It shakes vigorously, causing waves of rippling fur to twist to-and-fro. A multitude of fine water droplets spiral off in all directions. This is not the bear I saw while watching minnows at the creek. But it is large and has gigantic paws, claws, and teeth. An Alaskan brown bear has just landed on my island. *What should I do?* Before I have time to react, it walks into brush as if it owns this island. It is out of sight, but not out of mind. I realize now that my thought process is incorrect. This is not "my island."

Should I break camp and paddle away to make a new camp on mainland? That will require paddling in wind and whitecaps, which could result in a spill into cold, turbulent water. The cockpit opening is tight. Once tipped, exiting will be problematic, and drowning or hypothermia are likely. If I make it to mainland and setup a new camp, certainly bears will be nearby. After all, Katmai is a brown bear paradise. Or, I can stay overnight here, hoping the wind and whitecaps calm by morning. If I do that, there is a chance the bear will confront me. With either choice, there is an element of risk.

After some thought, I decide to stay and wait out the weather. With decision made, I organize my gear and kayak to allow for a quick exit. I return to my book but stay alert and look behind every few minutes. Evening comes. I make dinner and eat, then clean up. So far, the bear has not approached camp. I know it is on the island, hopefully on the other side, but with the thick vegetation here, it could be nearby. I store the dry bag with food at seventy-five yards from the tent, hanging it as high as possible in large brush. I could explore the island and find a high tree, but I don't want a chance encounter. It is best to stick to "my" side of the island. My hope is that with the food bag hanging near shore, the wind will push smells over the lake. The fresh air makes performing chores around camp invigorating. Good-sized waves continue to crash on shore.

There are few places in the world today where a person can walk along a beach and come across grizzly tracks in the sand. Here, Alaskan brown bears are apex—unafraid of showing themselves midday as they roam with impunity. This is the essence of "wild," where predators traverse the landscape as freely today as in the ancient past. All creatures, including *Homo sapiens*, yield to their dominance. The exhilaration of being here imparts a chill up and down my spine.

With the strong wind blowing, I enter the tent as evening light dims. At this time of year in the North, the night sky has a dim glow with only the brightest stars visible. After reading, I put the book aside and turn off the flashlight. Any untoward noises outside the tent are muffled by wind and crashing waves. My consciousness lets go of the fact that I am sharing this small island with a bear. The kayak is ready for a quick exit. Sleep is welcomed and delicious.

Day Four

Slept well. Getting out of the tent, I look to the sky and lake. Both are clear and blue. A warm breeze wisps across my face. Bright sparkles of sunlight flash off smooth ripples on the water. In the brightness of the morning sun, upon seeing no bear, I take a couple deep breaths and a sense of security sets in. After breakfast, I break down the tent and pack gear into the kayak's fore and aft holds. I neither heard the bear last night nor see it this glorious morning. It is a relief, and time to leave this island camp.

I squeeze into the kayak, shove off, and paddle away. As I circle the island, I look for but don't see the bear. The island is craggy with thick brush, so it is not surprising it is not visible. There are plenty of places to stay hidden, and it is probably bedded down. Pointing the kayak to the south, I paddle toward another island about a half mile away. The weather is calm, so I am not concerned about capsizing far from shore. After fifteen minutes, I paddle past the island and then toward a stream that enters the south shore of Lake Brooks. While floating offshore, I watch the stream. I rest, eat a few snacks, and wait to see if a bear comes for spawning salmon. Using the binoculars, I periodically scan along the shoreline looking for movement. The day is glorious and serene with sunshine streaming down and a cool breeze blowing. The motion of the kayak bobbing in calm water is soothing. I doze off but do not fall asleep. Refreshed, I point the kayak to the east and paddle toward the pick-up point.

Reaching the pick-up point, I disembark and unpack my bags of gear. At the appointed time, two workers from the lodge pull up with a vehicle. We put the pretty blue kayak into the back of the SUV along with my gear. The driver asks how I enjoyed the adventure. My reply: "Had a good time. It was an excellent learning experience." Then he asks if I paddled during the high winds and whitecaps. My reply is, "No, I waited it out on an island." Not sure why, but I don't mention spending the night on the island with an Alaskan brown bear. This is an experience that few people have and few would appreciate. It is an experience that is seared into my memory and one I will always savor.

SUPPLICATION

"Earth as an ecosystem stands out in the all of the universe.
There's no place that we know about that can support life
as we know it, not even our sister planet, Mars, where we
might set up housekeeping someday, but at great effort
and trouble we have to recreate the things we take for
granted here."

—Sylvia Earle

"The Journey" is part of the mystical transformation of one's emotional state while venturing toward a wilderness outing. If one is traveling by motor vehicle, the trappings of civilization fade in the rearview mirror. If traveling by aircraft, they recede when the plane becomes airborne. As we venture farther from the city and toward wilderness, towns get smaller and services become few. The tension of following a schedule and the noise of urban life evaporates. The mind begins to relax and is free to think whatever random thoughts that come to it. The priority of things that weigh heavily in town wanes. During "The Journey," a person's inner spirit is freed from its urban shackles. We are free to take in and inhale slowly and deeply. Instead of rushing to-and-fro, we allow ourselves to experience nature with all of our senses. It is at this point we are free to venture. Free to have one's senses and, indeed, one's body and spirit engulfed by the sensations and feelings created by nature. We are free to explore. Free to live in the here and now. Free to just be.

It is late October, and we are driving "Up North" to the Boundary Waters Wilderness for a hiking trip on the Kekekabic Trail. "The Kek" can be accessed by driving fifty miles up the Gunflint Trail from the town of Grand Marais on the North Shore of Lake Superior.

After leaving work in the Twin Cities earlier this Friday, my hiking partner and I had gotten a late start. After fighting traffic and a three-hour monotonous ride, we are getting tired. Currently we are traveling north on Highway 61 as it winds along the North Shore's rugged cliffs. My attention is focused on the twisty dark road and avoiding the sporadic deer whose eyes shine at us from the road's edge. Periodically, we pass a deer carcass—some of which have ravens pecking at them. As we pass another dead deer, I wonder why we don't see a wolf or two scavenging. Maybe wolves come out later at night when there is little traffic. My eyes are getting sleepy. I don't want to hit a deer or miss a turn and plunge into the lake.

The road hugs the face of Silver Creek Cliff north of the town of Two Harbors. As we circle around the cliff, along the right side is a minimal guardrail separating the vehicle from the cliff edge. My passenger gets a spectacular view overlooking the one-hundred-foot plunge into Lake Superior.

After passing through the town of Tofte, we pull off Highway 61, proceed north on the Sawbill Trail, then into a dirt turnaround. This is the Britton Peak trailhead for the Superior Hiking Trail. After a full day of work and four hours of driving, it is about 10:00 p.m., and we look forward to sleep. Instead of putting up the tent, we spread a tarp on tall grass. We want to get an early start tomorrow and still have seventy miles of driving to reach the Kek trailhead. We throw our sleeping bags onto the tarp and crawl into them for the night.

Tonight, I am experimenting with a lightweight homemade sleeping bag. My hope is the ultra-light fleece bag will reduce weight during our hike. It is late fall and there is a crisp—below freezing—chill in the air. After three hours of shivering, I concede defeat and retrieve a warmer sleeping bag from the car, throw it on the tarp and get inside. A partial moon is visible through golden birch leaves. Warmer now, I don't sleep well without a tent. For a while, I put my head inside the bag to warm my face. Later, I poke my head out to gaze at the stars and moon as they slowly trace arcs across the sky. My partner is sleeping soundly and snoring. At times, snoring loudly.

About 2:00 a.m., the sound of footsteps crunching brittle leaves reverberates through the forest. Not the slow, plodding steps of a human but the rapid padding of a four-legged creature. An animal is running on the slopes of Britton Peak. Each footstep disturbs the cold, quiet night with a distinctive crunch. I mull the sound over, wondering what it could be. Again, more crunching of leaves, followed by a quiet pause. Once more, the sound of an animal running through leaves. There are three animals. Then a fourth sound of leaves crunching. A few moments of silence. A fifth, a sixth, a seventh. *Do deer travel together in the middle of the night?* Now, the sound of an eighth, but this one suddenly stops. It is quiet. I wait motionless, listening for something to happen, wondering what it is doing. Silence. Whatever it is, it did not move on like the others. I feel its presence—not more than fifty feet away. There is a sensation it is aware of our presence. *But what is it?* After a few moments, there are more sounds of crunching leaves. This is not the sound of an animal running off like the others but of an animal slowly descending the hillside. My fear builds. Is it a bear? Was a bear chasing seven deer? The crunching footsteps get closer. It is coming to *investigate us.* Trepidation builds. Petrified, I hope staying still will cause it to lose interest. Lying next to me, my hiking partner does not stir.

An animal is standing twenty-five steps away, but in darkness and without my glasses, its shape is a dark, murky blur. My glasses are nearby, but I don't move to grab them. The night is pitch black, as the moon has fallen below the horizon. However hard I look, I cannot clearly see it, but I know it is looking at us splayed on the tarp. With neck craned, propped up on an elbow, I keep my eyes focused on the murky shape. Whispering to my hiking partner, "Hey, hey, wake up. Hey, hey, wake up." His reply is muffled breathing. Again, "Hey, hey, wake up." Nothing. Then with a very loud whisper, "Hey, wake up!" Finally, he stirs. I whisper, "Look over there, behind you." His reply is "What?" Again, I whisper, "Look over there," and he says, "What is it?" My response: "I don't know; I can't tell."

We both grab flashlights and shine them into the darkness. Two cones of light illuminate a wolf staring down on us! We are dumbfounded and motionless. We don't know what to make of it. It doesn't know what to make of us, two humans lying in sleeping bags in its territory. Perhaps it thinks we are wounded animals? Maybe we are vulnerable prey? Is this a curious young wolf? Perhaps it is a confident older wolf, bringing up the rear of the pack.

The dark shape of the wolf, standing tall with head held high, stares down at us on the tarp. We lay there in quiet supplication with necks craned upward, humbled and in awe to be in the presence of a monarch of the wild. It is confident and unafraid. One hundred million years of divergent evolution separates our genomes, yet still, we are kindred spirits on planet Earth.

After a few moments, the wolf turns and slowly meanders up the hillside. It peers back every few steps. It is not in a hurry. Its purposeful footsteps crunch dry leaves as it ascends. It is not anxious but cautious, looking back to see if we are following. Finally, it is gone, back into the darkness and wild from whence it came, to rejoin its pack. My partner and I, propped up on elbows with flashlights in hand, stare in disbelief into the empty darkness where moments before there was an apparition from the wild.

With the excitement of the encounter, the chill of the night is gone. I describe to my partner how I had heard seven other animals running over dry leaves while he slept. Finally, I grab my glasses and put them on, looking around to see if anything is nearby. Satisfied we are alone; we turn flashlights off and lay our heads down. He quickly falls asleep.

I stare into the night sky, looking at the shining points of light, brilliant in the darkness. I ponder the mystery of life on Earth, and perhaps other places in the Universe. It is awesome to contemplate life on other planets orbiting other stars. But here on Earth, the life forms are pretty awesome.

At morning's light, we wake up and pace off how far away the wolf stood. Roughly fifteen paces.

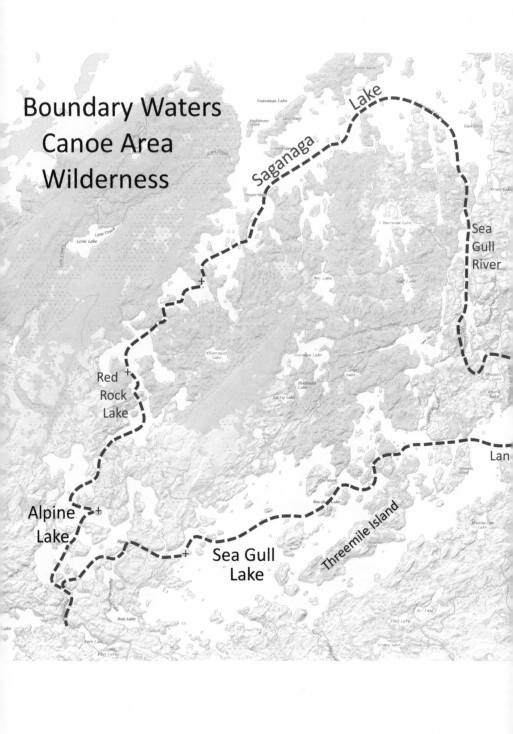

Boundary Waters
Canoe Area
Wilderness

Saganaga Lake

Sea
Gull
River

Red
Rock
Lake

Alpine
Lake

Sea Gull
Lake

Threemile Island

Lan

WINTER SOLITUDE

"I find it wholesome to be alone the greater part of the time.
To be in company, even with the best, is soon wearisome
and dissipating. I love to be alone. I never found the
companion that was so companionable as solitude."

—Henry David Thoreau, *Walden*, 1854

The lakes, streams, forests, and wetlands of northeastern Minnesota's
Arrowhead Region are bounded by the rugged cliffs of Lake Superior
on the south and the border with Canada to the north. The bulk of the
region is embodied within three million acres of Superior National Forest. Nestled within Superior National Forest are one million acres of
the Boundary Waters Canoe Area Wilderness (BWCAW). Touching
the northern borders of the BWCAW are another one million acres of
wilderness within Quetico Provincial Park in Ontario. Taken together,
the Quetico-Superior country is affectionately known as the Boundary Waters. This pristine forest and lake wilderness is where temperate
forest transitions to boreal forest of the North. Species such as eastern
white pine, red pine, red maple, and American basswood give way to
northern species such as jack pine, black spruce, white spruce, white
cedar, trembling aspen, balsam fir, and white birch.

The area was formed and sculpted by a series of geological and climatic events. A billion years ago, the area underneath Lake Superior
was an open wound caused by the North American continent splitting
apart—the 1,200-mile-long Keweenawan Rift. The rifting and fissure

process exuded vast magma outflows, resulting in the many dark basalt cliffs we see along Lake Superior's North Shore, one example being flows of basaltic lava at Gooseberry Falls. The main fissure is beneath Lake Superior. From the western end of Lake Superior, one arc of the fissure runs south and west through eastern Minnesota and western Wisconsin, then down through central Iowa and into Kansas. From Lake Superior's eastern end, another arc runs south and east through central Michigan.

Failing to rip North America apart, the rift's fractures and depressions filled with sediment. During the Pleistocene, repeated cycles of continental glaciation gouged depressions in the Great Lakes region. With each advance, the Laurentide Ice Sheet scoured the overlying sedimentary layers, thus exposing bedrock. In the Quetico-Superior Region, Earth's ancient geological core is laid bare. This is the Canadian Shield, which forms the foundation of the North American continent.

Here in the Boundary Waters, the bedrock dates to a time when Earth supported only unicellular life during the Precambrian eon, 2.7 billion years ago. As the continental ice sheet melted, the giant scoured depressions filled with meltwater, creating the Great Lakes. Smaller cracks and depressions in the bedrock filled with sediment and water, thus forming the numerous lakes in the Boundary Waters.

Coming out of the last major glaciation, as the Earth warmed and the ice sheet retreated, vegetation slowly reclaimed nutrient-poor rocky surfaces. The first to gain foothold were low-lying ground cover such as lichens and moss. These were followed by sedges, grasses, and ferns. After sufficient nutrients and soil had accumulated, larger brush and woody plants took hold. Over time, a succession of forest species migrated from the south, resulting in the tree species we see today. The Boundary Waters is now a patchwork of bogs, creeks, lakes, exposed bedrock, and mixed coniferous-deciduous forest.

As plant life flourished, animal life followed: first, small herbivores such as mice, muskrats, and ground squirrels. Eventually, larger herbivores such as beaver, caribou, and moose found suitable habitat. With herbivores came predators: wolves, black bear, badger, wolverine, cougar, and Canada lynx. Other species that migrated into areas exposed by retreating glaciers include mammoth, mastodon, saber-toothed cats, dire wolves, giant beavers, ground sloths, and short-faced bears. Humans have lived in the Quetico and Boundary Waters wilderness areas since at least nine thousand years ago and perhaps earlier. Today, even after more than ten thousand years of reclamation, the topsoil is not very deep; a meager two feet in lowland areas to none at all on large, exposed granite slabs that form many of the hills and shorelines of the pristine glacial lakes.

Before the melting of North America's continental glacier, caribou roamed south of the ice sheet, with caribou fossils having been found in Nebraska, Iowa, Indiana, Kentucky, Tennessee, Ohio, Georgia, Alabama as well as other states. At that time, these areas were not prairies, grasslands, or temperate forests but a mosaic of tundra, steppe, taiga, barren grounds, and boreal forest. While undergoing seasonal migrations across the landscape, caribou ate lichen, grasses, moss, sedges, and willow leaves. As the climate warmed, the ice sheet retreated. The tundra, taiga, steppe, and barren ground biomes migrated north, with caribou following. Prairies and grasslands replaced tundra and barren ground on the plains, with elk and deer replacing caribou. Until recently, caribou habitat existed in northern Minnesota, and as recently as the 1930s, boreal woodland caribou lived in the Boundary Waters Wilderness. Today, woodland caribou exist and thrive just two hundred miles north in Ontario's Woodland Caribou Provincial Park.

Besides fissures spewing magma and glaciers carving the landscape, as plants and forests thrive and reclaim land, another force of nature shapes the landscape—wildfire. With lightning strikes, swaths of forest burn, thus starting another cycle of vegetation and forest regrowth. Some species, such as jack pine, are dependent upon fire and regenerate only when their cones open during intense heat, thus releasing their seeds. When wildfires are absent, cedar, spruce, and fir take over, crowding out other species. After a fire, grasses and shrubs flourish, supporting snowshoe hare, beaver, porcupine, whitetail deer, and moose. Raspberry and blueberry bushes proliferate, providing food for birds and bears. Wildfires make way for a diverse mosaic of plant, tree, and animal species to flourish in the north woods.

Here in Minnesota's Arrowhead Region, there exists the remnants of a boreal forest mixed with tall, majestic pines, sprinkled with clear-blue bedrock lakes, sculpted by natural forces from an ancient time. Here lies the Boundary Waters Canoe Area Wilderness. Into this fire-forged landscape of glacially scoured bedrock, I embark on a snowshoe trek from ice-covered lake to ice-covered lake.

The trailhead is the terminus of a dead-end road known as the Gunflint Trail. The Gunflint started as a footpath used by the Ojibwa. Later, trappers and surveyors used it. Often, it was used as a pathway to Gunflint Lake where natives and voyageurs gathered Gunflint chert. When struck, the chert sparks, and it was used as a flint for a flintlock gun or to start a fire. With the onset of logging, the trail became a rough road into the forest. Today, the Gunflint Trail is a paved two-lane road starting in Grand Marais on the shore of Lake Superior and ending deep in the forest at Saganaga Lake.

The starting point for this journey is a landing on the eastern shore of Seagull Lake, just outside the Boundary Waters Wilderness. About five miles long, Seagull Lake runs roughly northeast to southwest; it is dotted with pine-studded granite islands, the largest of which is Three Mile Island. This area has been burned over from recent fires. The Cavity Lake Fire of 2006 was started by lightning. The Ham Lake Fire of 2007 was started when an unattended campfire spread. From the landing, vacant cabins are visible along the non-wilderness portion of the shoreline.

Navigation is by compass and map. Standing at the landing and looking out across the snow-white lake surface, I try to make sense of the tangled jumble of peninsulas, bays, and islands on the horizon. After several minutes, I identify Fishhook Island and scout a route that is west, toward a gap between Fishhook and the shoreline to the north. Now that I have my bearings, I strap on snowshoes and head onto the frozen lake surface, pulling the sled loaded with gear. Not entirely proficient with map and compass, I double-check my position on the map. Pulling the sled using two-inch webbing makes for a comfortable tow, unlike rope which cuts into hands and chest. The wind is blowing into my face and body but is not severe. Rather, it is invigorating. As I inhale the fresh air, purpose envelopes my consciousness and vitality spreads through my body. The going is tough through deep snow as the sled isn't tracking properly. It should be riding on the surface, but the sled is twisted with one corner plowing into snow. I stop to balance the load by reworking bungee cords; now the sled tracks true.

While passing Fishhook Island, I glance at the map and, indeed, it is shaped like a fishhook. It is a summer camp for retreats and has several buildings, but some of the structures burned to the ground when hot embers from the Ham Lake fire jumped across the lake. A footbridge connects Fishhook to a nearby smaller island.

Trekking west, I approach a small island with a sign at the top of two posts. It is engraved with the words: "Boundary Waters Canoe Area Wilderness" and "Superior National Forest." To the southwest are tree-covered islands whose inlets, bays, and peninsulas blur together. From this distance, it is difficult to know if an inlet is a bay or a passage between islands. I'm breathing heavily, and rising breath fogs my glasses. Should I head to the northwest or southwest toward an inlet between pine-covered points?

Towing a sled with snowshoes, while heading into the wind, I don't want to make a wrong decision that wastes time and energy. My plan is to follow the northwest shoreline of Three Mile Island. Scouting a path is required, so I abandon the sled to explore an inlet, but the inlet turns out to be a large bay. Retreating from the bay and veering west, I find a channel between Three Mile Island and an adjacent island. I go back to retrieve the sled.

Now pulling the sled, I enter the gap to where it narrows with flowing open water. Avoiding weak ice, I veer to the right, heaving the sled onto a snow-covered point. This would make a pleasant campsite, with water, tall pines, and shelter from strong winds. Momentarily, I consider making camp but push on, west and south. The goal is to reach the far end of Seagull Lake by late afternoon or early evening.

Many islands on Seagull Lake are burned over from the Cavity Lake and Ham Lake fires. Both fires were fueled by millions of dead and blown-down trees from the large-scale thunder and windstorm that struck Superior National Forest on July 4, 1999, with wind speeds up to 120 miles per hour. The derecho started in eastern North Dakota, raced through western Minnesota, and continued on a path 5 to 10 miles wide for 1,300 miles across the northern US and southern Canada. In the Boundary Waters, 300,000 acres were affected, and twenty-five million trees were blown down.

Despite windstorms downing trees and the countless fires that have burned this wilderness over hundreds of years, many islands in the Boundary Waters, including Three Mile Island, have white cedars that have survived and are quite ancient, with some groves between five hundred and a thousand years old. White cedar, with its flat, fan-shaped, aromatic leaves, is referred to as Arborvitae or the "Tree of Life." Tea made from its bark and leaves contains vitamin C and other beneficial compounds. A tea made from a conifer (likely white cedar) saved Jacques Cartier and many of his shipmates from scurvy during the winter of 1535–1536 while they explored the St. Lawrence River and the coast of Newfoundland. Extracts from white cedar also include anti-atherosclerosis and anti-cancer properties.

Traveling southwest, the gap widens to reveal a series of islands that recede into the distance. During wildfires, windblown cinders hopped from the mainland, igniting some islands while skipping others, leaving skeletal black pines on some while others still have tall majestic pines. Where there is no snow cover, glacially scoured pink-and-gray granite bedrock is exposed. Leaving the gap, the vista opens to a resplendent snowscape filling my spirit with joy and awe.

Trekking along, snowshoes and sled leave imprints as I zig then zag between islands. To the northwest is a view between two pine-covered islands. Framed between them and rising above the lake's frozen surface, dark craggy cliffs jut out. The cliff face is not the light gray and pink granite forming the islands. Rather, its dark color is likely the result of a different geological origin, perhaps volcanic. Gray-green moss and lichen cover its surface, while seepage from above darkens it. *What massive force sheared this cross section?* Perhaps tectonic faulting 2.5 billion years ago or glacial scouring 20,000 years ago. The top of the eighty-foot cliff is covered with snow, green pines, and spruce.

Trekking into the wind is pleasant. Concerns of civilization are abandoned, as being here engulfs my mind and body. The physicality of pulling a sled, the purity of fresh air, the white snowscape—release signals of a serene existence. The landscape is large and I feel small. Viewed from the sky, my form appears as a small dark figure slowly moving between islands on a vast backdrop of white forming the surface of Seagull Lake. My only concern is reaching the far end of the lake, making camp, and eating dinner before the sun goes down.

Through lightly falling snow, I see a gray-green jumble of islands on the western horizon. At this distance the islands are blurred together. Meandering between nearby islands, I am uncertain of my location. Using a compass tied to a string hanging from my neck, I take a reading and view the map, then focus on the next island and head toward it. Arriving at that island, I again check bearings and the map.

Self-doubt creeps in. I wonder if this trek exceeds my ability. Will I become confused and lose my way in this maze of frozen bays, lakes, and islands? What if I encounter thin ice and crash into water? Proceeding forward, I reassure myself, but at the same time realize that a bit of uncertainty is what makes an outdoor endeavor compelling.

To the south is an island with a semicircular bay which touches a long thin island with pines. Peering past these islands are more islands, and beyond those is Three Mile Island. This gives the snowscape richness and depth. The scenery engages my mind and body, evoking a feeling of quiet enthrallment and satisfaction.

As I travel west, islands become sparse. Plodding across an open white expanse, a blurry archipelago comes into view on the western horizon. Picking the closest island, I cut a path toward it. The wind whisks snow from the tops of drifts, blowing it in sinuous wisps. The sun, obscured by clouds, creeps closer to the western horizon. Although muted, it provides light, a sense of direction, and moral support. My goal is to find a semi-protected place to camp and eat dinner before sunset.

I approach the first of five islands. Navigating south for a distance, I turn west toward the mainland, a half mile in the distance—cutting between islands two and three. Along a pocket of island three, I pause. Here a patch of brown reeds and yellow grasses pierce upward through the snow. Beyond are lichen-covered granite boulders and cliffs, creating a protected area. It is a lovely scene. Standing here alone on a frozen lake in the Boundary Waters, I am thankful to view this exquisite microcosm of wilderness. Having expended effort to get here, taking in the quiet, serene beauty is satisfying.

Moving on, I tow the sled through a drift of deep snow, up onto the surface of island five. At its high point is a small northern white cedar, a few other trees, brush, and the blackened, burnt-out trunk of a pine. One of the trees has a hole chiseled into its base by a pileated woodpecker. After stomping down snow in a circular area and laying a tarp down, I set up the tent and put duffel bags inside to hold it in place. Having the tent erected provides a sense of security. If a sudden storm comes, say a freezing rain or blizzard, I'd be protected from the elements.

After attaching the fuel bottle to the stove, I set them in snow that has been compacted and unfold an aluminum windbreak around the stove. Tipping the sled on its side provides a full windscreen. I pump pressure into the stove, then flick the lighter; the hiss of hot blue flames comes to life. Lighting the stove provides another sense of security, knowing that hot water and food will soon be available. A working stove, hot food, and hot liquids are vital.

Using a pot, I scoop up snow and set it on the stove. The snow melts into a small amount of water, so I add more snow. After the water is brought to a boil, I add spaghetti noodles. In another pot, I heat sauce, slices of pepperoni, and Parmesan cheese. A bald eagle perched at the top of a burnt tree on the next island over watches my activities intently. While eating, I boil more water. Some is used for hot chocolate, the rest is poured into two water bottles, which I securely seal then insert into a sleeping bag. The lakes are frozen, so the eagle must hunt for fish and waterfowl on open water channels, streams, or nearby Seagull River.

The tangerine sun quietly sinks behind blackened trees to the southwest. Physical activity has kept my body warm, but with the onset of evening, cold seeps into my core. Silver-gray clouds obscure the last of the sun's rays as they diverge through translucent violet-blue sky. Then in a moment the sun silently blinks. It is out of sight below gray shadows on the horizon.

I make my way into the tent and unroll two foam sleeping pads and spread two sleeping bags onto the pads. Damp socks are removed and replaced with warm dry socks. I tuck my legs into sleeping bags where the heat of the water bottles is comforting. Opening a book and reading is relaxing and a good way to wind down from a day of physical activity. The night is calm and quiet. After putting the book down, sleep comes easily. Then in the darkness, I am awakened by booming sounds. Sharp cracking and thunder. I look outside the tent to see black sky and stars. The orange glow of a crescent moon hangs above the jagged black tree line to the west. There is no storm. The upper layer of lake ice, having thawed, is refreezing and buckling.

Day Two

The eagle is gone. Breakfast today is cereal and rehydrated milk and a cup of hot chocolate. I pack up camp and put on snowshoes, then pull the sled down the slope of the island and onto the frozen lake.

Pulling the sled away from the island, the next destination is Alpine Lake. Progress is west toward a narrows with flowing water that leads to a small bay. Veering left of the water, I pull the sled onto a point of land. Here is a big snowdrift where I struggle to pull the sled through deep, fluffy snow as strong wind blows into my face. I flounder, breathing heavily. Upon crossing the snow's crest, I pause to catch my breath behind shrubs and cedars which provide protection against the brunt of the wind.

From the peninsula, I follow the south shoreline of a small bay. Here, just a dusting of snow covers the lake ice and pulling the sled is effortless. To the west is the portage entrance; a white delta between green pines leading upslope toward a burnt-over forest. The portage itself is an indentation in the snow. Heaving the sled, I struggle uphill. Large trees have been reduced to ragged black snags rising out of snow. Rising amidst the burnt forest is fresh growth of birch and poplar. Hugging both sides of the trail are leafless brown branches of deciduous brush. Upon reaching the top of the rise, Alpine Lake comes into view.

With a howling wind blowing into my face, I follow the portage downhill through blackened forest. The sled easily glides as I breathe in cool, clean air. In contrast, some days Minneapolis has brown haze smeared across the horizon, but here the sky is crystal clear. Striding downward is exhilarating as fresh air fills my lungs, refreshing my vitality. Reaching the bottom, I pull the sled onto Alpine's frozen surface, then pause to rest, sitting on top of gear bundled on the sled.

Alpine Lake's shoreline and most of its islands are burned over. Although not as large as Seagull, Alpine has numerous islands and convoluted bays. Before traveling further, I want to get my bearings and identify islands in view. I reach into my left pant pocket to grab the map. The pocket is empty. I check other pockets. I check pockets in the backpack. No map. Darn. *What to do? Should I carry on, through the tangle of lakes, bays, and islands of Alpine and beyond?* One could spend hours exploring dead-end bays searching for the portage to Red Rock Lake. It would be a waste of energy and time taking a portage to a wrong lake. Planning this trip, I examined the map and route, but my recollection is imperfect. The maze of islands and bays on Saganaga Lake would surely be confusing. A worst-case scenario—getting lost, exhausted, and running out of food.

I know the route across Seagull Lake back to the trailhead: head northeast through the maze of islands. I could abandon this journey by backtracking but pause to think over options. Having decided, I abandon the sled and retrace my path back over the portage to Seagull Lake. Following sled tracks as they hug the shoreline of the small bay, I scan snow and ice looking for the map. Further backtracking, I come to the snowdrift I had struggled in this morning. There, in disturbed snow, is where I had fallen. Next to the snow crater is the map. The wind had not blown it away. *Whew!* Grabbing the map, I secure it in a zippered pocket and retrace back to Alpine, a third time over the portage.

With map in hand, I am prepared to explore Alpine Lake. Although most of the shoreline and islands are burnt-over, campers have gathered downed wood near a campsite on the closest island. Around the campsite, big pines have escaped the fires. Despite the ecological renewal created by fire, my aesthetics prefer tall green pines to black sticks.

As an alternate route for this trip, or in preparation for a future trip, I search for an inlet on the south side of Alpine Lake. The inlet leads to a bay where there is a portage to Jasper Lake. Mistakenly, I slog past the inlet and become disoriented. Consulting the map does not bring clarity. Scanning the south shoreline for several minutes, I discover the inlet behind me and backtrack. The inlet leads to a bay that curves around to the south. There is a tiny rock island with a small green cedar growing out of it—quite picturesque. It looks out of place, with most of the trees on the shore blackened. Trekking past the small island, I wind my way through the serpentine bay toward the portage to Jasper Lake.

On the southwest end of Alpine Lake, there is dark, ominous water where a large stream from Jasper cascades into Alpine. Trekking toward the portage, I stay on solid ice by keeping a good distance from the open water. Leaving the sled on the shoreline, I explore the portage which follows the cascade. Hiking over snow-covered boulders on the east shoreline of Jasper, I see open water where Jasper narrows. Proceeding along this route would require travel over snow-covered, rocky shore to avoid the open water. I head back to the sled on Alpine.

Grabbing the sled's webbing, I head toward a bay on the north end of Alpine where there is a portage to Red Rock Lake. This frozen kingdom of snow and ice looks remarkably different from my canoe trip here last summer when dragonflies and birds flew in a warm breeze and waves rolled past the canoe. Then the shoreline was engulfed in green vegetation.

The contrast is intense and is to be relished. In winter, this area experiences temperatures of -40°F and occasional blizzards. In summer, daytime can reach 90°F as storms whip up thunderheads, crackling bolts of lightning, and ninety-mile-per-hour wind.

Here at Alpine Lake are species at the southern fringe of their boreal range, such as moose, Canada lynx, boreal chickadee, Canada jay, snowshoe hare, snowy owl, spruce, white birch, and balsam poplar. Also here are species at the northern extent of their range, such as the ruby-throated hummingbird, snapping turtle, bobcat, great blue heron, green frog, monarch butterfly, sugar maple, and the majestic white pine. With climate warming, the range of boreal species is retreating north, while mid-latitude temperate species are advancing north.

What place in the Universe is so dynamic, has such a diversity of climatic conditions, and contains such a grand diversity of life? Astronomers are aware of planets and moons that have the right environment for liquid water. They *may* support life, but there are none that are known to contain life, except Earth itself.

It's been a good day to contemplate life on Earth with its glorious seasons. Having meandered among islands and bays, I have not traveled very far but have enjoyed exploring. With evening approaching, I set up camp on the north end of Alpine Lake. It is eerily quiet. The snow muffles every sound, except the hiss of my stove, while I sit on an ice-encrusted log making mac and cheese. If you are looking for solitude, this is it. I am completely alone, sheltered by cedar and pine on the shore of a frozen lake in the Boundary Waters. There are no wolves howling. No Canada jays yakking or trying to steal a morsel of food. My first winter snowshoe trip into the Boundary Waters was fifty years ago. On that trip, two Canada jays flew in to pick a morsel of food from a gloved hand. Their friendly presence added amusement.

Here and now, there is not a soul nearby; I feel unique and rich beyond belief. There are hundreds of miles of frozen wilderness surrounding my camp and not a single person nearby. Time spent in the quiet solitude of nature is precious. It allows one to listen to one's thoughts without interruption. Tranquil contemplation, especially while observing birds or wildlife going about their lives, is something to be cherished.

Evening's darkness envelopes my campsite. Between nearby trees, I see nothing but black void. I crawl into the tent. Pulling out a book, I light a candle for reading. Here in the frigid wilderness, the light and warmth from the flicker of a single flame is precious. Instead of reading, I stare intently at the flame's glow, at times cupping my hands near it for warmth. My mind drifts to worry. What if the tent catches fire while reading by candlelight? Being out here all alone, becoming engulfed in flames would be catastrophic. What if tomorrow I traverse a weak spot of ice that gives way? What if I lose the map again and must navigate through a maze of islands, bays, and portages? What if I run out of food? What if I twist my knee? What if I'm struck by appendicitis? I turn in for the night, convincing myself there is little to worry about. Snuggled in the sleeping bags, I am warm and comfortable and feel a glow of satisfaction after a day of exertion. I doze off, thinking about a meteorite crashing though the sky and obliterating the tent with me inside. Oh well, nothing a person can do about that. Then I think about the odds of a tree falling in the middle of the night and striking the tent. Now that could happen.

Day Three

After breakfast, the tent is disassembled, the gear is packed into duffel bags, and the duffel bags are loaded onto the sled. The day is calm with low clouds blotting out the sun. Leaving my campsite, I pull the sled onto the lake, trek west, north around a peninsula, then east toward a small island at the entrance to a bay. If I haven't made a wrong turn, at the north end of the bay is a portage to Red Rock Lake. Light snow is falling as I approach the shoreline where a trail of white leads into the green tree line. *That is the portage.* The green tunnel is inviting and confirms my location. Hiking alone in the wilderness under an overcast sky with snow falling is a magical experience. I feel a surreal sense of calmness and serenity that I will never forget and often reminisce about.

Hauling the sled along the portage, the snow is deep, thick, and crusted. The snowshoes do not sink as they would in fluffy snow. At the north end, the green tunnel opens to a view of Red Rock Lake. Pulling the sled onto Red Rock Lake, deep-green pines, cedar, spruce, and fir contrast against white snow. Further on, I trek past large boulders and cliffs. The black-and-gray crags have evergreen shrubs growing from cracks with large slabs covered with elegant sunburst lichen. Extracts from this orange lichen have been investigated for antioxidant properties and the ability to counteract DNA damage. Although many lichens are leafy and look like low-lying plants, they are fungi cohabitating with algae or cyanobacteria.

After traveling through a narrows with scattered islands, I pull the sled around a peninsula with an outcropping of tall pines. The trees form a windbreak which results in deep snow. Here, I set out to make camp in the deep, fluffy snow, stomping it down to form a circular crater. There, I put down the tarp and set up the tent. After putting bags of gear into the tent, I stomp snow in front of the door, creating an area to make and eat dinner.

After dinner, I put on snowshoes for a walk along the shoreline, zigzagging into the forest. The sun is setting behind trees to the west. Tree-shaped violet shadows slowly stretch across the white lake surface. It is a delight coming across tracks made by mice, shrews, and squirrels. Little mammals eking out an existence in a harsh environment. I follow a trail of larger tracks as they leave the forest, meander among snow-covered boulders, then into open terrain along the shoreline. The tracks have long, oval hind prints and closely placed smaller front prints. These are tracks of the snowshoe hare, which occupies northern Minnesota. I follow the hare's tracks about twenty yards, but they abruptly terminate.

This is curious. How can tracks suddenly stop with no trail leading away? I bend down to examine the last bit of trail. In the evening's last light, a silent chill hangs in the air. Looking closely, imprints of outstretched wings are on either side. I imagine a great horned owl, northern goshawk, or red-tailed hawk swooshing down to grasp the hare with talons, then lifting off, leaving imprints of its wing feathers.

Survival is difficult for snowshoe hares. If it isn't Canada lynx, it could be wolves, fishers, or coyotes threatening them. Either instinctively or having learned through experience, snowshoe hares are wary. A hare that escapes a four-legged predator gains a bit of wariness that is passed onto its offspring. But this snowshoe hare didn't evade the threat when it swooped in from above.

Day Four

After breakfast, I head north toward a line of trees on a narrow point. In the middle of the north end of Red Rock Lake, I encounter water and slush under surface snow. The slush freezes in thick chunks to the metal frame of the snowshoes, adding weight and making each step burdensome. Wary of encountering weak ice, I use a ski pole to test the ice before each step. Trailing behind are snowshoe prints filled with an inch or two of water and slush. With the weight of ice-encrusted snowshoes, I stop every twenty steps or so to catch my breath. After trudging for an hour through snow-covered slush, there is open water ahead, which I circle around, then proceed to the portage which leads to Saganaga Lake. Arriving at the portage, I am exhausted, drenched with sweat, and have an urgent thirst. Along the short portage between Red Rock and Saganaga is a frozen creek with a jumble of snow-covered boulders. Using a knife, I chisel a hole in the ice and fill up a small plastic water bottle. The water is freezing cold, quenching and deeply satisfying. Although it is a simple thing, years later, I have fond memories of drinking icy cold water from that creek.

After pulling the sled across the portage, it falls with a thud off an outcrop onto a rocky slab. Tipping the sled on its side, I see that the bottom has a long crack, although the crack is not severe enough to impede progress. This is a large bay of Saganaga Lake, lined with cedars and tall red and white pines—untouched by recent fire. There are twists, turns, inlets, and islands. Travel is north, then east, as I hug the east shoreline. Searching for the main passage, I become disoriented. It appears I have entered a cove with no outlet. Confused, I consult the map, then circle back, around a point and north. Beyond the point, travel is northeast toward a small island and another point. I veer to the island and then proceed between it and shore. On the inside curve of a narrows is a flat point mostly covered in snow. Forced to avoid open water and questionable ice in the narrows, I hug the shore, traveling toward the point where grass and brush pierce up through snow.

Much better than shoreline covered with thick brush and cedar or shoreline with rocky boulders, this is an ideal place to camp. It is level, has open water, and there are tall, beautiful green pines rising to the sky. Upslope is rugged with deep snow and dark crags and boulders encrusted with lichen and tree roots. *What is it about this landscape that is so appealing?* Pine-studded, rugged landscapes, especially those with snow, are appealing if not outright magnificent and inspiring. Maybe it is because they exemplify wilderness, wildlife, and adventure.

A common merganser stands on the ice next to open water. Its head feathers are rusty brown, jutting out like spiked hair. After the tent is set up, I throw duffel bags inside, then turn the sled on edge to serve as a windbreak for cooking. The sun is shining at a horizontal angle, illuminating pines on the far shore in shimmering gold, while trees at my campsite are shrouded in darkness. In the clear sky, an almost full moon rises majestically over the top of the dark forest to the east.

While I sit silently in the tent reading, the moon slowly shifts from left to right as purple twilight envelops my camp. The pines on the far shore are now in shadow. I leave the sled turned on its side with stove and pots nearby outside the tent door. Time for sleep. Waking up in the middle of the night, I peek outside into the cold and dark. The moon has shifted. Turning on a flashlight, I see my breath and maroon branches sticking up through white snow. Everything is quiet as I again fall asleep. Although there is no wind, the pots make clinking sounds. I open my eyes and listen. Yes, there is an animal moving around.

Quietly, I sit up and slowly open the door zipper a few inches. A red fox is licking the edges of a pot where drippings have frozen. The drippings have flavor and offer little nourishment, but the fox is persistent. I lie back down and attempt to fall asleep. How can a small animal less than fifteen pounds survive nights of -30°F or colder? With proper gear and clothing, I am warm but cannot imagine surviving a night here without them. Nor can I imagine finding food to eat. The fox is clever, has the right instincts, and is adapted to the harsh changes of seasons. Its sharp senses can hear a mouse through deep snow. Red foxes eat mice, voles, squirrels, and insects, but they also eat berries, small fruit, acorns, grasses, sedges, and tubers. I try to fall asleep.

The clinking sounds continue. Again, I look. Now there are two foxes. The second is shy, standing back. I watch for a few moments. Before I lie down, a deep howling comes from the forest. Both foxes look toward the howling. As the howling stops, the closest turns to the pot. The howling starts again—the deep, drawn-out sound of a wolf pack. Both foxes look into the distance. They don't want to be caught with their backs turned. I lie down, listening to wolves howling and drift off to sleep.

Day Five

Upon waking, I look outside. The foxes are gone and nothing has been disturbed. The merganser is gone. After breakfast, I pack up and load the sled. In the direction of travel, the shoreline has dark cliffs, boulders, and bedrock which have absorbed the sun's warmth and melted lake ice. I pull the sled through deep snow and rugged terrain along the shoreline, hoping to reach an area where solid ice touches shore. But the trek is exhausting as I flounder in brush and snow-covered boulders. Progress is minimal and exasperating. *Should I backtrack to Red Rock, portage to Alpine, then to Seagull and back to the landing rather than doing a circle route via Saganaga?* That would be safest.

Instead, I press forward, but carefully. There is no certainty of safety, whether one is trekking across a frozen lake in the Boundary Waters or crossing a street at an intersection.

Instead of abandoning the loop trip, I return to where shoreline meets solid ice on Saganaga. From here, there is a path through the narrows that bypasses open water. Using a ski pole, I punch it through snow and into solid ice. Satisfied, I slowly inch forward. Rather than having the tow webbing across my chest, I pull the sled onto lake ice with one hand extended behind my body, distributing the sled's weight away from my weight. Near shore, if the ice collapses, I will fall in up to my knees. Punching the ski pole, I test the ice before each step. Continuing further, water depth is five feet and deeper. If I were to crash through now, my full body would fall into frigid water.

With another step, ice heaves downward. Cracks radiate from the snowshoe like lightning bolts. Through the ice, I see air bubbles in liquid water gurgle away from my weight. For a moment I hold my breath, but the ice holds. With each step, ice heaves and cracks, and air bubbles gurgle. Fortunately, below the surface ice is a thick layer of solid ice. In between them is water. Still, it is unnerving and a feeling I won't forget.

If the ice doesn't hold, I will claw myself out wearing wet clothing, boots, and snowshoes. To help with that, I have ice picks dangling from cords at my wrists. *Could I claw myself out while heavily burdened?* Not sure. Continuing onward, I carefully check the ice before proceeding. The narrows widens and the ice becomes solid through and through, and I now proceed with greater confidence.

Crossing a narrows with unsure ice is a circumstance where group travel adds safety. One person proceeds while a second hangs back with a throw rope. Traveling solo, however, is my habit. It is a joy being alone while navigating wilderness. Wilderness is living in the real world, where safety is not assured, living in the here and now—moment to moment. With spending time in wilderness, a person develops satisfaction, confidence, and calmness. It is not the hurried and contrived world of walls, paved surfaces, and vehicles. Wilderness focuses one's mind on immediate concerns. Is a storm coming? Is a grizzly around a bend in the trail? Shall we trek on or camp? Where is the next supply of water?

As I wind my way through the bay, it opens to a frozen expanse dotted with small islands. It is starting to snow. Taking the map out of my pocket, the islands correlate to small shapes on the map. I trek toward an island with white pines whose branches are splayed like moose antlers. At the base of the pines are brush and birch trees devoid of leaves. Along the island's shoreline are rocks and boulders covered in snow. Nearby, another island has pines whose branches are windswept from right to left. The snowfall picks up momentum. Being surrounded by pristine nature in a snowstorm is like being in a snow globe's magical landscape. No one else is around. It is a serene and compelling feeling that is difficult to convey.

A number of people experience discomfort or anxiety in wilderness, especially if alone. Perhaps this is a response to being in an unfamiliar setting. With time and experience, a person becomes comfortable and realizes there is no immediate peril. Sitting quietly in wilderness and observing nature does not foretell that an avalanche will come or that a predator will attack. Yes, those and other tragedies happen, but the odds of something bad happening while watching birds flit about, wildlife graze, or the sun dip below the horizon are miniscule. Calmness in wilderness is knowing that if one is careful, they are generally safe. But of course, as in all of life, there is never a guarantee.

As I make my way past bays, small islands, and points, first Gold Island, then Long Island comes into view. Snow is falling heavily and obscuring distant views. Despite the snowfall, I see a small island that is burnt-over, perhaps the result of an errant campfire. Past this island, I come to another island that has endured fire. It has a tall pine with branches swept to the right. The rest of the trees are charred black and fallen. One toppled pine has fifteen-foot roots spread from its trunk. The roots cause the base of the trunk to be suspended ten to twelve feet above the island's granite bedrock, with some roots shooting upward from the trunk another ten to twelve feet. Before the pine toppled, the splayed roots clung tightly to its rock foundation, holding the pine upright, but now it resembles a giant spider web suspended in air.

Through the snowstorm, my trek continues east toward Sea Gull River. To the south is a tangle of islands, bays, peninsulas. To the north are dozens of pine-studded islands sprinkled about. Further north lies the great white expanse of frozen Lake Saganaga, and beyond the horizon is the boreal forest of Canada.

It is a long haul pulling a sled with gear, walking across a lonely landscape, experiencing and dealing with raw nature in its most rudimentary form. I imagine Will Steger traversing the Arctic or Antarctica—feeling the same wonder and awe, taking in the raw beauty of the landscape. Of breaking new ground, reaching new horizons, of seeing unexplored landscape for the first time.

Eventually I make my way to the Seagull River, ever closer to my starting point. There are cabins on snow-covered bluffs. Deep in thought, all is quiet except the rhythmic sound of snowshoes and the whispering of the sled as it glides across snow and ice. I glance back to inspect the sled and see a large dog. It trots alongside for ten minutes, sniffing the gear and keeping me company until it heads back to the cabins. Trudging back to my vehicle on Seagull Lake, my heart is serene; my soul is filled with gratification.

American
Creek

Lake Coville

Lake
Grosvenor

■ Cabin

Naknek Lake

Bay of
Islands

Iliuk Arm

Savonoski
River

Lake
Brooks

Katmai National Park

FRUSTRATED

"For me and for thousands with similar inclinations, the
most important passion of life is the overpowering desire
to escape periodically from the clutches of a mechanistic
civilization. To us the enjoyment of solitude, complete
independence, and the beauty of undefined panoramas is
absolutely essential to happiness."

—Bob Marshall

Katmai National Park is a remote wilderness park on the Alaska Peninsula. It boasts two thousand brown bears, the largest population of
unhunted brown bears in the world—thus they dominate the landscape.
Few people visit Katmai—40,000 to 80,000 compared to Yellowstone's
four to five million annually. Most people visit Brooks Camp to watch
brown bears fishing for salmon from viewing platforms. Some people
fish Brooks River for rainbow trout. Few people venture into Katmai's
vast wilderness for an overnight trip by foot, canoe, or kayak.

There is evidence of people having lived in the Katmai area for
thousands of years. Hunter-gathers migrated from northeast Asia
across the Beringia Land Bridge or along the North Pacific Coast. Their
descendants spread out, populated Alaska, and with time populated
both North and South America. The oldest evidence of Paleo-Arctic
people living in the Katmai area dates from about nine thousand years
ago, with the area sporadically occupied by various peoples and cultures
since then.

Three thousand years ago, people lived along the shores of Lake Brooks and Brooks River. Their artifacts have been found along with ground depressions where living quarters once existed. The homes were excavations with sides reinforced with logs that extended above ground level. The roof was timber overlaid with sod and moss for insulation. The villagers lived a subsistence lifestyle, surviving on nature's cornucopia of plants, berries, salmon, caribou, moose, and waterfowl. Many dugout houses cluster near Brooks Falls where salmonid teeth are found embedded in dirt, implying they used the seasonal runs of salmon. They competed with wolves, Canada lynx, wolverines, and brown bears.

Roy Fure was one of the last people to reside in Katmai. Born in Lithuania in 1885, Fure came to Alaska in the early 1900s and made a living as a trapper, hunter, and occasional laborer. In 1926, Fure built a cabin on the north shore of Naknek Lake on a mile-wide isthmus between the Bay of Islands and Grosvenor Lake. He lived in the cabin until 1940, then was forced to leave what was then Katmai National Monument. Fure built another cabin outside the monument's boundaries but continued to use the Bay of Island's cabin for short stays through the 1950s.

The bush plane service picks up me, my folding kayak, and my gear at King Salmon airport, and we drive to the floatplane base on Naknek River. While waiting for my flight, I sit on a tattered leather couch in a cabin that serves as the office. A handsome German shepherd walks in through an open door, carrying a branch in its mouth. I know this game, so I walk outside and throw the branch a few times, then pet and scratch its ears. The office manager tells me it was a stray found on the tundra. It probably would not have survived wandering the wilderness, and would've starved or been eaten by wolves. Lucky for this dog, a pilot brought him back, and it now resides here. After a few minutes, it lies in the shade of a spruce tree.

I meander around and encounter a couple of adventurers. Two young men are organizing and packing gear. They are heading out on a fishing and pack-raft trip on American Creek. Each has packed and will use a small inflatable raft to float the creek. Both are packing large-caliber handguns inside waterproof cases. I have pepper spray for protection. Again, there are over two thousand Alaskan brown bears in the Katmai wilderness. One can never be too safe in bear country.

Now it is my turn to depart. Walking onto a dock on the Naknek River, dockhands load my gear into a floatplane tied off at the end of the dock. Camping fuel and bear spray are not allowed in the cockpit so are stowed in one of the floats. I make a mental note to collect them at my drop-off point on American Creek. Getting into the aircraft, I sit in the copilot's seat. A multitude of dials, knobs, gauges, and buttons line the instrument panel. The pilot describes procedures in the event of an emergency landing. He is semiretired, working seasonally and then returning to California. The dockhands push the plane away and the pilot starts the engine with a roar. Conversation is next to impossible. The pilot hands me a pair of headphones to muffle the noise. The throttle is engaged, the engine revs, the plane surges forward, and we rise smoothly off the surface of Naknek River in an astonishingly short distance. We travel east, away from King Salmon and toward American Creek, flying low over verdant wetlands, ponds, and foothills. Over the roar of the engine, the pilot says he sometimes sees small groups of caribou. As the plane approaches American Creek, we first make a low pass. Circling around, we fly in and land smoothly on the water.

The pilot taxis the plane to the east shore and cuts the engine. He gets out of the cockpit, steps into the creek protected by knee-high wading boots, pulls a rope hanging from a wing, and brings the plane to shore. I get out of the cockpit to stand on a float and grab each bag of gear to hand to him on shore. Two duffel bags contain my folding kayak, which is my transportation for the next two weeks. After all baggage has been stowed on shore, the pilot opens a lid on a float and hands stove fuel and bear spray to me. It would not be good being out here alone with no fuel for cooking or the ability to dissuade an approaching bear. The pilot says, "Good luck and have a safe trip," starts the engine, taxis into the middle of the creek, and takes off. The roar of the engine fades as I watch the plane shrink to a dot in clear-blue sky. Then it disappears over the horizon. All is quiet. A warm breeze is blowing, which rustles three- to five-foot-tall grasses on both sides of the creek. I am alone in one of North America's largest, wildest, and most pristine wildernesses.

Completely alone. That was my choice. A conscious choice. *Was it the correct choice?* That is to be determined.

Quickly, it is apparent I am not alone. Within twenty minutes, a medium-sized brown bear walks on the opposite bank of American Creek. With the creek separating us, we cautiously eye each other. Glimmers of sunlight shine off its fur. It descends the bank into the water and angles my direction, wading closer, calm and unafraid. Perhaps it wants to check out my gear or test my resolve. Halfway across the creek, it veers upstream, periodically looking back to keep an eye on me. A female common merganser and her brood of ducklings paddle by a few feet away. I watch the ducks but keep an eye on the bear, which has now crossed to my side of the creek seventy-five yards upstream. It clambers up the creek bank, then disappears into brush and tall grasses. I unpack gear, erect the tent, and quickly assemble the folding kayak, all while looking out for the bear. Currently I don't see it, but I know it is not far away. The tent is erected five feet from the creek; behind it is a swampy wetland with tall marsh grasses mixed with bushy vegetation. Thirty yards downstream is an upland growth of birch, spruce, and aspen.

In early evening, I make spaghetti with pepperoni and Parmesan cheese while still keeping an eye out for the bear. After dinner, I wash dishes then hang the portion of food that does not fit into the bear-resistant canister in a nearby tree. The air is warm and calm; the sky is clear as I sit outside the tent on the sleeping pad, reading. The bear comes back. It wades into the creek in front of my camp, with nose and eyes under water—"snorkeling" for salmon. Its ears stay above water, which enables it to hear nearby movement.

It is 9:45 p.m., yet the sun is high in the Alaskan sky. Cooler now than when I was dropped off, I prepare for the night by setting the kayak next to the tent. It's as valuable as anything here, and without it I am pretty much stuck. My hunch is that an animal will be reluctant to approach human noises and smells. If the kayak were stored away from the tent, a bear might gnaw on its canvas-and-rubber fabric to see if it were edible. Holes gnawed into the kayak's fabric is not something I can allow. My intent is to scare away any animal that gets too close to the tent or kayak. Sleep is sound. Pepper spray lies within arm's grasp.

Day Two

While eating cereal with rehydrated milk and freeze-dried berries, I hear brush swishing. Standing up in front of my tent, I look along the creek bank to see grass and brush swaying. Emerging from tall grass, the vegetation parts to reveal a large bear a few yards away. Its powerful body is covered with fur mottled light and dark by patches of wetness. I grab the pepper spray from its holster and aim with my thumb on the trigger. The bear continues to advance and circles into tall brush a couple yards behind the tent. Its bulk and musculature reinforce its power and dominance. If it wanted to, it could destroy me in a moment. It glances in my direction and walks past the tent, again swishing through vegetation, and continues downstream. When it has travelled downstream to where I feel comfortable, I return the pepper spray to its holster and sit. The bear is focused on salmon in the creek. I continue with breakfast.

After breakfast, I break down the tent and pack gear into the kayak. I inspect the area for items that may have been missed, coming across a large mound of bear scat composed of grass and sedge. Putting the life jacket on and grabbing the kayak paddle, I enter the cockpit and push off. It is time to luxuriate in exploring wilderness—paddling a wild creek in Alaska! Before heading south toward Coville Lake, I paddle north up American Creek. The sky is blue.

Just fifty feet wide, American Creek meanders back and forth. After rounding a bend, on the left bank I approach a large jumble of branches piled eight feet high. A beaver lodge. Paddling further, there is a bear on the west bank, standing amidst tall grass and alders. I watch it while silently gliding several yards offshore. It looks to see me, then quickly recedes into thick brush. I remind myself, *Don't paddle too close to shore.* I come to a side stream. The thought occurs: I could explore it, but it is narrow. A bear on the stream bank would be just feet away. Continuing onward, the creek splits. Should I paddle the left fork or the right? Examining the map, it is clear. These are branches of American Creek that flow around an island.

Pushing the kayak onto the island, I exit cautiously. Walking a few steps among tall grass and willow, I encounter a four-foot-wide excavation. After gorging on salmon, a bear's stomach becomes so full its belly bulges. The bear digs a bowl-shaped hole where it can comfortably rest and sleep. Looking around, I see uneaten salmon parts strewn in the grass. In front of me lies a salmon head—its mouth forming an aggressive hook, its jaws lined with sharp teeth. Being cautious, I spend just a few minutes here. There could be bears hidden in brush.

After getting back on the water, I take the left fork. The right fork is narrow, which could get tense if a bear is encountered. Paddling no more than a few minutes, I approach the island's north end. To my surprise, in the creek sits an enormous bear. Its shoulders, head, and front paws are above the water surface—its paws hold a salmon to its mouth. Floating silently in the kayak with the massive beast forty yards away, I listen to its heavy breathing while it devours the salmon. Now, it looks in my direction. I can tell it sees me but continues to eat. With this salmon consumed, it submerges into the creek to look for more. I consider exploring farther upstream, but if this bear wades into the middle of the creek, my return will be blocked. Sweeping the paddle in a circular motion, I spin the kayak around and head downstream. In a few minutes, I again near the island's southern end. This is where I had pulled ashore and explored earlier. As I float past the end of the island, I look back on the fork not taken. As Frost penned many years ago, "And that has made all the difference." There in the right fork is a large bear eating salmon, just feet away from where I had disembarked.

It is time to escape the confines of the creek and head to Coville Lake. Continuing downstream, I paddle past last night's campsite and encounter marshland. Here, on its way to Coville Lake, the creek forks around an island. Taking the wider right fork, I paddle through tall grasses, alders, and reeds, encountering several species of ducks and gulls. Finally, the creek widens to a full view of Coville. Paddling onto open water, I veer right, hugging the west shore. If a storm blows through, I can quickly pull ashore. Paddling south, I find a break in dense shoreline vegetation where camp can be made. Gliding the kayak toward the opening, I nudge the bow onto pebbles and gravel, avoiding wear on the fabric hull. Then, in an unbalanced and awkward maneuver, I disembark and pull the kayak onto land.

There is no rush or reason to make a great effort paddling long distances in this supreme wilderness, so even though it's early I make camp. The tent is set in the forest on soft moss and grass, inches from the narrow gravel beach. It is a privilege being here and inhaling pristine freedom. Tonight's camp is not far from yesterday's camp on American Creek. The weather is mild, the scenery awesome, and the wildlife compelling. I have plenty of reading material, food in a bear-resistant container, and more food in a dry bag that must be hung in a tree at night. Dinner is kung pao chicken, rice, and noodles. Sitting on a sleeping pad at water's edge, I read through the evening. Scattered along the shore are freshwater clamshells. If this were the Mississippi River, it could be raccoons or river otters leaving broken shells, but there are no racoons here.

There is a dark object moving where American Creek flows into Coville. Grabbing the binoculars, I see it is a bear precisely where I had paddled earlier. It is far enough away that I am not concerned, so I return to reading. As evening unfolds, I notice movement to my left. A bear has emerged from the shoreline and wades into the lake. Now I have two bears to watch. The wading bear is much closer. It is either cooling off in the lake or searching for salmon. In open water, it is unlikely to catch a swimming salmon, but maybe it will come across one that has spawned and expired. It snorkels with its eyes and nose underwater. Entering deeper water, now it stands on hind legs with head and neck exposed. It looks in my direction, water dripping off its face. The only part of the bear not wet is the top of its head and big fluffy ears. I return to reading, but now the wading bear makes its way to shore, clambers onto the rocky beach, and disappears into the woods. Back to reading. There is a shorebird in the water in front of my camp, maybe a greater yellowlegs or Hudsonian godwit.

9:10 p.m.

The bear that was wading emerges from the woods and walks along the beach, headed for my camp. It is close enough now that it sees me sitting, so I stand. It continues to approach but at twenty yards veers into the forest and circles around. I watch it walk amidst trees and past camp. Then it travels to the lakeshore and ambles along until it wades into the water and submerges its head up to its ears to search for salmon.

10:25 p.m.

The wind shifts from the south to a north wind. Getting into the tent, I zip closed the door but leave the mesh window open for a view of the lake and breeze to enter. Crawling into the sleeping bag, I fall asleep.

11:45 p.m.

Asleep, I hear the sound of footsteps on the gravel beach. Opening my eyes, I stare into darkness and listen. The footsteps grow louder. If this is the same bear that circled by earlier, it knows I am here. This time it is approaching the tent and not circling. It sounds about ten feet away and getting closer. While prone in the sleeping bag, I exclaim, "Get up, get up, get up!" Leaning over to look out the window, there in the gloam is a dark silhouette of a bear on the beach four feet away. It slows for a moment and motions its head in my direction. After a pause, it continues up the beach. After lying back down, I fall asleep. In the middle of the night, it may have walked past again, but I did not wake.

Day Three

From across the lake, the sun shines warmly on my campsite. I walk down the beach to a tree where my food bag hangs, retrieve it and the bear-resistant food container, and eat breakfast. While sitting on the sleeping pad in the tent door, I read and soak up the sun. Looking to the right, a bear walks along the shoreline from the south, coming this direction. It doesn't hesitate a bit as it approaches. With no more than five feet of gravel between the tent and the lake, I back into the tent. The bear advances, now just feet away. I hear footsteps while sitting in the tent. Through the open tent door, I see it, perhaps a female or young adult. As it walks past the tent, it does not so much as glance in my direction. It is not frightened of me and my camp, but at the same time it shows no interest. Its beautiful golden-brown fur sweeps from head, shoulders, and sides, back and down, as if combed. There is the distinguishing brown bear hump behind its head and above the shoulders. The bottom of its paws have thick black pads. The claws on the front feet are visible and pronounced. The rear paws look like hairy human feet but with claws. As the bear walks by the open tent door, I say in a calm voice, "Hey there," to make sure it knows I am here. It ambles away along the beach. It is becoming apparent that some bears here are tolerant of people. However, being that they are massive, powerful, and unpredictable, one cannot assume they will always be tolerant.

After a little more reading, it is time to break camp. The weather has changed to partially overcast. I hug the west shore of the lake, paddling past volcanic cliffs. Along this stretch, there is nowhere one could pull ashore in stormy weather or make camp. A bald eagle perched high in a white spruce intently watches my progress. Some of the cliffs are composed of volcanic conglomerates. A common loon floats nearby. The water is flat and calm. The loon calls a few times before diving beneath the water's surface. Upon surfacing, it calls again, its eerie tremolo echoing across the lake, bouncing off cliffs and reverberating in the silent wilderness. Along the shoreline, I see a bear snorkeling for salmon as I silently paddle nearby; the top of its head and ears are above the water's surface. Eventually its head breaks the surface and it sees me floating in the kayak. It looks directly at me. I paddle away and it goes back to snorkeling. Ahead is a small island with a beach which I point the kayak toward. Perfect. I decide to make camp on this island covered in birch and balsam poplar trees. Its volcanic rocks are covered in palegreen lichen.

The sun has come back full strength and the afternoon has warmed. From the island, I see the bear that I had paddled past is out in the cool water, still looking for salmon. I decide it has the right idea, so I put on my swimsuit and wade in. The water is extremely cold, so I slowly inch forward until it reaches my waist. The slow method is torturous, so I do a full plunge, diving beneath the surface. The shock of cold water is quite ghastly. Reflexively, I burst to the surface with a whooping exhalation. The bear may have the right idea, but I am not covered in fat and fur. Quickly, I exit the lake and head to camp. Sitting on the sleeping pad, I let sunlight and a warm breeze dry my body. Wanting to take a nap, I put the pad into the tent and lie down, but the gravel is lumpy and has sharp rocks. Removing all gear from the tent, I move it to a grassy area and crawl in again. In the sunlight, the shadows of poplar trees wash across the tent wall. After the nap, dinner is macaroni and cheese with pepperoni slices. The evening is spent reading; then sleep.

Day Four

The night was quiet and uneventful. I start with my usual breakfast of cereal and rehydrated milk, then clean up and break down the tent. The gear is stowed in the kayak. I push off for another day of exploration. Paddling south, I make my way to the channel between Coville and Grosvenor Lake, where forested hillsides slope down to meet at a narrows. Beyond the narrows, Grosvenor opens up with large mountains on the horizon obscured by thin clouds. Pulling ashore, I pause at the narrows before proceeding. There is a fishing lodge here but it is shuttered and vacant. After stretching my legs, I paddle along the east shore of Grosvenor toward a group of islands about three miles distant. The weather is calm—the water is smooth as glass. Upon reaching the islands, I circumnavigate them, exploring each from the water, looking for a good landing and campsite. Finding one, I pull ashore, set up the tent, and make dinner, which consists of brown rice, red and black beans, dehydrated vegetables, and tuna from a foil pouch. From my campsite is a view of a green mountainside to the east. Cutting through and down the side of the mountain is a valley with a stream running along the valley bottom. Sprinkled on both side of the valley are meadows filled with pink and purple fireweed. The lingering light and calm weather beckon me to the water for an evening paddle. I explore the pristine beauty of the islands, returning to camp about 9:00 p.m. Around 10:00 p.m., I get ready to turn in but hear chattering and squeaking. Walking over to a small cliff, I peer over the edge to view the water. A family of five river otters swim alongshore. They frolic in the water awhile, then swim around a point and are gone. It is getting darker, so I return to the tent to read for a while, then retire for the night.

Day Five

The morning is routine as I start the day. The water is calm under an overcast sky. I point the kayak east, travelling along Grosvenor's north shore. After five miles, I approach a tree branch sticking out of the water near the shoreline with a raven perched on top. The raven's upside-down reflection shimmers on the water. As I get closer, the scene unfolds. The raven is perched not on a branch but the upper tine of a palmate antler. The antler is attached to the head of moose whose carcass is partially submerged. As I paddle closer, the raven flies off. Fur has been torn off, exposing aged and graying meat. Some of the carcass is scavenged, but the majority is still here. Ravens can't tear the hide and fur off a moose carcass. Cautiously, I paddle a little closer but change my mind and hold back. There may be a bear nearby protecting its food.

At first, I think it unlikely to have stumbled across a bear guarding a cache of meat, but on rethinking, there are a lot of bears here. Scanning the shoreline, to the left is a trail worn into the hillside. My eyes follow the trail up the hillside. Not more than thirty feet up is a large bear sleeping in a hollowed-out bed of earth, obscured behind trees and vegetation. My naivete is jolted to reality.

Such is the subtlety of paddling a canoe or kayak. One can quietly and intimately explore a lake or river without disturbing wildlife, whether it is a loon, swan, deer, moose, eagle, blue heron, or a sleeping bear.

Quickly, I back-paddle away from the carcass. Now at a distance, the kayak hovers in calm water while I inspect the scene. It is possible the bear attacked and killed the moose along this rocky stretch of shore. Or the moose attempted to swim across Grosvenor, got caught in a williwaw, drowned, and washed ashore. Either way this bear has plenty of food for the next several days. The antlers on this bull moose are large; its remains are large as well.

The wind has picked up and the water has become choppy. The sky has become dark and gloomy. It's time to move on and find a place to camp. With the bear unaware, I quietly paddle away toward a nearby island. Reaching the island, I paddle to the lee side to get out of the wind, then angle to a point. Disembarking, I pull the kayak on shore and set up the tent in a thick bushy area that offers protection. I'm relieved to be off the water as there are now whitecaps.

This afternoon is the first time that there has been significant wind. With my shelter erected, I peer through binoculars to view the moose carcass. The bear has woken and is on the carcass, pawing, chomping, pulling chunks of meat off with its jaws. It starts to drizzle, so I hunker down in the tent and relax. At about 7:00 p.m., I exit, fire up the stove, and make dinner. Chicken is marinated in a spicy sauce, warmed on the stove, and stuffed into flour tortillas. The fajitas are delicious. Both the bear and I have full stomachs and we will sleep well. The wind is becoming quite intense, so before turning in for the night I go down to the shoreline and pull the kayak farther onto the island. I don't want the kayak blowing into the lake and floating away.

Day Six

Today I am greeted by a strong wind, drizzle, and whitecaps. The sun is trying to peek through clouds but just can't seem to do it. I watch the bear feeding on the moose from my island home. A bald eagle flies by. Gulls caw and flit about. The wind gathers strength; the drizzle turns to rain. Returning to the tent, I read and contemplate. With extra time on my hands, I recall math and physics from bygone college days. Trying my hand at poetry results in a difficult struggle. To relieve boredom, I exit the tent to walk and stretch my legs during a pause in the rain. Exploring the island, I find back in the woods a flat rock which makes a perfect table. Returning to the tent and gear, I gather food and cooking gear, bringing them to the rock. Lunch is spiced mashed potatoes and hot chocolate. The wind is relentless, with whitecaps pirouetting on the lake. I retreat to the tent, resigned to more reading.

I open my book about the origin of the Universe and the evolution of life. The current chapter discusses the Universe's structure and composition. This is intriguing to contemplate while alone on a small island in the middle of a remote wilderness with a storm blowing through and a bear eating a moose carcass nearby.

For most of history, humans had no inkling of the vastness of space or its grandeur. But now, we know the sun is one of billions of stars in the Milky Way and there are billions or perhaps trillions of galaxies. We also know distant galaxies are moving away from us—thus the universe is expanding following the Big Bang. One mind-expanding sentence from the book stands out: "Thus the big bang was not an explosion in space; it was more like an explosion of space." Sitting alone in the tent, the sound of wind and waves fade as I attempt to grasp the concept and wonder—*What is space expanding into?*

The Milky Way, Andromeda, and Triangulum are the major galaxies in our local group. Our local group, along with other galactic clusters, form the Virgo Supercluster. The Virgo Supercluster is a portion of an even larger structure, the Laniakea Supercluster, which contains over 100,000 galaxies. Laniakea, along with other superclusters, forms gigantic filaments and walls of matter that stretch through space, creating a cosmic network that permeates the Universe. I visualize glistening dewdrops on a three-dimensional web. Or, within the human mind's fragile and limited ability to comprehend, perhaps the Universe is a cosmic mass of bubbles, floating like foam in space. I picture the interconnected cosmic web of superclusters. Might the cosmic web be analogous to the web of neurons within the brain? Now . . . that thought surely leads to madness. It is time to take a break.

Standing outside the tent door, the wind continues to howl as I peer over low brush. Looking over to the shoreline, the bear is engaged with the carcass. I can't think of a reason why it might swim to this island, so am not concerned.

It is obvious the Universe exists on a scale so vast and resplendent that it is unfathomable in its boundless and everchanging intricacies. During our short existence, we will not absorb or understand all there is to know about the Universe's full breadth and majesty. Maybe it is enough to live as all of Earth's creatures do. To breathe, to eat, to reproduce, to care for each other and the young. To be as content as possible and at peace during the life we have; immersed within the wonderous four-billion-year stream of life on Earth, but an infinitesimal part of the Universe's greater grandeur.

My earthly concern is the cool, dreary weather and strong wind blowing mist and drizzle sideways. Exiting the tent, I behold the lake whipped into a froth of whitecaps. I crawl back inside to find the tent walls flapping wildly and near collapsing. I brace the tent with my body, hoping the poles don't snap. Growing weary, I move the tent further onto the island to an area protected by balsam poplar. Concerned the kayak will blow off the island, I tie both ends to brush. Optimistically, I hope the wind will die down, but instead it grows stronger. At least now the tent is semiprotected in the woods. With the severe weather, I skip breaking out the stove and making dinner, instead eating snacks before returning to my book. Even in the protection of the woods, the tent shakes. More rain. Finally sleep.

Day Seven

Slept well. A little less wind this morning, but dark threatening clouds are moving over the mountains. It doesn't look good for getting off the island today. There are cresting waves on the water, and the wind is blowing strong from the southeast. If I were to pack up and start paddling, I would be paddling into wind and whitecaps. Better stay safe and continue reading in the tent.

My book greets me with a chapter on the origin of life. There are multiple theories as to how life started. Charles Darwin hypothesized in 1871, "The original spark of life may have begun in a warm little pond, with all sorts of ammonia and phosphoric salts . . . " In 1966, Graham Cairns-Smith theorized it may have started among clay crystals by providing a matrix-like structure. An alternative proposal by Jack Corliss is that life emerged near oceanic hydrothermal volcanic vents called "black smokers," after he dived in the deep-sea vehicle *Alvin* off the Galapagos Islands. There, he discovered an astonishing diversity of life including white clams, shrimp, and giant seven-foot-long tube worms. In 2016, Jack Szostak wrote: "Remarkably, lakes in a geothermal active area provide just such a fluctuating temperature environment, because lakes similar to Yellowstone can be generally cool (even ice covered in winter), but they contain numerous hydrothermal vents that emit streams of hot water," and "this could be the most likely scenario for the early Earth environment that nurtured the origin of life."

Outside the tent, the wind gusts and whitecaps continue to swirl. Once primitive proto-cells formed, they competed for free-floating nutrients. Proto-cells that were efficient at absorbing nutrients survived and reproduced. Those that were not became rare and disappeared. Later, some microorganisms evolved to latch onto or engulf one another, stealing nutrients from other cells. These were Earth's first predators. Not quite a bear eating a moose, but that will come later.

To pass the time, I copy a picture from the book into my journal of a cell, including its organelles. With an abundance of time on hand, the drawing is quite intricate, showing the nucleus, DNA within the nucleus, endoplasmic reticulum, Golgi, mitochondria, chloroplast, microtubules, peroxisomes, lysosomes, intracellular vesicles, cytoskeleton, secretion granule, flagellum, and ACTW fibers. I have no idea what all these organelles are or what they do, but the complexity is astonishing and mesmerizing.

5:45 p.m.

Outside the tent, the wind gusts and whitecaps continue to swirl. This will be my third night on the island. Using the binoculars, I see the bear again feeding on the moose.

Back to my book. Earth life is categorized into three groups—eukaryotes, bacteria, and archaea. Eukaryotes are large cells with organelles and DNA in a nucleus. Bacteria and archaea are smaller, do not have organelles or a nucleus, and have DNA that floats throughout the cell. Eukaryotes may be unicellular or multicellular, while bacteria and archaea are always unicellular. Humans, bears, trees, salmon, and mushrooms are multicellular eukaryotes. The shape-shifting amoeba is a unicellular eukaryotic predator with pseudopod arms which it uses to engulf prey. Giardia are single-celled eukaryotes. Backcountry hikers and campers that drink untreated water containing Giardia may develop stomach distress. An example of a bacterium is streptococcus, which causes strep throat. *Sulfolobus acidocaldarius* is an archaean which flourishes in hot thermal pools such as Grand Prismatic Spring in Yellowstone. Another archaean, but at the other end of the thermal spectrum, is *Methanogenium frigidum*, which is found in the frigid waters of Antarctica.

7:45 p.m.

Despite my protected position in the woods, extreme winds are whipping the tent. Looking up at the sky, clouds are flying by. *Maybe I should move the tent further into the trees for protection?* Optimistically, I think the wind will calm down; it can't continue to sustain this intensity, can it?

8:15 p.m.

The storm is relentless—the wind doesn't calm. The tent shudders at a crooked angle as its aluminum poles flex. I hope they don't snap. Inside, I brace the tent with my arms and back, holding it upright. But growing weary, I move it further into the protection of trees. The kayak is tied to small brush. Still, I worry it may be blown into the lake. If that were to happen, I would have to put on my dry suit, wade into the water, and swim to retrieve it. Again, I skip dinner, as it is too windy to fire up the stove. Being stuck on this island for a few days, it is best to conserve food to ensure there is enough for the duration of the trip.

9:30 p.m.

Now it is even windier. The tent flaps strongly even deep in the protection of the woods. I worry about trees falling on the tent with me inside. I look out the tent door to check. There are small trees nearby, but no large trees.

10:50 p.m.

More rain and intense wind. Worried the kayak may be blown away even though it is tied to brush, I strap dry bags with gear to it. I can't afford to have it blown away. Sleep finally comes but isn't peaceful.

Day Eight

After three days of storms, I wake to silence. My head aches from a lack of sleep. Everything outside the tent is wet. The sky is overcast and mist hangs in the air. Wasting no time, I pack up and paddle away on choppy waters. Feeling a little stir-crazy, it is good to get away from the island. Finally, the breeze dies down and the lake calms. A common loon follows nearby as I paddle, offering companionship. The loon's haunting calls echo across the lake surface. It repeatedly dives, later to resurface in a seemingly random location. It is nice to have some company. Finally, the sun shines in full brilliance and the lake surface becomes a flat mirror reflecting blue sky. I am thankful for good weather. My direction of travel is southeast, following Grosvenor's northeast shore to where Hardscrabble Creek empties into Grosvenor.

Reaching the southeast corner of Grosvenor, I pull ashore to look for a campsite. The vegetation is thick, sometimes overhanging the lake; hence I explore the wooded area, bushwhacking along the muddy shoreline. Just to the south is where Hardscrabble Creek drains. As it flows into Grosvenor, it sweeps sand and gravel from multiple braids, creating a broad, shallow delta. At one of the creek's mouths, there are two bald eagles feeding on salmon scraps on the beach. If I were to camp here, I would have a good view of Hardscrabble Creek. The area is protected with trees and vegetation, which would provide shelter from the wind. Looking for a level area to set the tent, I discover that much of the shoreline is heavily trodden with bear tracks as well as piles of dinner-plate-size scat. Further exploration reveals several large bear beds dug into the soil. With the abundance of bear sign, I decide not to camp here.

Returning to the kayak, I paddle east past Hardscrabble Creek and head to the southwest corner of the lake. In a protected cove, I find a good area to camp, but it does not have a view of Hardscrabble Creek. Paddling out of the cove and moving down the shoreline, there is a five-foot margin of gravel beach with a view of the creek outlet. I like having a view, so I paddle to shore, set up the tent, and organize camp. From the island to this campsite, I have paddled fifteen miles following Grosvenor's shoreline. It feels good to have made decent progress.

For dinner, the menu is spaghetti and Parmesan cheese, which is satisfying. While cleaning dishes, I notice the lake water is cloudy with silt. This seems peculiar. The north end of the lake was clear. Glacial meltwater contains silt, which clouds lakes, but Grosvenor doesn't have glacial water as a source. Perhaps the wind and storms of the last few days stirred the lake up? The clear-blue sky that provided such excellent paddling during the afternoon is gone. A dark storm with drizzle and wind comes rushing in from the north.

Getting protection from the storm, I sit in the tent vestibule watching clouds stream across mountain peaks on the lake's far shore. In the direction of Hardscrabble Creek, I expect to see bears on shore or wading into the shallows, but there are none. The two eagles are still there, but soon they fly off. A few moments later, an immature bald eagle lands where the two eagles were. A duck paddles offshore. After washing my hands and face with cold lake water, I pack my remaining rations of food inside the bear-resistant container and seal the lid. While relaxing on the sleeping pad in the tent doorway, I watch storm clouds go by. With the brunt of the storm having blown through, it is calm and quiet except for ripples caused by salmon. Occasionally their dorsal fins are visible skimming above the surface, or there is a loud splash when they jump.

6:05 p.m.

I move the kayak next to the tent. More clouds drift over the lake, moving west to east, bringing rain and drizzle. Seagulls squawk and quickly dart about. To pass time, I read about ancient sea life and watch the clouds. I copy a diagram of an ichthyosaur into my journal. It is a predator that looks and swims like a shark but is an air-breathing reptile. The drawing is an accurate reproduction from the book. With no distractions here in the wilderness, my ability to deeply focus without interruptions is much enhanced. I continue reading but get tired and my eyes close. The silence of the night allows for a deep sleep.

Day Nine

This morning, the sun tries to shine from behind clouds but does not quite make it. My food supply is getting low. Everything fits into the bear canister now, with room to spare, so there is no need to hang extra food. While I relax in camp, a belted kingfisher flies by as it searches for food. It is blue-gray with a white underside, sports a crest on the back of its large head, and has a large beak. Such a delightful bird. Kingfishers feed by diving into water and catching small fish with their long, sharp bills, but they also eat other small prey.

Returning to my book, this chapter describes the evolution of feathers and birds. The first fossil of a feather was found in Germany in 1861, and a few months later a rock slab was unearthed showing a bipedal reptile adorned with feathers. Unlike modern birds, the fossil had claws on its wings and sharp teeth in its jaws. Named archaeopteryx, it was a birdlike dinosaur that was transitional between dinosaurs and birds. Thus, the lineage of the little blue kingfisher that flits around my camp can be traced back to feathered dinosaurs.

This afternoon, I take the kayak out for a paddle to Hardscrabble Creek, enjoying sunny weather and glorious scenery. The water at the creek's delta is shallow, only a foot or two deep even two hundred yards from shore. A bear could easily wade out to this location. Beyond the creek outlet is an inspiring view of Serpent Tongue Glacier as it cascades down the flanks of Snowy Mountain Volcano. Considering that Serpent Tongue is twenty miles distant, its size is quite impressive. The last time Snowy Mountain erupted was in 2001, so there is no immediate danger, although Fourpeaked Mountain had volcanic activity earlier this year.

Tonight's dinner is soup with brown rice, black beans, dehydrated vegetables, spices, and chicken. The beans take a long time to cook, but I have plenty of time sitting on shore, reading and watching salmon splash. Hearing splashing sounds, I look over to Hardscrabble Creek to see a bear running in shallow water chasing salmon. A flock of twenty common mergansers paddle by. When they notice me, they wildly flap their wings and "run" across the water's surface. The evening passes peaceably while I read about Earth's early life.

For the first three billion years, life consisted of single-celled organisms and simple multicellular organisms. It was during the Cambrian Explosion 540 million years ago that animal life radically diversified. As already mentioned, evidence for the Cambrian Explosion can be found in the Burgess Shale of the Canadian Rockies. It is during the "explosion" that multicellular animal life evolved novel body plans—in as little as twenty million years.

One animal, pikaia, was a flat worm an inch and a half long. It swam by undulating through the ocean. Along the length of its body extended a primitive nerve chord. Thus pikaia, or similar life forms, established chordates 530 million years ago. Chordates led to vertebrates, including fish, amphibians, reptiles, mammals, and primates. Humans would not be here had pikaia and its kin not survived fierce competition swimming the oceans of the Cambrian. Ancient seas were a dangerous place filled with predators such as *Anomalocaris canadensis*. Anomalocaris grew to three feet in length and had two frontal appendages tipped with barbed spikes used to pull prey to its disk-like mouth.

Day Ten

Today the weather is cool and overcast, gusty, with drizzle. I consider leaving this camp but wait to see how the weather plays out. As the day wears on, the wind gets stronger. I don't have a fixed schedule, so there is no need to paddle in rough weather. Lunch is snacks. The food supply is slowly and relentlessly being consumed.

While I read about the Cambrian Explosion, a tiny red dot crawls across the page. It appears to be a red spider, likely a clover mite. If it is a clover mite, then it is female, as the species has no males.

During the Cambrian Explosion, animals with eyes start appearing in fossils. Trilobites were one of the first animals to evolve complex eyes. Generally, predators have eyes on the front of the head, enhancing depth perception and their ability to focus on prey. Prey species usually have eyes on the sides, for a wider predator-detecting field of vision. The development of eyes allowed predators to efficiently find prey, while prey species with eyes can detect predators, retreat, and are more likely to survive. Thus, eyesight may have initiated a visual acuity competition between predators and prey and facilitated the Cambrian Explosion.

The dreary day plods along with wind, drizzle, a rough lake surface, and gray clouds. By afternoon, there is a gale and high whitecaps. My food supply dwindles; thus, dinner is a meal of crackers and chocolate-covered raisins. I hope the food lasts the duration of the trip. Before I turn in for the night, I watch rain clouds rush past mountain peaks across the lake.

Day Eleven

I wake to drizzle and a howling wind. Big waves crashed onto shore all night, making sleep difficult. Out on the lake, waves are swirling in every direction, even into the wind. The wind catches wave tops and sprays mist in the opposite direction the wave is traveling. *How is that possible?* The water is thick with silt. On the exposed beach, the tent shudders violently. To ensure it doesn't blow away, I fortify the corners with logs and rocks. Inside, I brace the tent with my body and a paddle. After skipping breakfast, lunch is a granola bar.

Two bald eagles are again perched on the ground near the outlet for Hardscrabble Creek. Big logs and entire fallen trees are circulating not far offshore. The logs and trees carried by wind have been pulled upstream, out of the Grosvenor River and into the lake, travel *against* surface waves. The situation is chaotic and confusing. My intentions were to stay at this site for two nights, but this will be my fourth night. Ramen noodles for dinner are very good. Hot chocolate for dessert is a treat.

Hopefully the wind tomorrow will be kind enough to allow me to paddle the Grosvenor River to its confluence with the Savonoski River. Once on the Savonoski, it is twelve miles downriver to the Iliuk Arm. My food supply is almost gone, so my daily rations are sparing.

Day Twelve

Thankfully, the weather is reasonably calm. I anxiously pack up and look forward to paddling to the Savonoski. With the Savonoski's remoteness and its swift cold water, I put on my dry suit. The sun is beautiful with silver rays of light shining through a jumble of stacked white-and-gray clouds. The Grosvenor River is peaceful to paddle, with forested bluffs and wetlands embracing its curves. A kingfisher—maybe the same one I saw in camp—chatters and flits from branch to branch along the river-bank, paralleling my progress and providing companionship for several minutes. Looking down into shallow portions of the river, I see large bear tracks embedded in the mud. My mood has improved with the opportunity to be on the water, but food intake has been insufficient to maintain my weight. At times, when getting up to stand, I feel dizzy and lightheaded. Knowing that I have unstable balance, I am trying to be careful. But my strength and stamina are not what they should be. I become deliberate and hopefully prudent in my exertion.

The three-mile paddle is peaceful. Upon reaching the confluence with the Savonoski, I pull ashore, get out, and look over mudflats and islands covered with thick brush at the junction. The mudflat I'm on is covered with bear tracks zigzagging to-and-fro. Some tracks are enormous. Across the Savonoski, either on an island or the far shore, a couple of brown splotches slowly lumber about. My binocular-enhanced eyes confirm they are bears. Large bears.

In all my travels, it is here at this confluence that most awakens a sensation deep in my gut that I am in a primeval world. On the horizon are snowcapped volcanoes with glaciers creeping down their slopes. Immediately in front of me is the relentless power of the Savonoski, its braided channels twisting, merging, splitting, with logjams aggregating on gravel bars. Here I am alone in a vast wilderness, sharing existence with two Alaskan brown bears, with a multitude of bear tracks scattered at my feet. I am a small, frail being surrounded by living, breathing predators, alone in the elements, with powerful forces at work. Very carefully, standing quietly, I scan the area. The vegetation is thick and dense. Large willows and alders dot the shoreline, mudflats, and islands. There could be a large bear nearby, hidden by brush. My attention is supremely focused on the here and now. The rest of the world does not exist. It is just me in a wild, untamed wilderness. The 7.5 billion other people on Earth do not exist. Cities and traffic jams do not exist. Electronic communication does not exist. The only communication is the distance my voice can travel—and there is nobody here but the bears to hear it. This is nature—raw and authentic, where rules of wilderness prevail.

The Savonsoki converges on the Grosvenor at a right angle. But, the Savonoski is overflowing its banks, swelled by glacial melt and heavy rainfalls. Flooding is pushing the Savonoski's silty water three miles up the Grosvenor River and into Grosvenor Lake.

Having surveyed the area, I get back into the kayak and paddle toward the confluence. Once I make it onto the Savonoski, it will be twelve glorious miles downstream to Naknek Lake. With high confidence and high expectations, things are looking up. But to get there, I must contend with the force of the Savonoski's upstream current. My arms and torso paddle swiftly with powerful strokes. Progress is made, but after several minutes, my arms ache and my breathing is heavy. At a certain point, the kayak remains in place, as if on a treadmill of water. Making progress toward the confluence is not happening. The counter-current is too strong!

Floating calmly backwards in the kayak, I rest and gather strength. Determined to persevere and knowing that I will succeed if I paddle hard and fast enough, I try again. Again, I have an epic struggle against the current. The effort was colossal but ultimately wasted. Exhausted, I allow the current to push the kayak backwards and up the Grosvenor. After resting while floating in the kayak a few minutes, I pull ashore.

I need to think this over. I am surprised at the strength of the Savonoski's current and at my own lack of strength paddling against it. Now with dogged determination, I make another enormous effort, paddling as hard and fast as my body allows. But to no avail; I am beaten back. Now I know what it feels like to be drained and demoralized in a vast wilderness with no one to turn to for help. It is no use. I can't make progress by paddling. In full surrender, I give up as the current pushes the kayak backwards and up the Grosvenor. With the Savonoski in a deluge, the force of the current is too much for my meager body.

Endeavoring to be resourceful, I try another angle of attack. I paddle along the east bank of the Grosvenor for a distance as it approaches the Savonoski. Then, getting out of the kayak, I explore the marsh and mud flats, walking toward the Savonoski. With each step, my legs sink to my shins in muck, causing a large effort with every step. Now, I lose a shoe. It takes a minute of digging in soupy mud to retrieve it. I struggle forward, but with every third or fourth step, one of my shoes is sucked off. I abandon the shoes and walk with dry-suit footies covering my feet. Now each step feels like walking in wet cement. I put a foot down and it sinks into muck. The rear foot must then be pulled out of the life-sucking muck. After about seventy-five yards of meandering in and out of marshy wetlands and through tall brush, the Savonoski is finally in sight. But still, it is agonizingly distant. The effort to get through the marsh is huge. I cannot envision lining the kayak while walking along the riverbank; I would surely lose control, lose my balance, and get pulled into the river. Nor can I visualize successfully portaging the gear and kayak through the muck and tangled brush. While portaging, the sounds of my struggle might arouse the interest of a bear.

A combination of factors are taking a toll on my body and mind: a lack of food and not getting enough sleep because of storms crashing waves onto shore. Whatever the factors, I am haggard, sapped of strength, and alone. I have to be very careful in proceeding. After retreating through the marsh and retrieving my shoes, I am back at the kayak. *Darn it!* It is frustrating to be so close yet having such difficulty getting there.

Getting back into the kayak, I shove off and float out onto the Grosvenor to think. There is an alternative path to Brooks Camp. If I backtrack eighteen miles, I could portage my kayak and gear to Fure's Cabin on the Bay of Islands. Then, twenty-three miles of paddling to Brooks Camp. How long that takes depends on the weather, of course. Maybe two nights with good weather or maybe four nights with poor weather. But here I am, so close to completing the intended route. Taking the Savonoski River is the route I told my family.

I try another tactic to attain access to the Savonoski. This time, I approach by paddling along Grosvenor's west bank. Things go well, but there is thick alder and willow overhanging the river, with the Savonoski pushing the kayak into the brush. Using this to my advantage, I grab branches and pull the kayak hand over hand against the strong current. This is making good progress! Pleased that I had not given up,

I congratulate myself on persistence, intelligence, and resourcefulness. Paddling down the Savonoski will be achieved! But then, Robert Burns said this about the struggles of mice and men: "The best-laid schemes o' mice an' men Gang aft agley."

Repeatedly grasping branches, the kayak inches closer to the Savonoski's main flow, now only thirty feet away. Success is imminent.

Here the countercurrent is powerfully surging, pushing the kayak into overhanging brush and tilting it at a forty-five-degree angle. With shock and horror, I watch water pour into the kayak in slow motion. In a moment the hull will fill, and I will be pushed beneath the current. Grabbing the coaming with my left hand and a branch with my right, I level the kayak. With the immediate emergency nullified, the current drives the kayak and my body into the brush. Now I am stuck. Sweat builds as branches press into my face. I work intensely to extricate the kayak and my body, all while the current pushes. With several minutes of intense effort, I break free of the entanglement. Now, I grab overhanging branches, pulling the kayak backwards and into calm water. I breathe a sigh of relief. But where is the paddle? I look around, but it is nowhere to be found, lost in the melee. I am stuck in the middle of a vast and primeval wilderness with a kayak and no paddle.

Before leaving home, my daughter gave this crucial advice: "Dad, don't you think it would be a good idea to bring a spare paddle?" At first, I brushed it off, but on reconsideration, she was correct. Twisting around toward the stern, there, strapped to the back of the kayak, is the spare paddle she suggested. After assembling the paddle, I spin the kayak around and paddle away from the Savonoski, relieved to be above the surface and still breathing. My daughter is a wise person who still has a father.

In three attempts to reach the Savonoski, I was beaten back. Each used a different approach, and each resulted in a struggle. *Maybe the Universe is trying to tell me something? Perhaps it is best to not continue the battle.* Thus, I decide to alter my route and paddle to Fure's Cabin. This is disappointing. Now I must backtrack up the Grosvenor River and northwest along the coast of Grosvenor Lake. This is different from the route my family expects, but with my GPS device, I send a message each day with my location saying, "Everything is OK." They also know my food supply is close to empty.

Paddling up the Grosvenor, I see an object bobbing on the surface. As I approach, I recognize it as the paddle I lost while fighting with the alder brush! This bolsters the case that it is silty glacier water from the flooding Savonoski that is pushing three miles up Grosvenor River and clouding Grosvenor Lake. Reaching over the side of the kayak, I pick the paddle out of the water, disassemble it, and secure it to the kayak deck. It is good to have a spare paddle again.

Having regained a semblance of composure, I replay in my mind the tipping of the kayak and its filling with water while entangled in brush. What occurred thirty minutes ago could have resulted in a tragic outcome. It is fortunate that the kayak was righted immediately. Once rushing water starts flowing into a boat, the entire craft can quickly fill and submerge or be pressed against an obstacle with tremendous force. *What would have happened to me had that occurred?* It is an uncomfortable thought, and I cringe when thinking about it.

Today I got lucky and live to paddle another day, hopefully wiser and a little more experienced. Experiences in the outdoors and gaining knowledge, that is an interesting component of wilderness travel. But one must survive the experience to learn the lesson. In our day-to-day lives, infrequently do we make decisions of consequence based on the natural elements, and there are few circumstances where a decision can have instantaneous and catastrophic results. The exception that comes to mind is driving a vehicle. Wilderness travel, however, requires decisions that are consequential every day. Should we travel or stay put during a storm? Should we hang food in a tree and keep a clean camp? Should we carefully track our location so we don't get lost? These and other questions routinely come up in the wilderness. It is these types of questions that make wilderness travel compelling and authentic.

Heading to Fure's Cabin, I paddle up the Grosvenor River as wind picks up from the southeast. Paddling into Grosvenor Lake, I am weary and demoralized to be backtracking. On the unprotected lake, wind pushes whitecaps from the rear splashing over the kayak's deck. Water sloshes at my feet. The weather was calm and sunny for the first part of the trip, but now the days are filled with a relentless procession of clouds, rain, wind, and whitecaps. After a strenuous morning, I need to get off the water and out of the squall, lest an unexpected large wave upsets the kayak, plunging me into cold water. I look for a place to pull ashore, but the shoreline has volcanic ledges and boulders with no level place to land. I paddle along a rocky point jutting into the lake. As the point is approached, I paddle away from calmer water and take the full brunt of wind and cresting waves, then to the point's lee side. Once around point, it acts as a breakwater and provides protection. Hugging the shoreline, I paddle into a bay. The bay curves outward and, again, a rocky outcrop juts into the lake forcing me to paddle in wind and whitecaps. As each wave approaches from behind, first the stern of the kayak rises with water splashing at my back, then the bow is raised as the wave progress forward. Following the shoreline of bays and paddling around exposed points repeats several more times. Hugging the shore is safer than crossing mile-wide bays but adds much time and distance.

It is dangerous being on the water. Paddling past more volcanic cliffs, there is a narrow sand-and-gravel beach. Waves crash onto it, but it is a flat place to land and a haven in the storm. Fatigued, I paddle ashore as waves smash the kayak, tipping it sideways and onto the gravel shoreline. Surveying the area, it is not wide enough to set up a tent, but here I am. Crawling out of the swamped kayak, I stand and feel dizzy. After regaining balance, I take gear out of the kayak and pull it further onto the beach and away from waves. Lifting the stern of the kayak, I tip it upside down, letting water drain.

From the beach rises a steep muddy bluff. Grabbing a bag of gear, I begin crawling upward. It is a struggle pulling the bag up the bank while my feet slide backwards in mud. At the top, I set the bag in thick, lush grass, descend, retrieve another bag, and crawl back up. Then a third bag is retrieved and finally the kayak. The food supply is down to a few items, but it has to last. Several days of travel are still required. I set up the tent and put gear inside.

In the wind and drizzle, I explore the mossy forested area around the tent and find plump red watermelon berries. The juicy berries taste like cucumber and have seeds inside. They take time to gather and are not filling, but they are fresh food and may contain vitamin C. Still munching on watermelon berries, I come across bright-red bunches of baneberries, which have a superficial resemblance to watermelon berries. Although baneberries are harmless to birds, they are poisonous to humans, causing heart problems, so I leave them be.

Next, I come across curiously shaped purple flowers. The flowers resemble the hood on a robe worn by a monk; thus, the plant is named monkshood. This plant is extremely poisonous, containing aconitum, which is one hundred times more lethal than strychnine. People of the North Pacific extracted the deadly toxin from the plant's roots, dipping arrowheads and spear tips into it, which were used for hunting sea lions and whales. Since you are reading this, you know I didn't eat any.

Another purple flower here is the arctic lupine, which produces pods that look like edible peapods and are in the same family. Since they look like the peapods I am familiar with, I wonder if they are edible and am tempted to try some. But not taking chances, I don't eat any. That was a good decision, because once back home I learn they are toxic. One thing is certain: I could not survive here by gathering edible plants. Most of the plants I know anything about are poisonous. Since plants cannot flee from herbivores, creating toxins is one of their defense mechanisms. Avoiding the toxic plants, I have been gathering and eating watermelon berries, but the amounts have been minuscule.

I return to the tent, and my impatience grows waiting for better weather. The storms have delayed my progress. There were three nights on the island watching the bear eat the moose. Then four nights on Grosvenor Lake near Hardscrabble Creek. The detour backtracking to Fure's Cabin is taking unplanned time. *But what can a person do when there is stormy weather?* It feels safer going slowly and carefully, even as food dwindles. With nothing to do, I reread a chapter in a book, then take a nap. Then reread another chapter. Sleeping and sitting in the tent causes restlessness. Knowing that I am overdue and food is minimal generates urgency. My urge is to be on the water paddling, making progress. Looking at the map, I make rough estimates. There are twelve miles

Arctic Lupine
(*Lupinus arcticus*)
by Sven Bellanger

left to reach the portage. Then gear bags and the kayak must be portaged one-and-a-half miles to Fure's Cabin. From the cabin, the paddle through the Bay of Islands is seven miles. Then it's eight miles of open-water paddling to a point that separates Naknek's North Arm from its South Arm. After paddling around the point, it is nine miles hugging the coast to Brooks Camp. According to my calculations, and depending upon the weather, all food will be gone, even while eating only tiny amounts each day. If the weather is stormy, I will be forced to remain on shore with no food. If the weather is cooperative, I can make good time but will still run out of food.

Evening comes. The weather has settled down. A chickadee chirps. The sun dips below the horizon but I'm not sleepy, having spent much of the day and evening resting, reading, and napping. The thought occurs that I could paddle in darkness, but that doesn't seem like a good idea.

Day Thirteen

Getting up this morning at 6:00 a.m., I look out onto the lake to see an overcast sky and calm water. I quickly bring the gear and kayak down from the bluff. After packing gear into the kayak, I am on the water in short order. There is only a slight breeze. I paddle northwest toward the big island. Approaching it, my route is through the narrows on the west shoreline. Now past the island, I paddle around a bend and proceed westerly, hugging the jagged shoreline.

The sun is rising behind me. An almost full moon is eerily shining through low-lying clouds in front. The lighting seems curious; there is a diffused glowing in the clouds. To the left, a bear walks through brush on the side of a hill. It doesn't know that I am observing it as I silently paddle by. A rainbow is visible in the mist of clouds on one side of the moon. This is a positive sign. It feels surreal—inspiring. I am hungry, tired, and paddling in wild natural beauty, in misty glowing weather, with a rainbow, all alone, except for a bear foraging on the side of a hill. The wind picks up and whitecaps splash at my back. I don't know why; maybe it is seeing the rainbow, but besides the birth of my children, this is one of the best days of my life. Maybe it is the lightheaded sensations I have been experiencing. Maybe it is the struggle to survive. Maybe it is the surreal beauty of the area and the primordial aura. It feels like this day was meant to be. To be one with all of nature's elements. The sun, the moon, the Earth, the clouds, the sky, the rainbow, the water. Like the bear on the hillside, I have purpose, struggling while immersed in Earth's natural beauty and dealing with its elements. That is how humans evolved, and by returning to wilderness, it is returning to where we came from. It causes my body and mind to feel at peace with contentment—even happiness. It is invigorating having these feelings, even though I know survival is not assured.

It appeared the sun would be victorious in burning off the cloud cover, but the clouds not only prevail, they thicken. The wind picks up and it starts to rain. As water collects in the bottom of the kayak, everything gets wet. I am making good progress despite the weather, but the water is cold, and I am alone. I cannot take a chance being on the water in these conditions. Survival would be fifteen minutes or less. My estimate puts me four miles from the portage. Very close, and in good conditions, an hour of paddling. But four miles in this weather while in gaunt physical condition is risky. Capsizing would be fatal. Thus, despite my optimism, the weather doesn't relent. I consider continuing or pulling ashore.

By 10:30 a.m., it is too rough. I pull over and make camp to wait it out. In the tent, I pass time by making notes in my journal and rereading a book. 11:10 a.m.—drizzle and wind, reading the book's acknowledgments. 12:00 p.m.—whitecaps and more wind, reading footnotes. 1:25 p.m.—whitecaps, cool, breezy, reading the bibliography. 3:15 p.m.— whitecaps, cool, breezy. reading the preface. 4:20 p.m.—drizzle, whitecaps, wind, reading the copyright page. 6:45 p.m.—whitecaps, drizzle, reading the index. 7:05 p.m.—a little bit of sun peeking out but still whitecaps. 7:20 p.m.—looks like I am going to spend the night here. 8:35 p.m.—whitecaps, overcast. Small snack for dinner. Night. Restless sleep.

Day Fourteen

Today I wake early, antsy to get going and make my way to the portage. My plan is to portage to the old trappers' cabin, spend a night there, then continue my journey through the Bay of Islands. A mist hangs over the tranquil lake as I paddle four miles to the portage. It is a relief coming to a small island and then a bay where the portage should be. After exploring the shoreline, I see a trail that leads into the forest. That must be the portage! After pulling the kayak onto the trail, I explore, making sure I know my way before expending effort moving gear and the kayak. This could be a game trail that leads deeper into the woods. Following the trail, there are side trails and alternate paths, some of which are bear trails. It is confusing, and I am not exactly sure where I am or if I am on the correct bay. With further exploration, the trail leads to a beaver pond. The pond appears on the map, thus confirming my location. Satisfied I know my way around, I carefully retrace my path back to the kayak and gear. At this stage, it would be horrible to get lost in the woods, with no gear and no food—that's when tragedies happen. I am getting concerned though. With the rationing of food this past week, I have stretched the supply out. There are just a few snacks left. That will have to last three to five days.

Today I will portage to Fure's Cabin and spend the night. Tomorrow, if the weather is good, I'll be paddling on Naknek Lake. Then, two or three nights will be needed to paddle to Brooks Camp. Despite having lost weight, a low energy level, and little food, this seems doable. At least in theory.

Sitting on shore beside the kayak, I contemplate the facts. After thinking for a while, I look out onto Grosvenor Lake. There is an object moving. A small motorboat is in the distance—coming this direction. As the boat gets closer, it is evident it is coming into the bay and to the portage. The pilot cuts the engine and the boat silently glides onto the gravel beach. The man piloting the boat is the first person I have seen in two weeks. After we say hello, he asks my name, how I am, and if I have any food. I respond by telling him, "I am tired and hungry." He is the manager for a fishing camp on Grosvenor Lake. The camp is closed; however, he was doing maintenance when contacted by radio from Brooks Camp.

My family has been monitoring the multiday storms over Katmai and they are tracking my GPS way points. When they saw my slow progress and deviation from the Savonoski River route, they became concerned and asked Brooks Camp for a welfare check, which relayed the message.

After talking a few minutes, he offers a water taxi to Grosvenor Camp. Once there, a previously scheduled float plane is going to Brooks. I can hitch a ride on the plane if I am interested. Gaunt and haggard, having little food, and with Brooks my intended endpoint, I accept. We load the kayak and gear into the boat and motor across Grosvenor. This will cut several days off my journey.

While crossing the lake, he tells me that my family had requested the welfare check several days ago. Because of the severe storms and the lake being agitated, he dared not be on the water. He asks how I passed the days on shore waiting for better weather. "A lot of time reading and writing in my journal." He asks what I was reading. My reply: "Some interesting stuff on the structure of the Universe and the evolution of life."

Back home, my family tells me I'm underweight and look too skinny. It was frustrating waiting day after day, stuck in the tent. After weighing the risks, I stayed on shore rather than paddling on a remote cold-water lake subject to storms. I know it was a good decision to accept help, however, after accepting the taxi, there is a part of me that regrets the decision. *I wanted to continue the struggle.* I don't know if it was ego or a reluctance to accept help. Or proving that I am self-reliant and can survive adverse conditions. Years later, while looking back on the adventure, my soul yearns to return. Indeed, I will.

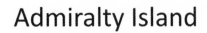

Admiralty Island

Oliver
Inlet
↓

■ Cabin

Swan
Island

Seymour Canal

KOOTZNOOWOO

"I will argue that every scrap of biological diversity is priceless, to be learned and cherished, and never to be surrendered without a struggle."

—E.O. WILSON

Flying into the Juneau airport on the Alaskan panhandle, my expedition partner and I look out the window to see a small portion of the seventeen million acres of old-growth rainforest—part of Tongass National Forest. Adjoining and ecologically connected to Canada's Great Bear Rainforest to the south, together the Tongass and the Great Bear Forest form the largest intact temperate rainforest on Earth. Sustaining the area's rich biological productivity, the rainforest blankets coastal mountains receiving one hundred inches of rainfall annually. Most tourists visit Juneau by cruise ship along the inside passage. Cruise ship, however, is not *our* intended mode of transportation. Our wilderness endeavor will be kayaking a protected bay of Admiralty Island. Admiralty, along with Baranof and Chichagof, are known as Alaska's ABC Islands.

After exploring Juneau, we meet our outfitter, who supplies us with a hard-shell tandem kayak and provides a water taxi to Admiralty. The outfitter gives us pepper spray and two emergency flares so that we can signal rescue or fend off an aggressive bear. All the food and gear for our nine-day excursion is contained in two large duffel bags. With the two-person kayak and gear loaded onto the outfitter's boat, we cross Stephens Passage and head toward Oliver Inlet on Admiralty. We could

191

have paddled from Juneau across the channel to Admiralty, but with our lack of sea kayaking experience and the potential for winds, rough seas, and currents, we use the water taxi.

About five hundred Tlingit, "People of the Tides," live in Angoon on Admiralty Island's southwestern edge. Tlingit, who have lived in the archipelago region of the Alaskan panhandle for ten thousand years, call the island *Xootsnoowu*, or the "Fortress of the Bears." The majority of the island is protected as the Kootznoowoo Wilderness. The island is home to 1,600 bears that are a subspecies of Alaskan coastal brown bears endemic to the ABC Islands.

The brown bears of the ABC Islands have a peculiar ancestry that has confounded scientists and is still being studied. They appear to be related not only to Alaskan coastal brown bears but also to polar bears. It is a mystery how this came about. Their mitochondrial DNA, which is passed down from female bears, matches polar bear mitochondrial DNA. Perhaps, after the last major glaciation, a group of polar bears were stranded on the ABCs. It may be that mainland subordinate male brown bears in search of territory and mates swam to the islands, inter-breeding with female polar bears. Thus, over time, repeated hybridization created this subspecies. Despite DNA evidence of their ancestry, the bears of the ABC Islands do not retain white polar bear coloration but are usually dark brown.

Admiralty Island brown bears are omnivores. They feed on salmon, squirrels, grass, sedge, roots, and berries. There are healthy populations of Sitka black-tailed deer, a subspecies of mule deer, on all the ABC Islands, and they are preyed upon when a fawn is found hidden in understory or when an adult can be ambushed. Admiralty Island brown bears also feed in intertidal zones on clams, crabs, and whatever they find by turning rocks over or checking pools at low tide. Being that Admiralty Island encompasses an area of 1,646 square miles and it has 1,600 brown bears, that works out to one brown bear for each square mile. This assumes they are distributed evenly, but they aren't. Some areas contain more, some less.

Both black bears and wolves are good swimmers and occasionally swim the channel that separates Admiralty from the mainland. Despite this, there are few, if any, wolves or black bears on Admiralty, Baranof, or Chichagof, even though there is plenty of food for them. The ABCs have black-tailed deer that wolves could prey upon, just as they do on the mainland. But competing with large predaceous and densely populated brown bears precludes black bears and wolves from creating resident populations. When they can find them, brown bears may dig out a den, kill, and perhaps eat black bear cubs and wolf pups.

Day One

Crossing Stephens Passage, we approach the north end of Admiralty Island. We cruise along its north shoreline to where an opening appears and the captain turns the boat toward it. Entering Oliver Inlet, we travel three miles to the inlet's southern end. Here the captain veers the boat to the right and we come to a stop on shore. After unloading the kayak and gear onto the gravel beach, we watch our water taxi pull away and head back to Juneau. The captain has promised to return in nine days to pick us up. We are alone and all is quiet. We have landed on Admiralty Island, the Kootznoowoo Wilderness—the Fortress of the Bears.

Now we need to transport the kayak and gear across a one-and-a-half-mile wide isthmus of wetland and bog to our paddling destination. Forty miles long, Seymour Canal is an ocean inlet that cuts through Admiralty Island, providing protection from rough weather on its north, east, and western edges. Its southern extant, however, is open to Stephens Passage. Thus, we hope to have safe paddling as we explore the inlet's bays, estuaries, and islands.

Connecting Oliver Inlet to Seymour Canal is a mile-long rail and pushcart tram. Built in the 1950s by Juneau area residents, the tram allows easy transport of gear and material. Without it, hauling gear across the wetlands would be a slog. Across the horizon is muskeg sprinkled with short pines.

We load the tram with our two duffle bags and center the ninety-pound kayak between them, then begin pushing the tram. Scattered about the bog and shrouded in mist are stunted lodgepole pine somehow surviving the low-nutrient, acidic conditions. It looks and feels like a primeval landscape of the Jurassic Period, quite foreign to my modern sensibilities. As we push the tram, we step on railroad ties which raise the rails above the marsh. Nearby are groups of low-lying plants with giant leaves. These are western skunk cabbage, which grow in clumps and have large, oval leaves. Out across the bog are tall grasses and hummocks rising out of murky water. Not feeling any particular anxiety, we continue pushing the cart toward Seymour Canal. Eventually the rails bend to the left and we reach the end of the line.

From here we shoulder the gear and portage into thick forest, finding a Forest Service cabin. Refusing to use the cabin, we make camp, waiting for rainfall to stop. Our tent is pitched under the shadows of giant, old-growth western hemlock and Sitka spruce. These, along with western red cedar and yellow cedar, make up much of the coastal rainforest. Another tree species, the Pacific yew, grows at the southern edge of the Tongass and along the Northwest coast. Its bark contains the compound Paclitaxel, which is used to treat ovarian, breast, lung, cervical, pancreatic, and other cancers.

Throughout much of the understory is a ubiquitous plant standing three to five feet in height, with a stalk topped by giant maple-leaf-shaped leaves. The leaves and stalk are covered with hundreds of noxious irritating spines—thus the name devil's club. Although it is painful to touch the spines, compounds produced by devil's club have been found to inhibit tuberculosis microbes and may be therapeutic for leukemia.

At the cabin, we encounter a man and woman hastily cleaning up, packing gear, and preparing to depart. They are Alaska Game and Fish employees, terse and not friendly. The man marches around with a rifle slung over his shoulder. My partner later hears their story. A few days prior, they had been transporting equipment to the cabin using the tram. A bear came at them, charging aggressively. With repeated charges coming closer, they shot and killed it. Its carcass lies nearby in brush. They returned to Juneau to inform their supervisor and file a report. Because of the encounter, or because they are uneasy, the project has been aborted and, with gear packed up, they are returning to Juneau. My partner and I have the area around the cabin and our camp to ourselves. Except, they warn us . . . there are other bears in the vicinity, coming to feed on the carcass.

Day Two

Our tent sits under the widespread boughs of towering old-growth. A steady rain comes down, so we string up a tarp as shelter for cooking and eating. Pale-green lichen—old man's beard—hangs from tree branches. Several compounds in old man's beard have been studied and are found to have antibiotic and anticancer properties. Deep-green moss covers the lower portions of tree trunks and the ground. Today it rains and drizzles, so we wait for the weather to clear. We read quietly in the tent. Avoiding devil's club and the thick of the forest, we explore the coastline, finding bald eagles and nests. Among tall grass laden with dew, we find an eagle feather. My partner holds the feather, feeling its delicate balance. We discuss keeping it but know we cannot. With one thousand eagle nests sprinkled along Admiralty's 860-mile coast, there is more than one nest for each mile of shoreline. But there are eagle nests inland as well. Thus, Admiralty Island's rich bounty supports over 2,500 bald eagles.

Admiralty Island's abundance supports one of the highest densities of brown bears found anywhere in the world, with one brown bear for each square mile. This is similar to brown bear density in Katmai National Park, which, like Admiralty Island, supports copious runs of salmon. Away from the southern coast, inland and north, Denali National Park has brown bear density at one per twelve to eighteen square miles. In Alaska's far north, on the arctic coastal plain and in the mountains of the Arctic National Wildlife Refuge, brown bear density is estimated at one per thirty square miles. In comparison, brown bear density in Montana's Glacier National Park is one per thirteen square miles. For the Greater Yellowstone Ecosystem, brown bear density is difficult to estimate because the population has fluctuated, with a low-point estimate between 136 and 312 grizzlies in 1975. That year, grizzlies were listed as threatened in the lower forty-eight states under the Endangered Species Act. Since then, the number of Yellowstone Ecosystem grizzlies has risen to 757 bears in 2014. Inside the 2.2 million acres within Yellowstone Park, there are an estimated 150 grizzlies, which works out to one grizzly per twenty-three square miles.

One motive for us to kayak here is to see humpback whales. During late fall and early winter, humpbacks congregate where Seymour Canal opens to Stephens Passage, and although this is August, we hope to get lucky and see a humpback or two. Some years over one hundred humpbacks come to the mouth of Seymour Canal. By the end of November and early December, most migrate south, some crossing the North Pacific and journeying to the Hawaiian Islands, while others follow the coastline to waters near Mexico.

Beyond bald eagles, brown bears, and humpbacks, Admiralty Island and southeast Alaska support rich biological diversity. Coastal waters support vast congregations of krill, Pacific herring, fishes, and five species of salmon. Herring spawn in sheltered bays and estuaries in the springtime while preying on krill. Krill—small crustacean filter feeders—sift plankton, diatoms, and algae with feathered combs on front appendages. The translucent pink krill gather in tight swarms, with densities of 10,000 to 60,000 individuals per cubic meter of seawater. Of the five species of salmon that spawn on Admiralty Island, the pink, sockeye, and coho especially feed on krill, which contribute to their pink flesh. Pink salmon are also called "humpy salmon" because males develop a pronounced hump on their back as they migrate up streams to spawn.

Humpback whales come to feed on krill, herring, and small fishes using their great gaping mouths and baleen filters. Bears eat luxuriant sedges and bulbs during the spring and summer, berries in the fall, and capture spawning salmon as they migrate up freshwater streams in summer and early fall. Eagles eat herring, other fish, and the remains of salmon after they have finished spawning. And of course, like all large mammals that inhabit the woods, bears expel digested fish in the forest, thus fertilizing the forest floor with nitrogen and other nutrients. Within the tops of old-growth trees, bald eagles build nests and fledge their young. A perfect example of an interdependent web of life.

Day Three

Today the rain lets up. After consulting tidal charts, we put on dry suits, with rubber seals at the wrists and neck, and haul the kayak and gear to Seymour Canal. We avoid putting the kayak into the stream which runs in front of the cabin, not wanting to disturb the multitude of spawning humpy salmon or crush eggs in the streambed. At high tide, we shove off and paddle into Seymour Canal on our sea kayaking expedition. It feels exhilarating to be out on the water. And what an exquisite paddle it is, gliding on the blue water's surface, each ripple glinting sunlight as it rolls by, surrounded by green-clad mountains. We peer down into the clear depths of the water and with almost every stroke of the paddle, we discover something new. There is a crab easily seen on the seabed. Over here is a pink sea star. Float-ing by is a large orange sea jelly, likely a lion's mane. Now, here are several translucent sea jel-lies with four clear, semicircular organs within them—moon jellies. At the fringe of many sea jellies' bells are sense organs with primitive eyespots (ocelli). Despite their deli-cate, gelatinous nature, sea jellies have survived on Earth for over 500 million years, and perhaps up to 700 million years, thus making them one of Earth's first multior-gan animals.

For a couple of paddlers accus-tomed to freshwater canoeing in the Boundary Waters, sea kayaking is foreign to our Midwestern expe-rience and sensibilities. Paddling

Lion's mane jellyfish
(*Cyanea capillata*)
by Sven Bellanger

onward, we come across several long, green, multi-tentacled "things" floating on the surface. Curious, we paddle over to one, snag a tentacle with a paddle, and pull it to the kayak. My partner grabs it with his hand and lifts it out of the water. To my relief, the tentacle does not wrap around his arm. This is not some beast, but kelp. He grabs a knife and cuts open the long stalk, finding it hollow. Knowing that kelp is generally edible, we sniff it and eat a portion. Inter-esting. At the end of the stalk is a hollow bulb, where numerous leafy structures emanate. This is bullwhip kelp. Bullwhip forests thrive off the northern coast of Baja California, along the West Coast, on Alaska's south coast, and along the Aleutian Islands. It can grow up to ten inches a day with its stalk reaching upwards of one hundred feet from seabed to surface where thirty to sixty leafy blades float. Bullwhip and other species of kelp contain extracts that have been shown to have anticancer properties.

We are on the lookout for a source of fresh water to top off our supply. Having bypassed a stream cascading down a cliff face several miles back, we turn to the right around a rocky point, then paddle up an estuary. Consulting our map, we locate a freshwater stream at the far northwest end of the estuary. The now lower tide causes the bottom of the kayak to scrape bottom. Pulling to the side, we are forced to disembark precariously on a slick muddy bank. Walking the beach, we sink into mud as we follow a brackish stream one hundred yards to its outlet at the edge of the forest. As we approach the forest, I am nervous. The mud is slick. Maneuvering is cumbersome. Now would not be a good time for a bear to come charging out of the brush at the forest's edge. We arrive at a point where the stream runs downhill, so is unlikely to be brackish. We test it and find it is fresh.

Using a gravity-fed water filter, we replenish our supply, then walk along the intertidal stream back to the kayak. We explore the water's edge while glancing at the tangle of thick dark forest to our left. The air is still and quiet, and with the treacherous footing, I can't shake feeling vulnerable. Our kayak is just a minute or two walk, but in this place called Fortress of the Bears, I'd rather not dawdle.

Halfway to the kayak, my partner stumbles across a large heavy bone. Walking over to see what he found, I come across bones. This was big, whatever it was. Searching about, we find bones scattered in sand and hidden in clumps of grass. A rib here. A femur there. Over here is a fully articulated spine. A large pelvis. Gathering them up, we place them into their proper positions. We lay out the vertebral column with ribs on either side, put the pelvis at the bottom, then both femurs below the pelvis, and a tibia and fibula forming a leg. Standing back, we look over the skeleton. This was either a bear or maybe a moose. We need the skull to know for sure. We search further, even into the forest, but can't find the skull. Admiralty doesn't have a moose population, but sometimes a moose swims from the mainland. This is likely the skeleton of an Alaskan coastal brown bear, or more specifically, the subspecies with polar bear genetics mixed in. Either it did not survive a territorial conflict with another bear over fishing rights, or a hunter took a trophy home, including skin and skull, leaving the rest.

Having topped off our supply of fresh water, we paddle toward a small unnamed island with a rocky beach. One hundred yards away, a cute little gray face with black eyes bobs in the water. That is something we don't see in the Boundary Waters. The harbor seal keeps an eye on us but stays at a distance. It is wary in part because Tlingit from Angoon do subsistence hunting and fishing, and that includes cute little harbor seals.

As we approach the island, it is evident that its craggy shore is submerged at high tide. Rocks and outcroppings along the beachfront are encrusted with tens of thousands of razor-sharp, filter-feeding bivalves. With the shore blanketed by blueish-black mussels, I feel pangs of guilt after exiting the kayak as I put my foot down and crush them. These are northern Pacific blue mussels, also known as common mussels. The predators of blue mussels are Dungeness crabs, green sea urchins, five-arm ochre sea stars, and sunflower sea stars, which have anywhere from sixteen to twenty-four arms. Being that we're using a tough, hard-shell kayak, we aren't concerned about the mussels' sharp edges cutting its hull. Had we brought folding kayaks or a folding canoe with a fabric hull, the mussels' sharp edges would surely cut the fabric to shreds.

Generally, I find a campsite before evening because pulling into a new camp in twilight and setting up a tent in low light, not knowing the lay of the land, creates an uneasy feeling. It is during early evening with darkness descending that wildlife, including brown bears, become active. Finding a campsite before evening allows us to explore and get to know the area. There is a boulder here, a log there, a bush over there. Human smells and noises are established. We understand we are visitors and that wilderness is home for wildlife. But, for this evening and night, we are going to be here. This allows wildlife to become aware of our presence before inadvertently stumbling into our camp.

If a bear comes into camp, we will defend ourselves. The plan is to gather outside the tent, stand together, look formidable, and have pepper spray ready. If the bear continues to advance, we may be forced to retreat down the beach or into the forest. In a worst-case scenario, we haul the kayak to the water and paddle away, no matter the weather or darkness. That would not be pleasant, abandoning our gear and food to be pilfered or destroyed.

The island's shoreline has stones, large rocks, rocky slabs, and downed trees. Farther inland is a cutbank that rises about ten feet where high tide doesn't reach. We make and eat dinner on the rocky beach. When high tide comes in a few hours, we are not sure how much of the beach will be inundated, so we set up the tent on mossy ground above the cutbank and pull the kayak up next to the tent. We don't explore the island because the terrain is uneven, steep, and thickly vegetated, and darkness will soon be encroaching.

Away from camp, about a hundred yards down the beach, we find the base of a tree with a tangle of exposed roots and branches that dangle high over the cut bank. Over the highest branch, we toss a rope and hoist our food bag into the air. From above the cutbank, a bear would have difficulty reaching out to get our food without tumbling downward through the roots and branches. From below, the bear would have to reach twelve feet into the air.

My partner and I retire to the tent to settle down for the night and do some reading. The air is still. It is eerily quiet. With flashlights focused on books, each of us is in his own world. We hear a slight and unidentifiable noise, then silence. We look at each other, say nothing, and return to reading. Several minutes later we hear another noise. Again, we ignore it. But now, once more we hear something. It is the sound of cracking; maybe branches breaking? My partner says, "Did you hear that?"

"Yes," I answer, putting on my boots.

He looks at me with a perplexed look on his face and says, "You're not going out there are you?"

"Yes, I am," I reply. "We're here. We can't sit in the tent like frightened mice. If it is a bear, I don't want it milling around, getting closer and closer, then sniffing our tent while we hold our breath. That is a recipe for disaster." I want to make our presence known, and let "it" know we aren't a prey species. We are human beings that stand tall and will defend ourselves. That is the message that must be conveyed. There is no other choice. I crawl out and stand, peering into the darkness. Nearby I see trees and murky blackness. Nothing stirs. There are no more sounds and nothing is moving. I calmly call out, "Hey there, hey there, anybody out there?" Waiting for a reply, we listen, but there is only silence. For all we know, the noises could have been a squirrel chewing nuts. I get back into the tent and we continue reading and writing in our journals. We hear no more noises nor any sounds that go bump in the night. Eventually we tire and fall asleep.

Day Four

Waking up, we retrieve our food from the tangle overhanging the cut-bank. After breakfast of cereal, freeze-dried berries, and rehydrated milk, we take down the tent, then lower the kayak down the bluff and bring it to the water's edge. In the midst of packing gear, we come across a purple sea urchin shell. Likely a sea otter had brought it here, used its teeth or a rock to crack it open, and consumed the insides. Purple sea urchins can regrow tissue, spines, and tube feet and can live up to fifty years. The red sea urchin, which also inhabits these waters, can live up to two hundred years. Proteins found in sea urchins have been found to kill cancer cells, and its genome has provided insights into Alzheimer's and diseases related to aging.

The purple sea urchin is an omnivore but feeds voraciously on kelp. If a sea urchin population grows unchecked, they decimate kelp forests. A kelp forest provides shelter and habitat for sea creatures just as a terrestrial forest does for birds and land animals. Sea otters and other predators such as fish, crabs, lobsters, octopuses, and sea stars keep urchins in check. When predator numbers are low, urchin populations explode, eradicating kelp, creating a kelp-free area called an "urchin barren." Without the kelp forest, species that depend upon it for shelter and forage leave or their numbers suffer.

The impacts of predators on prey, and prey on vegetation, are well-known. The most notable example is the natural recovery of cougars and grizzlies in Yellowstone while at the same time wolves were reintroduced. Increasing numbers of cougars, grizzlies, and wolves preyed upon elk, deer, moose, and bison or bighorn sheep. The predators limited herbivores, which alleviated stress on Yellowstone's grasses, forbs, alder, willow, cottonwood, and aspen. Whether in the sea or on land, for many ecosystems, apex predators keep prey species in check, allowing kelp forests to thrive in the sea or terrestrial forests to thrive on land.

The air is calm and, thankfully, it is not raining. To pass time, we challenge each other to a rock-skipping contest on the placid water of Seymour Canal. Deciding we should take advantage of the weather, we pack our gear into the kayak and shove off. It is mostly cloudy, but here and there cerulean sky shows between gray clouds. Leaving this unnamed island, we paddle south and west, crossing King Salmon Bay. At its head, King Salmon River feeds freshwater into the bay and is a natal river for chinook salmon, also known as king salmon—the largest of Alaska's salmon species, with some reaching fifty pounds or more. Paddling west, we approach a mountainous peninsula then head south, hugging the shoreline. After rounding the southern point of the peninsula, we turn west again, this time heading toward the northern end of Swan Island. Having voyaged seven miles, we decide to camp on Swan Island. Seeing a grassy area, we pull ashore. My partner gets out of the kayak, then steadies it while I extract myself, stepping onto a hard, irregular rock outcropping. We pull the craft ashore, unload our gear, and set up the tent in tall grass, which backs up to high brush. After lunch, we turn our thoughts inward, pulling out books to immerse our minds—surrounded by a million acres of raw, spectacular wilderness. There are no distractions. Only pure and utter focus, living vicariously in worlds created by authors.

I can't help but be impressed by my expedition partner's reading choice: *The Brothers Karamazov* by Fyodor Dostoevsky. Over eight hundred pages in length, the novel is set in nineteenth-century Russia. It involves ethical and philosophical debates dealing with free will, God, and morality. Heavy stuff. It is a book he happened to come across at a bookstore in Juneau. Being we are dealing with rain and long periods of time cooped up in the tent, having reading material is essential.

This late afternoon, we replenish our cooking and drinking water by paddling three miles to Swan Cove, where several streams converge after cascading down the mountains. The sky is clear blue with a scattering of small white clouds. Approaching the estuary at low tide, interwoven streams flow across the tidal flats. We abandon the kayak and walk three-quarters of a mile on seaweed-covered mud toward the forested shoreline. Hundreds of humpy salmon are swimming up streams, their humped backs protruding and wriggling above the surface as they undulate. As we proceed, we also see hundreds of dead and dying humpies on the flats. When we are within forty yards of the forest, we judge we are beyond brackish water. Evening is approaching, and we are in the shadow of the island's high peaks. Bears will be active and this is an ideal place for them to feed, so we avoid getting close to the forest.

We promptly filter water into our containers and take a sip. Half expecting it to taste like salmon soup, it is clean and fresh. The filter is doing its job. As we turn back toward the kayak, a dark shape emerges from the shadows of the forest. Sure enough, a bear is coming to devour salmon. It sees us, raises its head, and sniffs the air. It wants to identify what type of creatures we are. Cautiously, we watch each other. After a few minutes, we leave to let the bear feed. As we retreat, the bear warily walks onto the flats and wades into the largest stream.

While we paddle back to the island, I wonder if our campsite has been disturbed. Bears are excellent swimmers, and there might be one or more on the island. A bear could be curious, start sniffing around, and perhaps rummage through our gear or rip up the tent. The food, however, is safe hanging high in a tree. If the tent is shredded, I know we can survive without it but will have an interesting story to tell. Upon arriving back at Swan Island, we see that our camp is just the way we left it.

We settle down at camp and make dinner. Nothing too fancy. Sometimes it is freeze-dried camping food. Often it is dry goods: mac and cheese, powdered mashed potatoes, spaghetti, or a rice dish, maybe with pepperoni, tuna, or chicken from a foil pouch. Drinks may be hot chocolate, coffee, tea, a flavored powdered drink mix, or just water.

When undertaking backcountry camping and travel, my mood invariably improves. Perhaps it is not having the stress and obligations of everyday work and life. But that is just part of it. Studies show that being in nature, enjoying fresh air, and spending time in natural sunlight enhances mood. After spending time in the outdoors, my outlook improves, and I have seen its positive effect on other people. It is magical. Nature's mood improvement slowly and subtly engulfs a person's spirit. Whatever it is and however it works, I feel an afterglow after spending time in the outdoors.

After dinner, a campfire sets a serene mood while we enjoy our view of Swan Cove. Dark-green mountainsides fill the vista. At their base lay glassy, calm waters, silently reflecting emerald-green forest. Misty, low-lying clouds obscure middle elevations. Higher up, the uppermost reaches of mountain peaks touch steel-gray clouds.

While we slowly feed the fire, darkness encroaches on our camp-site. Here on this island, two human beings sit by the glow of a fire surrounded by a million acres of wilderness. Beyond our island lies millions of acres of rainforest. But we are not alone. No. We are surrounded by life brimming with exuberance. Bears and salmon and eagles and whales and giant trees live here. The trees are covered with moss and lichen. In their uppermost branches are nests where eagles lay eggs, bringing forth another generation into the world. Millions of salmon struggle upstream to spawn, laying eggs in gravel nests. In the sea are crabs, sea stars, sea jellies, otters, sea urchins, kelp, and mussels. We are very much not alone. We are surrounded by life.

The fire keeps burning. The clouds dissipate and stars come out. We identify familiar constellations. We talk. We sit in silence. We quietly add branches to the fire. We talk. We sit in silence some more. There is an unspoken truth here. The fire flickers. The stars shine. We stare into the fire. We look to the stars. Silence, except for the crackle of the fire. There are mysteries on Earth and in this Universe that humans will never fully comprehend. The fire flares and crackles, then there is more silence and calm. The fire shimmers off my partner's face. The sum of human knowledge and understanding is great. In the context of geological time and within the realm of distant stars and galaxies, our understanding is minuscule. The fire dies down, but the embers continue to glow and throw off heat. In this moment and in this place, despite our lack of understanding, we are at peace and feel content. We feel at home on this island. We feel at home in this wilderness. Sleep is sound this night. No rain. No wind. No strange noises in the middle of the night.

Day Five

Today is sunny with a few crisp-white clouds sprinkled here and there. It feels good to have the sun shining on our faces. After breakfast, we sit around camp enjoying the scenery, the weather, and lush green splendor, all while immersing ourselves in books. After lunch and feeling the need for activity, we embark in the kayak toward Pack Creek. Pack Creek is a high bear-activity area, where they can be seen fishing for salmon and digging for clams on tidal flats. With the proper permit, a person can charter a float plane from Juneau, spend a day watching bears at Pack Creek, then return to Juneau for dining in a fine restaurant.

We, however, are traveling by time-honored tradition, propelling a kayak stroke by stroke. With each pulling motion of the paddle, whirlpools of water swirl behind our path. In a dual kayak, we synchronize. The person in front sets pace. The person in the rear matches rhythm so that paddles do not bump. Our aim is not to paddle into and up Pack Creek, as there are a multitude of salmon spawning and bears will be fishing. Instead, we pull ashore and disembark at a distance and walk onto exposed tidal flats. At low tide, Pack Creek meanders into the estuary. At high tide, the flats are immersed by the sea. We spot a mother and cub on the far bank. Taking turns with the binoculars, we watch them move back and forth along the creek. The mother paws at salmon. At this distance they are not aware of our presence. Looking beyond the creek, there are white splotches on tidal flats. *Maybe the splotches are conglomerations of sea foam.* The weather is too warm for snow. I use the binoculars for a closer look. These are seagulls sitting in groups. A few are flying around, and even at this distance we hear their squawking.

After an hour watching the mother patrol the creek, catching and eating salmon with the cub shadowing, we paddle back to camp. The day is turning into evening. More bears will be coming out to feed. Looking at the map, the scale of features on shoreline compared to their rendering on the map is deceiving. Small features on the map are surprisingly large in reality. We have to adjust our expectations as it takes much longer to paddle an inch on this map compared to an inch on a map for the Boundary Waters. As we paddle north, there is a large bear walking south on the shoreline toward Pack Creek. The bear sees us, but we are at sufficient distance that we have no concern. The bear ignores us and trundles along the beach past a large boulder. The trees along the mainland are deep green in shadows. Past the bear, we continue paddling north.

It is an exquisite evening. The dark silhouette of Admiralty Island's mountains tilt down to meet glassy, smooth water. The water reflects deep-green mountain slopes and layers of clouds. As we silently glide forward, small ripples spread away from the kayak in an ever widening V. Miniature galactic whirlpools spin away from paddle blades. We are mesmerized by wild splendor, quietude, and rhythmic paddle strokes. Not wanting to break the spell, neither of us say a word. We arrive at our camp cloaked in dark shadow. This evening, our moods reflect calm water and tranquility. We prepare and eat dinner. It is dark and time to turn in. It has been a gratifying day in the wilderness.

Day Six

Peeking out the tent door, the sky is gloomy. Heavy clouds have moved in during the night. The day brings drizzle and rain. We spend the day in camp. We huddle in the tent and read. Between rain, we stretch our legs, exploring Swan Island on foot. Walking along the water's edge, we come across a geodetic survey marker embedded in rock. Engraved into the marker are the words "National Ocean Survey. For Information Write to the Director Washington, DC." We explore further the shoreline and along the eight-foot-high cutbank. Jutting out over the bank are gnarly lichen- and moss-covered trees, branches, and roots. On a grassy area below the bank is a tree stump covered in moss. Crouching to look closely, the moss has clinging drops of dew sparkling in the sunlight. Past the tree stump are the green, verdant mountains of Admiralty Island. Nature's grandeur great and small.

Rain resumes, so we retreat to the tent. The incessant rain and drizzle continue through the day. Puddles of water collect on the tent floor. The bottoms of our sleeping bags are wet. This old tent is a cheap one, bought twenty-five years ago, but has served its purpose well. The tent and I have survived storms which bent and buckled its poles, with a third of its pole sections now replaced. We have shared nights in

Yellowstone's frigid cold with wolves howling nearby. One night in the Boundary Waters, a black bear poked its nose into the screen mesh of the door, nudging my back. In Denali, setting it up in the rain, I encountered a grizzly. On another trip, sitting in the tent at the base of Mount Robson, I watched icebergs calve off a glacier into Berg Lake. This tent is like an old friend. You can't replace a longtime friend. Only reluctantly do I accept the notion of getting a new tent.

My partner and I continue to read into the evening while rain patters on the roof and water collects on the floor.

Day Seven

The day is overcast with more showers. We stay in the tent and read, wondering when the weather will clear. But it never does. Between showers, we scramble out and get something to eat but quickly return to the tent. It is cramped inside the small tent. There is not a lot of conversation. That is good because we don't want to drive each other crazy with endless chatter the other doesn't want to hear. Thus, our thoughts are to ourselves and inside the world of our books. Things are wet and damp, but the temperature is mild, so we are comfortable. Evening comes. We are getting stir-crazy. We discuss leaving and paddling back to the cabin. Once at the cabin, we can spend a day or two drying out. We consult the tide chart and look for the best time to depart. We agree to ignore the tide and plan to depart in the morning regardless of low or high tide.

Day Eight

The morning is partly cloudy but with changing conditions. Thick clouds and showers are moving in. We stuff the tent away soaking wet. The rest of the gear is packed into dry bags, then stored in fore and aft compartments of the kayak. We put on our dry suits.

After walking around our campsite looking for any remaining gear, we leave Swan Island. The water is calm as we paddle in drizzle. Hugging the coast, we paddle twelve miles, reaching the north end of Seymour Canal at low tide—just as the tide charts predicted. Now we are stuck. There is a mile-long tidal flat exposed by the low tide. To avoid a long portage, we discuss paddling up the creek, which runs through the flats toward the cabin. Where the creek becomes too shallow, we consider dragging the kayak while walking in the creek. But there are hundreds of salmon spawning. Walking up the creek would disturb the salmon and crush millions of eggs. Instead, we remove dry bags from the kayak and carry them across the flats to a luxuriant grassy area. With each step, our feet sink into mud. It is raining heavily now. Returning to the kayak, we pick it up and slog through mud and rain to the grassy area. After hard, physical work, our shoes and dry suits are coated with mud. From the grassy area, we move the gear to the cabin. Again, we go back to the kayak and take turns pulling it through tall, wet grass, with my partner doing the heavy lifting and hauling.

Finally, we bring the gear into the cabin and sort through it. It is comforting changing into dry clothes, and it feels good to stretch out in the cabin without being pelted by rain and drizzle. The cabin has a pro-tected porch where we cook and eat a hot meal. After dinner, we tinker with an oil-fired stove but cannot get it fired up. Along the back wall of the cabin are spacious bunks. My partner climbs into the upper bunk with his book. I grab the lower with my book.

This evening, I walk down to the stream to where humpy salmon are engaged in a primeval struggle. The water boils with activity as the salmon swirl back and forth with the males' backs and dorsal fins break-ing the surface. Even though everything is in shadows, it is an energetic show. I keep my distance to avoid disturbing them. They are oblivious of my watchful eyes as I silently contemplate their struggle. This is raw and pristine nature at its finest. Vigorous life engaged in a compulsory strug-gle to survive and reproduce. I am mesmerized by the motion. If I were not here, their struggles would continue independent of my existence. I wonder for how many years, how many generations of salmon have struggled up this stream to reproduce. *Possibly since the last Ice Age?* I wish them well in their struggle. Today is but one day in their struggle for renewal, linking this generation on this evening with thousands of generations into the past. May this area remain pristine and available for them to continue their struggle for thousands of generations into the future. Turning away, I walk back to the cabin and check in with my partner. He is deep in thought, reading in the dark with a flashlight shining into his book. I decide not to disturb him and quietly climb into the lower bunk for the night. I fall asleep in the darkness with thoughts of a multitude of salmon spawning and creating a new generation just a hundred yards from the cabin.

Day Nine

It is time to pile the kayak and gear onto the tram and push it to Oliver Inlet for our pickup. My partner has finished reading *The Brothers Karamazov*. Today we leave Admiralty Island—the Fortress of the Bears. But this island is much more than that. This island might more aptly be called "the Fortress of Life."

The
Thundere+

Mount
Norris+

Lamar River

+
Amethyst
Mountain

Cache Creek

+
Death
Gulch

Yellowstone National Park

DEATH GULCH

"Do I dare to believe that one of my great-grandchildren
may someday journey to Sheenjek and still find the gray
wolf trotting across the ice of Lobo Lake? Yes, I do still dare
to believe!"

—Margaret E. Murie, *Two in the Far North*, 1957

Cooke City, Montana, is located just outside the northeast corner of Yellowstone Park. It is one of the most isolated towns in America. From the end of May through September, one can travel from Red Lodge to Cooke City along the Beartooth Highway, which switchbacks perilously through the Absaroka and Beartooth Mountains and over Beartooth Pass. From mid-October through May, deep snow closes the pass. Thus, for most of the year, the only access to Cooke City is by driving fifty miles through Yellowstone. Despite its isolation, Cooke City retains a small number of hardy, year-round residents. For eight months of the year, they live at the end of a long dead-end road. What an extraordinary place to live.

The route to Cooke City from Gardiner winds over the Blacktail Plateau, through the Lamar Valley, along Soda Butte Creek, and up Ice Box Canyon. Along this route, across Yellowstone's open valleys, wolves and wolf packs are highly visible. Here, a person can step out of their vehicle and observe wolves behaving naturally in the wild: hunting, mating, raising pups, forming packs, asserting territorial boundaries, and at times attacking one another for control of territory or mates.

211

During winter, when the foliage from deciduous trees and brush has fallen, wolves are particularly visible against the backdrop of snow.

Along this route are broad vistas of glacially carved river valleys, brush-covered foothills, deep forests, and plateaus covered with grasses and forbs. The landscape supports one of the last great remnants of an intact North American ecosystem with a full complement of predator and prey species. Sprinkled across the landscape are abundant prey such as whitetail and mule deer, elk, pronghorn, moose, bighorn sheep, bison, and mountain goats—in addition to smaller prey such as beaver, snowshoe hare, pocket gophers, yellow bellied marmots, golden-mantled and red squirrels, and least chipmunks. The predators are black and brown bears, red fox (more correctly omnivores), gray wolves, cougars, bobcats, coyote, river otter, badgers, marten, wolverine, and lynx. Birds of prey are bald eagles, red-tailed hawks, ospreys, great horned owls, golden eagles, and peregrine falcons. Magnificent birds include trumpeter swans (the heaviest bird in North America, reaching up to thirty pounds), sandhill cranes (reaching almost five feet when standing), and white pelicans (with wingspans up to nine and a half feet). Yellowstone, and the greater region surrounding it, is an intricately woven ecological system with incredible biodiversity.

Thus Yellowstone, and specifically the Lamar Valley, is sometimes called the American Serengeti. Becoming increasingly rare in the modern world, large intact ecosystems such as Yellowstone with high diversity of life tend to be relatively stable and resilient during periods of ecological stress, such as severe drought, extreme rain and flooding, or largescale fire.

In addition to abundant predators and prey, *Homo sapiens* have lived in the Yellowstone area for the last eleven thousand years. Mummy Cave, named after the 1,200-year-old naturally mummified inhabitant found within, sits outside Yellowstone's east boundary, on the Shoshone River's North Fork. Not actually a cave, the shelter shows almost continuous use for nine thousand years. Multiple layers reveal a long history and multiple types of projectile points, indicating its inhabitants were big-game hunters. They hunted mule deer in river valleys and bighorn sheep among eroded rock formations at higher elevation. During my visit to Mummy Cave, I look out over the river valley and imagine living here with plentiful wildlife, among the weird volcanic formations of the Absaroka Range. Standing in solemn silence, one can still hear their spirits singing joyously in the wind.

One of the more recent native peoples to live in the Yellowstone area is a subgroup of Shoshone known as Tukudeka—sometimes referred to as "sheep eaters." The Tukudeka lived high in the mountains as well as in valleys in and around Yellowstone Park's northern border. They often followed the seasonal migrations of bighorn sheep, but they also hunted deer, elk, bison, and pronghorn; caught fish; and foraged for seasonal plants.

I drive south through aptly named Paradise Valley toward Yellowstone's north entrance. As winter envelops the Yellowstone Plateau, hundreds of elk, bison, pronghorn, bighorn sheep, and mule deer migrate into Paradise Valley to escape deep snow and cold at higher elevations. Across the Yellowstone River is an intriguing geological formation. Two immense vertical rock walls ascend 1,500 feet up the side of Cinnabar Mountain—testament to ancient layers of Earth's surface laid down eons ago—then folded and tilted by geological forces into an upright position. Along the valley floor are scattered groups of deer, elk, and pronghorn that have made the migration, with more to follow as winter progresses. While thrilling to see wildlife, my attention is focused on driving as they occasionally wander near the road or attempt to cross. Pulling into the town of Gardiner, a mule deer and its offspring meander among residential buildings. An impressive bull elk with a full rack of antlers causally saunters in front of the post office as pedestrians take photos, walking around it. After crossing the Gardiner bridge over the Yellowstone River, I drive under the Roosevelt Arch, whose cornerstone was placed by President Teddy Roosevelt in 1903. Silently, I express gratitude to its inscription: "For the Benefit and Enjoyment of the People." Five miles later, I arrive at Mammoth Hot Springs and follow a snowplowed road toward Cooke City. Within a few minutes, I am surrounded by the snow-encrusted landscape of the Blacktail Plateau, turn at Roosevelt Junction, pass by Slough Creek, then through a canyon and into Lamar Valley.

Halfway through Lamar Valley are log buildings which have historically been called the "Lamar Buffalo Ranch." For years the ranch was used to breed genetically pure bison to augment Yellowstone's wild population. The need was dire. By 1900, there were only twenty-five wild plains bison roaming North America, all of them living in Yellowstone.

About a mile before reaching the cone-shaped hot spring named Soda Butte, I pull into a parking area. From here I embark on a five-day exploration of the Cache Creek drainage on the far side of Mount Norris and its sibling mountain—The Thunderer. There is snow on the ground, so I have snowshoes and a sled, but since the snow is only four inches deep, snowshoes are not needed. Lightweight winter boots will suffice. A tarp is spread on the sled, and duffel bags with gear are set onto the tarp. The duffel bags are wrapped like a package and secured with bungee cords.

Pulling the sled, I cross a footbridge over Soda Butte Creek, then up onto sagebrush-covered flatland. Two miles to the west is the Lamar River. In front is the western flank of Mount Norris. To the left is The Thunderer. It is an epic landscape of big mountains, big trees, and big views, all blanketed with snow. The route goes around the western base of Mount Norris, then follows the Lamar River upstream to Cache Creek. There are groups of bison scattered about, grazing in thick alder brush. The bison ignore me as I plod along, pulling the sled above the Soda Butte Creek floodplain. The weather is pleasant, in the upper twenties with little wind and an overcast sky. Nighttime temperatures are forecast to dip down to 0°F. I have packed two sleeping bags and two sleeping pads to insulate my back from the frozen ground. A couple nearby coyotes are not concerned with my presence. The mountains and overcast sky project rich shades of white and gray, reminiscent of an Ansel Adams photo.

Rounding the western base of Mount Norris, I travel south, up a gully and onto a rise. Here I pause to look over the horizon as a moderate wind hits my face. About a mile in the distance is a dense line of evergreens. That is my next goal as I endeavor forward. It is exhilarating and a privilege exerting oneself, pulling a sled, alone and isolated from the trappings of civilization on a lonely landscape amidst snow-clad mountains and expansive vistas.

I envision myself an explorer of North America during the Ice Age, complete with groups of bison grazing in brush and snow. Perhaps I am traveling with a small band of people. We have migrated from Northeast Asia across the Beringia Land Bridge, then south along an ice-free corridor between two colossal embankments of ice. To the west is the Cordilleran ice sheet spilling out of the Canadian Rockies onto the Great Plains. To the east is the Laurentide Ice Sheet, stretching for thousands of miles, covering central and eastern Canada. Travelling south between immense walls of ice, we venture onto a fresh landscape to arrive in the fabled Yellowstone country, where human footsteps have seldom trodden and wildlife is naive to human hunting. As fascinating as this scenario is, early peoples likely lived in North America before the ice-free corridor route was viable. An alternative route follows the Pacific coast using watercraft.

Towing the sled through deeper snow at elevation, my efforts turn strenuous. My core is overheating, but my face and neck are chilled by the bitter headwind. Forging forward, the stand of evergreens slowly inches closer. Reaching the evergreens, I pull the sled over downed trees into a protected area to catch my breath. Here, the air is still and there is silence and calmness. Now concealed, no person or creature knows I am here. This is a good place to make lunch. Between ice-encrusted fallen logs, I stomp down snow to make a place for the stove. After setting out a sleeping pad, I place cooking gear and a food bag nearby. Sitting on the sleeping pad, I ignite the stove to melt snow. With the water now heated to boiling, I pour it into a foil pouch of dehydrated food and into a cup for hot chocolate. Eating hot food in cold weather is especially satisfying. It feels safe and comforting sitting in snow—hidden from predators and protected from the wind. Perhaps this sense of security is instinctual or a primeval response.

I pack up gear and explore to the south. Leaving the evergreen thicket, I move on to an eerie landscape with no ground vegetation. The trees are dead and toppled, with some standing but dying. Little snow covers pink, cream, and gray granular soil. Leaving my gear, I travel upslope to explore a ravine where steam is rising. Hot mineral water seeps from the hillside at the ravine's top. The odor of sulfur permeates the air. The hot, acidic water trickles down the hillside. Where it flows with sufficient intensity, trees and vegetation are killed or stunted.

Encircling the thermal area is a microclimate where the evergreen thicket thrives.

Living within Yellowstone's ten thousand hot springs and geysers are many unique forms of microscopic life—thermoacidophiles, or heat- and acid-loving bacteria. Discovered by Thomas Brock, one bacterium named *Thermus aquaticus* thrives in hot water up to 175°F. Because it lives in thermal pools, *Thermus aquaticus* produces an enzyme allowing it to replicate its DNA when the bacterium divides. Biochemists, recognizing the enzyme's unique properties and stability under heat, have found a useful purpose for it. In the lab, they use it to make copies of any kind of DNA, whether it is from bacteria, plants, animals, or humans. The process, called *polymerase chain reaction* (PCR), takes a single or small number of DNA strands and, during cycles of heating and cooling, duplicates the DNA. During each cycle, the number of DNA strands doubles. After thirty cycles, millions of identical DNA strands are created.

Wherever people are, they often leave behind sweat, hair follicles, saliva, and other bodily residues. Swabbing a residue and putting it through the PCR process multiplies trace amounts of DNA found in the residue. After the PCR process has completed, sufficient DNA has been created, thus allowing comparison to an individual's DNA. If a crime has been committed and the residue is from the crime scene, the evidence is unambiguous. If the DNA matches, it indicates that the person left the residue. Of course, DNA evidence may help convict someone or may be used to exclude them.

Leaving the hot spring at the top of the ravine, I return to the sled. Grabbing the tow strap, I pull the sled across the dead zone toward dense evergreen trees to the south, then follow a game trail through a gap. Leaving the hot spring behind, I'm now travelling in open terrain. Approaching an overlook, I see snow-covered Cache Creek Valley, with the frozen, meandering creek at the valley bottom. Letting the sled lead the way downhill, I walk behind while holding onto the tow rope and guiding it around rocks and trees. At the valley bottom, I pull the sled onto a rise near the creek and set up camp. While I'm setting up the tent, a pole snaps. At this point, I recall the aluminum tube packed with the tent stakes. The six-inch tube is slightly wider than a tent pole. Sliding it over the snapped pole, it mends the break almost magically.

With the tent set up, I haul cooking gear and food away from camp. The air is still. The sky is blue, but the sun inches closer to the western horizon. After dinner, I explore the area before returning to the tent to read.

Day Two

Starting out the day, I hike toward a hill north of my campsite, passing a Douglas fir with a big gash in its bark—probably made by a bison or perhaps an elk rubbing velvet off an antler. Hiking uphill in snow at altitude of 7,500 feet in frigid temperatures is a struggle. Upon reaching the hilltop, I sit in snow and enjoy a view across Lamar Valley. There are periodic whiffs of sulfur in the mostly still air. The little black dots sprinkled about the valley floor are bison. Using binoculars, I scan the valley and mountainsides for anything that moves or looks like a group of dark objects, which could be a wolf pack napping. When viewed at a distance, wolves are difficult to identify, especially if they aren't moving. Several dark objects stand out against the white valley floor. They could be wolves! But when viewed through binoculars, they turn out to be boulders, rock outcroppings, or tree stumps. Since it is late morning, any wolves or packs are likely napping, with wolves being most active during early morning or evening. But being an optimist, I am determined to put in time sitting on this snowy hilltop. So, I continue to glass the valley and hillsides, hoping to find a pack somewhere in the valley.

After spending a couple hours scanning the valley floor and surrounding hillsides, I am getting chilled; thus I get up on my feet and start moving about. Walking downhill toward the Lamar River, I find an elk skull partly covered in snow. The skull has a full set of antlers with each antler having six tines. An adult male elk can carry thirty to forty pounds of antlers on its head. Examining the tines, some are almost fifteen inches long and quite formidable. I would not want to be stabbed in the chest with one. For wolves searching for prey, a seven-hundred-pound bull elk can feed a pack for several days. This elk skull has healthy antlers attached but nevertheless likely succumbed to wolves. If no wolves or other predators are around, male elk can live

217

twelve to fourteen years in the wild, and females a bit longer. But with wolves in the Lamar, few elk die of old age or chronic disease. Wolves pick off the weakest first.

Walking downslope, I come to a steep bank which overlooks the Lamar River. Sprinkled here and there are Douglas fir. At the base of one, there is no snow, so I sit on dry grass with my back against the trunk and scan the river. Scattered bison browse in the lower river valley. Here, Douglas fir live four to six hundred years. The bark is gray and brown with deep, rough fissures. Its soft, thin needles are one inch long and stick out like a bottle brush. In this area, the Douglas fir are sporadically growing in the open, but one grows next to a boulder. There are many places in Yellowstone where trees grow next to boulders. Boulders provide shade, moisture, act as a windbreak, and protect seedlings from being trampled by wildlife. From my view here at the base of this Douglas fir, I can scan west toward Amethyst Mountain and Specimen Ridge.

Both Amethyst Mountain and Specimen Ridge have Douglas fir on their slopes. But they also have other species, with some not being found in this area for millions of years. Fifty million years ago, volcanic eruptions engulfed forests in Yellowstone. As volcanic ash and mud eroded away, the ancient forest was uncovered, exposing fossilized trees, some standing in an upright position. Many different species of plants and trees have been identified, including sequoia and redwood trees, whose closest living relatives live one thousand miles away on the Pacific coast. After eating some snacks and contemplating ancient forests, I decide it is time to leave.

Heading back to camp, I cross tracks in the snow made by my sled and boots during yesterday's trek. Embedded on top of my tracks are canid tracks. Crouching down, I form a fist with my hand and put it next to one. It's as large as my fist; therefore, it was made by a wolf. Pausing to scan the wider scene, two wolves traveled in the same direction as I did. Yesterday, while breathing heavily and floundering in deep snow, perhaps I appeared to be in distress. When trekking, I should pause to look behind more often. The wolves, however, could have been following my tracks at any time in the last twenty-four hours. They were not necessarily tracking me but may have used my tracks as an easier route for travel. If they were following my tracks, how did they know which direction the sled was traveling? Wolves are clever creatures.

Back at camp, I make and eat dinner while watching the crescent moon. In the moonlight, nearby trees cast gray shadows onto silvery snow. Cleaning up, I notice a bright celestial object below and to the left of the moon. Wondering what it is, I grab the binoculars. It appears to be distorted. Certainly not circular. Adjusting the focus, I cannot get it to resolve to a point, which would make it bright star. A crescent would be Venus or Mercury. A circular shape with small adjacent dots would be Jupiter and its moons. It doesn't have a shade of red, which would be Mars. The binoculars might be out of alignment, but they focused fine earlier today. The fuzzy shape must be Saturn and its rings. Galileo was the first to note Saturn's odd shape. He thought Saturn had two large moons, one on each side, or perhaps it had two "handles." Five decades later, Christiaan Huygens published *Systema Saturnium*, explaining the "handles" as rings that circled Saturn, but never touched it.

The temperature is dropping. It is time to turn in for the night.

Day Three

After breakfast, I pack a daypack with emergency gear and snacks to hike east on a trail that parallels Cache Creek south of Mount Norris. There are wolf prints in the snow, indistinct and melted, likely days old. Hiking a couple miles, I look across Cache Creek to the south. Getting out binoculars, I see there are gray, white, and pink ravines that drain into Cache Creek—another thermal area. Like the first one, this one has standing dead trees, giving it a ghostly appearance. Harvard geologist Thomas Jaggar explored this hot spring in 1897. He found eight dead bears. One was a black bear; the others were grizzlies. He also found a dead elk and dead squirrels, rabbits, and butterflies. They all died from gases that had collected in a gulch. Evidently, as the bears came to feed on the carcasses they also perished. It makes me a little nervous being here, but I detect no smell of sulfur at the moment and am determined not to meet my own demise at Death Gulch.

Hiking back to camp, I take a break and have a snack. This afternoon, I follow Cache Creek downstream to where it converges with the Lamar River. Following a game trail that winds through thick alder brush, I come to a steep hillside to the right. The alders, encrusted with ice, sparkle in the sunlight. At the base of the hillside, obscured by thick brush, I discover a bison skull with several neck vertebrae attached. Horns protrude from the skull and curve backwards. The right horn is missing its sheath, but the left has its dark keratin sheath. I can't tell if this was a male or female since both have horns that are never shed. Looking closely, I see that desiccated skin covers the back of the skull and the neck vertebrae. It must have been too tough for wolves or coyotes to gnaw off. Continuing, I hike toward the Lamar, then circle around a snow-covered gravel bar and back to camp.

Back at camp, I enjoy sitting on a log watching four bison on the hillside. The sky is glowing translucent blue, gray, and pink. The sun is behind Amethyst Mountain to the west. The bison sway their massive heads back and forth, pushing snow out of the way, exposing edible grasses and small plants. The bison are at peace, doing what they need to do to survive. They have every right to be at peace. A healthy, full-grown bison has few predators. One exception is a wolf pack, which prey upon bison when they are weakened in late winter or if they are young or injured. After making and eating a hot meal, I make a special dessert of water and snow mixed with a packet of cherry-flavored powdered drink. The improvised snow cone is excellent and thirst quenching. The moon is out. This evening it is closer to a half moon.

Day Four

Today is Thanksgiving. I consider exploring the Lamar River Valley to the south, which would require crossing Cache Creek. The creek isn't completely frozen over, so I will have to walk through icy water, which will spill into my boots. When I reach the other side, I will have to take them off and dump the water out. Spending the day hiking while wearing frozen boots and cold, wet socks will not be pleasant. Of course, crossing back will require a repeat. I could cross barefoot, dry my feet, then put socks and boots on again. But stepping on slippery, sharp rocks with bare feet seems unsafe, and I could fall into the creek. Exploring the Lamar Valley to the south is scratched off the list.

The views are spectacular on a couple hikes not far from camp, but I am spending much time in the tent, especially in the morning when it is coldest. Frigid temperatures are taking a toll, and the novelty of cold-weather camping is wearing thin. This may be my last winter trip. Dreaming, I envision a tropical expedition. A canoe or kayak trip exploring the Zambezi or Nile would be an exhilarating challenge. Then again, Nile crocodiles prey upon and kill dozens of people every year. There are certain advantages to cold-weather trips to Yellowstone—no crocodiles! No matter my self-doubt, the situation is here and now. I am cold and hungry. Dinner is nothing fancy: corn and hot mashed potatoes.

In the tent this evening, I distract myself by making a list of natural sources of light. Sun, stars, lightning, fire, aurora borealis, fireflies, glow worms and other creatures of the deep sea, magma, a spark or static electricity, meteorites, moonshine, light from planets. *Moonshine and light from planets are reflected light from the sun, so should they be on the list?* After settling down for the night, I bury myself in the warmth of the sleeping bag. Nights in a tent during the winter season are long. Some nights I spend twelve hours in the tent, reading and thinking. My thoughts focus on why winter camping and travel is satisfying. With that thought in mind, warm and content inside the sleeping bag, I fall asleep.

That is, until 10:00 p.m. when I hear a wolf growling. Listening to its growls and agitated whimpers and whines, I can hear that it is very close. Just a few feet away, on the other side of the tent wall. The growling and whining continue. Slowly and quietly, I sit up. In darkness I stare at the tent wall, almost forcing my eyes to see through it, but there is nothing but blackness. After several minutes of growling, I expect it to lose interest and move on, but it does not. Now, I get concerned. *Is it going to come tearing through the tent fabric?* I review in my mind reports of wolf attacks.

In North America there have been few documented attacks of healthy wild wolves on humans. Knowing this is reassuring, but I do not want to be put on the short list. I continue to listen to the wolf's eerie growls, snarls, whines, and whimpers. Growling signals aggression. *But whimpering and whining are noises of submission, correct?* More time passes. My anxiety continues. It is difficult to pinpoint the wolf's distance, but I continue to try. It sounds like the growls are a couple feet away, just on the other side of the tent wall.

A second wolf howls in the distance. This wolf is to the west, toward the Lamar River. The wolf outside my tent howls in response. The distant wolf howls again. They are communicating, but what are they saying? *Is the near wolf telling its mate it has found vulnerable prey?* I wonder if the second wolf will approach.

Again, I review my knowledge about wolves attacking humans. A hunter carrying a dead deer was lunged at by a wolf in northern Minnesota. Once the wolf realized a person was carrying the deer, it ran off. A wolf pack that fed on garbage at a landfill in northern Saskatchewan was habituated to humans as trucks pulled up and dumped garbage. In that case, one person was killed by a wolf or wolves in November of 2005. A person near Chignik Lake, Alaska, was killed and partially devoured by a wolf or wolf pack when they went for an evening jog in March of 2010. There have been several cases of penned wolves or wolf-dog hybrids that have killed people. But in the wild, in North America, there are few cases of healthy wolves attacking humans. There are records in Europe of wolves having killed and eaten people—probably precipitating the story for "Little Red Riding Hood." In India, there are modern-day instances of wolves attacking villagers as they tend fields, and occasionally a wolf enters a village and attacks a child. But in North America, *there are very few wolf attacks on humans.*

The wolf outside my tent continues to growl, whine, and whimper. With concern, I wonder what it intends and what it wants. *Should I do something?* I resolve to make my two-legged human presence known. Getting out of the sleeping bag, I unzip the tent door and crawl into the snow. Not wanting to appear as four-legged prey, I stand next to the tent. The moon has set, so it is dark except for meager starlight. Turning to the left, I look toward the growling. The silhouette of a black wolf crouches in silver snow. It faces me. I face it. Time stands still while two creatures contemplate each other's existence in the dark of a frozen, wild landscape under the shimmering light of distant stars embedded in black sky. Then, in an instant, it darts off like a bolt of lightning.

Day Five

Today I wake happy to be alive. There have been occasions when I have dreamed about wolves. Last night was not one of them. It was real. I exit the tent, then march nineteen paces to the print in the snow where the wolf was crouched while growling and howling. Nineteen paces. I double-check the distance. No more. No less. In the dark of the night, it sounded closer, as if it were on the other side of the tent wall, just a few feet away. Yes, it was a little farther away than I estimated, but then again, it was close enough.

Two hundred years from now, I wonder if people will be able to have an experience like this.

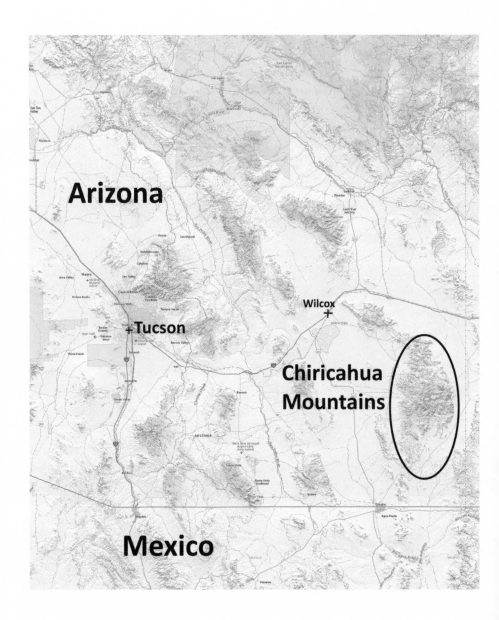

SOMBRA

"When you realize the value of all life, you dwell less on what is past and concentrate more on the preservation of the future."

—DIAN FOSSEY, LAST JOURNAL ENTRY
BEFORE HER MURDER, 1985

Today I wake near Wilcox, Arizona, to the sound of sandhill cranes cackling and trilling. Instead of a winter trip to Yellowstone's Lamar Valley, my objective is to hike a warmer climate in the Chiricahua Mountains of southern Arizona, named after the American Indian people who live here. The Chiricahua are culturally related to many bands of this area, which together are known as the Apache. Looking upward into the clear southwestern sky, I see a dozen cranes fly in formation. While driving south through the Sonoran Desert, greater roadrunners scurry across the road in front of the vehicle. As I approach, they lift off, fly a distance, then land just beyond the roadside post-and-wire fence. As a predator, greater roadrunners eat pretty much anything they want, including tarantulas, scorpions, black widows, mice, small lizards, and even small venomous snakes. Apart from mice, none of these species would be encountered in the Lamar Valley in the wintertime.

Ubiquitously sprinkled about the desert landscape are soap tree yuccas. Besides yuccas, what catches my eye are sotol plants. The base of the sotol is composed of pale blue, spiky leaves which radiate outward forming a spherical shape. Its flowering stalk rises fifteen feet into the air, terminating with soft bottlebrush flowers; white flowers are male, pink are female. The other plant that strikes my attention is agave, especially one called the century plant. It also shoots a stalk into the sky from a base of thick, waxy, gray-green, tooth-edged leaves. Calling it a century plant is an exaggeration as it matures in fifteen to thirty years. At maturity, it throws the stalk upward, with some stalks reaching twenty-five feet in height. Small side branches emanate from the stalk at intervals of six inches to a foot in a balanced but not symmetrical pattern. At the end of each branch are pods which, when dry, will open—dispersing small, flat-black seeds into the wind.

Century plant
(*Agave americana*)
by Sven Bellanger

I slow my vehicle as it approaches a dead deer along the road's gravel shoulder. Several ravens are pecking at it, with two perched on the pavement in my lane. Despite steering into the empty oncoming lane, the ravens fly off as I approach. Looking further afield, I see that sitting atop a nearby post is a large brown raptor which probably was feeding on the carcass. Stopping the vehicle, I back up, shift to park, and grab the binoculars. That is a very large raptor, perhaps a hawk but more likely a golden eagle, although it could be an immature bald eagle, even here in the desert. Its plumage is mostly dark brown, but with a few lighter-colored flecks on its folded wings. The tip of its beak is black, then fades to gray and white near the head, whereas a bald eagle's beak is yellow. This bird has feathers down to its feet, unlike a bald eagle whose feathers stop above the feet. This makes evolutionary sense; bald eagles swoop low over the water and pluck fish with their talons, a behavior golden eagles do not have.

A female golden eagle can weigh over twelve pounds and may have a wingspan up to seven and a half feet, similar in size to a female bald eagle. A female peregrine falcon weighs up to three pounds with a wingspan of up to four feet. The peregrine falcon can dive over 200 miles per hour, while the hefty golden eagle can dive at 150 miles per hour. Quite remarkable for such a large bird.

Here in the desert, golden eagles eat carrion and prey on black-tailed jackrabbits, desert cottontails, and black-tailed prairie dogs, as well as venomous creatures such as prairie rattlesnakes and even Gila monsters.

It is pretty much settled—this is a golden eagle. The last time I saw one was thirteen years ago in Denali National Park. After a moment or two the eagle, with eyes several times more powerful than mine, notices me at the side of the road observing it with binoculars. It flies off in the opposite direction low over the terrain. A couple of ravens fly after it and swoop in toward its tail, attempting to nip it. As the group flies off, I recall the golden eagle in Denali. A golden eagle can live twenty years and migrate 2,500 miles between summer and winter range. It is possible, but unlikely, this is the same one. If it is the same one, what a remarkable disparity in habitat. Its breeding range is the glaciated mountains and tundra of Denali and its winter range the Sonoran Desert.

As my vehicle slowly and carefully ascends the winding gravel road into the Chiricahua Mountains, vegetation on either side of the road transforms. Low-elevation desert plants at first intermingle with, then give way to, oak woodlands. At higher elevation, Ponderosa pine, Douglas fir, and white fir dominate. Pockets of Engelmann spruce—a tree more commonly found in the northern Rockies, the Cascades, and British Columbia—live on cooler north-facing slopes.

The Chiricahua Mountains are part of the Sky Island ranges of southern New Mexico and Arizona. Tree species found in the Sky Islands at high elevation can't survive in the hot, arid regions between islands; thus the "islands" are separated by a sea of desert. How did these forest islands come about? Did high-elevation forest species hop from Sky Island to Sky Island? Maybe, but the accepted scenario is that in the not-too-distant past, forest species existed at lower elevations when the climate was cooler and wetter. As climate warmed at the end of the last major glaciation, species retreated into the mountains, thus creating the Sky Islands.

Evidence for a cooler, wetter past is provided by fossilized pack rat middens and soil core samples extracted from the Sonoran and

Chihuahuan Deserts. The middens and cores have pollen containing varieties of oak, pine, spruce, and Douglas fir—trees not found in the desert.

Further evidence for a different climate and ecology is found at archeological sites. Mammoths, mastodons, and other large mammals once roamed the valleys between Sky Islands. The Clovis people, of about thirteen thousand years ago, created unique, fluted stone spear tips, using them to kill camels, bison, mastodons, and mammoths. Lehner, Naco, and Murray Springs are kill sites in southern Arizona that today is desert. The Lehner site contained thirteen projectiles and the fossilized remains of nine mammoths. The Naco site contained a Columbian mammoth and eight Clovis projectile points.

The Chiricahua Mountains were formed by multiple episodes of volcanic activity between 35 and 27 million years ago. One of the largest eruptions occurred 27 million years ago when a giant magma chamber formed below the area. The volcano eruption was one thousand times greater than the Mount Saint Helens eruption of 1980. It expelled 120 cubic miles of magma and ash, generated massive pyroclastic flows, and shaped 1,200 square miles of landscape, leaving behind the twelve-mile-wide Turkey Creek Caldera.

The last grizzlies in Arizona were extirpated in the mid-1930s, thus I am not in the Chiricahua Mountains to search for grizzlies. By the late 1970s, there were no more Mexican wolves in the wild. Starting in 1998, Mexican wolves have been reintroduced into the White Mountains in eastern Arizona and western New Mexico. As of 2022, there are about two hundred Mexican wolves in the wild. Searching for Mexican wolves, although fascinating, is not the reason I am here.

This trek is a quest to find jaguar tracks. If I'm lucky, despite the odds, perhaps I'll encounter a jaguar. There are one, maybe two jaguars living in the wild in the United States. Trail-cam video and photos provide conclusive evidence that jaguars periodically live in southern Arizona and New Mexico. The photos and video are not grainy, in low light, or in shadow. They are clear and unambiguous. In fact, trail-cam photos show that a jaguar named Sombra (Spanish for "shadow") is alive and well, roaming the wilds of the Chiricahua Mountains.

Jaguar range includes northern Mexico near the US border and north-south corridors along Mexico's Pacific coast and Caribbean coast.

Jaguar corridors run through Central America and into South America. In South America, countries with substantial numbers of jaguars include Columbia, Venezuela, Peru, Brazil, and Bolivia. At their southern extent, jaguars live in northern Argentina.

Since 1996, and as of this writing, there have been seven jaguars documented in southern Arizona and New Mexico, all males. No female is known to have crossed the border recently, and thus no reproduction is known to have occurred. Historically, however, jaguars lived and reproduced in the southwestern United States and have ranged as far north as the Grand Canyon, four hundred miles north of the international border.

Jaguar is the third-largest feline behind the lion and the tiger. Jaguars are stocky, muscular predators, capable swimmers, and well adapted to water environments. Jaguars, however, are adaptable creatures and can survive in deserts and semi-mountainous areas. The fur of a jaguar has a pattern of dark rosettes against a tawny orange background, similar to African and Asian leopards. Unlike leopards, jaguar rosettes are larger and may have dark spots inside the rosette. While hunting, jaguars, like other big cats, often go for the throat and windpipe when taking down prey, but jaguars may also bite the base of the skull or the back of the neck. Being an apex predator, jaguars eat whatever they find, including nine-banded armadillo, agoutis, and Earth's largest living rodent, the capybara, which can weigh up to 150 pounds. They also prey on green sea turtles, caimans, tapirs, and anacondas.

One of the jaguar's primary prey species in the Chiricahuas is javelina, which is also known as the collared peccary. Javelina resemble the wild boar found in Europe and Asia, but the javelina is smaller. Other jaguar prey species are mule deer and a subspecies of whitetail deer called Coues whitetail. Coues whitetail are smaller than northern whitetail deer and live in southern New Mexico, Arizona, and Mexico. There have been some reports of jaguars attacking humans, but such reports are extremely rare, even in the tropics where jaguars are abundant.

Here in the Chiricahuas, the odds are one in a million that I will come across jaguar tracks. Nevertheless, the idea of hiking in the vicinity of a jaguar stirs the imagination. In the remote chance that I observe a jaguar, now that would be spectacular. Certainly, I will be observant and hike with heightened senses.

I drive on a gravel road through Pinery Canyon that leads thirteen miles up into the Chiricahua Mountains. Arriving at Rustler Park trailhead, the elevation is 8,500 feet. Vegetation has changed from yucca, sotol, and century plants to a cool, semi-open forest of ponderosa pine and Douglas fir. The hiking route is not determined. It is whatever whim, direction, and duration I feel on any given day. Having learned from past painful experience, attempting off-trail travel or taking what is perceived as a shortcut often leads to confusion and frustration. The result is wasted time and energy spent bushwhacking, sometimes in circular patterns though unknown territory. Sticking to trails keeps a person correlated with a location on the map. There are no people or other vehicles here at the trailhead, thus I am unlikely to encounter people while hiking. I will be alone in the wilderness, and my plan is to stay on trails and stay found.

My aim is not to be hiking great distances. Spending time in an area with a jaguar is satisfaction enough. Water is a valuable resource in the Sky Islands. Locals have told me there has been no rain at low elevation for three months. So, I have a map with freshwater springs marked, but there is no guarantee the springs are flowing. Therefore, I will be hauling four liters of water. Since I am not bringing a stove or fuel, my food consists of cereal with dry milk, apples, oranges, vegetables, nuts, tortillas, peanut butter, guacamole, and tuna in foil pouches.

There are thirteen species of rattlesnake in Arizona. But, folks in town tell me that rattlesnakes will be hibernating this time of year. With little expected rain, I am not carrying a tent. Instead, I will lay my sleeping bag and pad on a tarp. If rain comes, my plan is to fold the tarp over the sleeping bag. By not sleeping in a tent that is zippered shut, it is possible a wayward rattlesnake may seek warmth inside my sleeping bag.

There are more than thirty species of scorpion that call Arizona home. With no tent, my boots will be sitting in the open next to the sleeping bag. A scorpion could crawl into one of my boots during the night. The Arizona bark scorpion is nocturnal and is the most venomous scorpion in North America. If it injects sufficient venom, it is extremely painful and is the only North American scorpion that can pose a threat to human life, having killed hundreds of people in Mexico.

Another venomous creature is the giant desert centipede. Up to eight inches long, it is the largest centipede in North America. Its black head, orange body, and yellow legs warn not to meddle with it. This nocturnal predator not only preys upon insects but also mice, lizards, frogs, and snakes. In the morning, I will check my boots before putting them on.

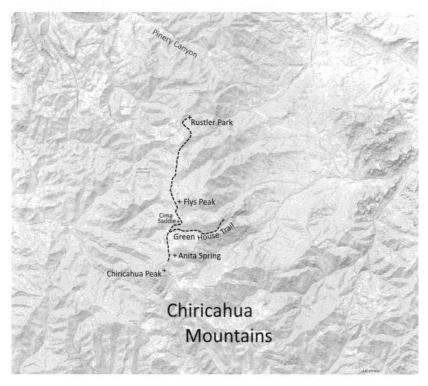

This trek starts on a winding trail from Rustler Park, which leads south through a hillside of dry yellow grass. From my vantage point and at this altitude, I look out over the horizon to see expansive views of the golden desert. Out in the distance and beyond the ocean of desert is a dark silhouette on the horizon—another Sky Island. Above, the sky is translucent blue with wispy white clouds swirling at high altitude. On both sides of the trail is brush with thorns that lean into the path. The thorns snag my pants and scratch the back of my hands. The trail ascends to the bottom of a cliff face. At the top of the cliff, I imagine a jaguar silently looking down on me. If it is up there, it is evaluating whether the upright, bipedal mammal matches its image of an acceptable prey species.

I wonder how many times wolves, lynx, or other wildlife have been aware of my presence while I am unaware of theirs. Likely they quietly trot away into the forest just before coming into my view. Years ago, while hiking the Kekekabic Trail in the Boundary Waters Wilderness of northern Minnesota, I paused to take a break. Alone in the wilderness, I sat for fifteen minutes, quietly observing and contemplating the wild beauty all around. Unexpectedly, a large female moose rose from behind nearby brush and nonchalantly lumbered off. Had it not revealed itself, I would have been totally unaware of its presence.

Now past the cliff, I continue onward. A small animal scurries in thick grass and through tangles of brush. Unable to get a good look, I can see only that it has sandy-colored fur and a long thin tail. The small rodent is likely why I am seeing scattered groups of burrow entrances. It could be a pocket mouse, kangaroo rat, or a white-throated wood rat— all of which dig burrows with multiple entrances and separate chambers for sleeping, living, and food storage.

Continuing on, I come to a fork in the trail and decide to explore the side trail; the map shows it leads to Hillside Spring. Although I have packed plenty of water and the air is cool, I want to see if the spring is flowing. Following the trail downhill, I find that the spring is flowing. Actually, it's more of a trickle. Since I don't need water, I don't take any, but it is good to know this is a source of water. As I am about to return to the main trail, I notice a trail camera strapped to the trunk of a tree. Someone is photographing wildlife that comes to the spring. It is exciting to think that this trail cam may have snapped photos of Sombra.

Back on the main trail, I come across hoofprints made by Coues whitetails. Looking over the landscape, I have a view of rugged terrain covered in conifers. Downslope are burnt-sienna foothills, and at the lowest elevation is an arid sea of tan, ivory, and gold. After two hours of unhurried trekking, I come to a sign: "Chiricahua Wilderness, Coronado National Forest." Besides the fir, spruce, and pines I am accustomed to in the northern Rockies, the Sky Islands are home to the Apache pine, a tree with long, luxuriant needles ten to fifteen inches in length. It is native to the Sierra Madre Occidental Mountains of northwestern Mexico but spills into the Chiricahuas and other Sky Islands. Further along the trail, I come across an elongated scat composed of hair. It's not particularly large but is sign of a small predator.

A few hundred yards further is the track of a feline. Not all of it is visible, but three ovoid toe pads and part of the hind pad are apparent. The rest is missing because of pine needles and gravel. Here I am, hiking for a couple hours in the Chiricahua Mountains. *Have I come across a jaguar track already?* It is unlikely, but then again, a jaguar does lives here. It was most likely made by a mountain lion or bobcat, although jaguarundi and ocelot are possible. Mountain lion range includes most of the western United States, southwestern Canada, Central America, and almost all South America. Bobcat range is pretty much throughout the lower forty-eight states, southern Canada, and most of Mexico. This track appears too large to have been made by a bobcat, ocelot, or jaguarundi.

Hiking past Fly's Peak, I come to Round Park, a luxuriant flat area with soft golden grasses situated on a mountain saddle. I consider camping here because it is so nice, with exquisite views both to the southwest and northeast. But it is an open area, with wind blowing quite strongly from the southwest. Finding shelter on the lee side of the saddle, I sit and have a lunch of broccoli, carrots, and cauliflower with guacamole dip, followed by an apple. After lunch, I explore a side trail to a spring named "Booger Spring." Leaving the pack on the main trail, I hike downslope through a burnt and charred ghost forest. As always, the hike is farther than anticipated, but with persistence I come to a cement trough meant to capture spring water. The spring is not flowing and the trough is bone dry. Having left the pack, it would not be good to become lost and have to survive without food and gear. Fortunately, I easily follow the ravine upward and towards the southwest and back to the main trail.

Picking up my pack, I sling it over my shoulders and trek on. There is no destination or goal in mind. No need to travel X number of miles. I am in the wilderness with a living, breathing jaguar. My satisfaction is in knowing that I share these mountains with a jaguar. *How cool is that?* From Round Park, I hike slowly, taking in scenery, looking for a campsite as the sun sets. At Cima Saddle, an unnamed peak to the west gives protection from the wind.

Hiking off trail and uphill through semi-open forest, I search for a soft, level area to lay out the sleeping bag. From a slight rise, looking back to the east, I see a pleasing view. Finding a grassy area surrounded by rock outcrops and large pines, I set the pack down. This will make a pleasant place to spend the night. Pulling a tarp out of the lower compartment of the backpack, I spread it on the grass, then roll out the sleeping pad and bag. The bag is rated for temperatures down to 55°F. It is lightweight and compact but ineffective for keeping a body warm. In the morning chill, I will pay the price. I pull the food bag out of the pack along with reading material. Here is my bivouac.

Dinner is vegetables and tuna wrapped in a tortilla. With the wind having calmed, the evening is strangely quiet. Sitting in my bivouac, I silently read as shadows of ponderosa pines slowly creep across the forest floor. Hidden by rock outcrops, I look up to scan the perimeter. In the back of my mind, I can't resist the expectation of seeing a jaguar sitting in the distance, staring back with golden eyes. The evening rapidly cools. With the last of the sun's light receding, the trunks of ponderosa pines glow red. Now, as the sun dips below the horizon, reading requires a flashlight. I put on all my clothes, but still, I am cold. Here in southern Arizona, it is colder than I expected. But then again, my elevation is 9,300 feet.

I put the book down and snuggle into the sleeping bag. The sky is pitch black. It doesn't bother me spending long periods of time staring into the sky looking at stars, listening to the wild, thinking over the day's events. I reflect on family and relationships present and long gone, and the vastness of time and space. It is all a mystery worth contemplating and trying to understand. There is a glow rising from the east, causing the black outline of treetops to become visible. A full moon is rising. After a half hour, it is light enough to read without a flashlight. But it is too cold and there is much to contemplate. I take my glasses off and put them into one of my hiking boots at the side of the tarp, then scrunch down into the sleeping bag to hide my face from the light of the moon There are no scorpions in my boots, at least not yet, nor have any rattlesnakes slithered into my sleeping bag.

Day Two

It is early morning and I am shivering. My core muscles are involuntarily contracting—struggling to generate heat. Water in the water bottles isn't frozen. There is no frost on nearby grass and shrubs, but I suspect the temperature is near freezing. The sun will not be rising for two more hours. Darn it, being cold in the morning is miserable, but there is nothing "perfect" in life, especially in the wild where uncomfortable conditions often occur. Putting on my hat and gloves helps a little. To generate additional heat, I try performing isometric exercises inside the sleeping bag—pressing one foot against the other and flexing my leg muscles, or pressing my knees together with force. It is not clear that it produces any heat, but it passes the time.

Despite the cold, I doze off for an hour, but later wake to glimmers of sunshine. Sticking my head out of the sleeping bag, I tilt forward, open my eyes and squint into morning light. To my astonishment, the sky and forest are glowing red. Rays of sunshine stream through the forest, illuminating the air. Looking behind my campsite, I see the ponderosa pines have their burnt-orange bark glowing with a translucent reddish hue. But the effect only lasts a minute. Soon the sun rises slightly and the light show is over. We are back to normal lighting conditions. But for a moment or two, it was glorious.

Sitting up while still in the sleeping bag, I look up through the trees. The sky is mostly overcast, but little patches of blue peek through. Low-altitude gray-and-white clouds stream eastward at a brisk pace. My body is not shivering, but it is still quite cold. Maybe it is because my elevation gives a closeup view, but I don't recall ever seeing clouds rush by so rapidly. Looking around, I check to see if a jaguar is watching me from a distance. If it is, I don't see it. With my clumsy and groggy movements this morning, if a jaguar had been watching, it surely left without making a sound and before I noticed. I grab a nearby bag of food and a bag of gear. Pouring cold water into a bowl, I stir in dry milk and add granola with dehydrated blueberries. While eating, I open my book and quietly read until the sun burns off the morning chill.

Reading allows a person to be silent while observing nature and wildlife. Being quiet in nature allows a person to listen to the swish of wind in trees, the cracking of ice, the babbling of a brook, thunder in the distance, or the patter of rain. People thousands of years ago survived by instinct and intimate knowledge of the wild. They expended considerable effort in their struggle to survive. Unlike them, my packed gear and food allow me to survive for a few days at a time. Early people lived a semi-nomadic way of life, living off the land, gathering edible plants, hunting game, and catching fish. Later, as people built permanent shelters and lived in villages, crops were planted and tended, domesticated animals were herded. These activities preoccupied early people. For my sojourns into the wilderness, none of these activities occupy my time, so I spend time reading.

After reading for a couple hours, the morning has warmed. I remove extra layers of clothing and pack up gear. As I hike toward Anita Park, there are striking views of the desert valley. On the horizon are dark ripples of distant mountains. The most remote ripple fades into the atmosphere, nearly indistinguishable from low-lying clouds. My location is forty miles from the border; thus, those distant mountains are in Mexico. Here at Anita Park, the wind pushes clouds eastward at a rapid pace.

Leaving my pack and gear behind, I take a side trail to see if Anita Spring is flowing. The trail twists around an outcropping, slightly uphill on the side of the mountain, then down and around into a ravine. Yes, the spring is flowing. On the return hike back to my gear, I come to an impressive ponderosa pine. Here, exposed to the wind, its windswept branches whorl eastward.

Possibly it is a lack of sound sleep, the cold night, or elevation that is catching up with me. Maybe age is as well. Sleeping in the open on a tarp has resulted in a groggy and creaky feeling. Had I used a tent, however, I would have missed the glorious light show. Over the years, I have spent much time being cold and don't care to spend too many more nights that way. I turn back and start looking for a place to camp. Traveling further would require spending three nights out.

Backtracking, I come to Cima Park where the main trail intersects the Greenhouse Trail. The wind is blowing fiercely. I hike down into the valley of the Greenhouse Trail, seeking protection from the wind. I come to a colossal, fire-scarred ponderosa pine; the setting provides a rustic place for lunch. Sitting on a bed of pine needles, I take food out of the pack. Lunch is nuts, vegetables with guacamole, and an orange. This site has a cozy feeling. It is protected, has large trees, and has views into the valley. So rather than hiking more, I decide to spend the night. *This is about being in the area of a jaguar.*

I don't know its location, but I do know it's somewhere in the Chiricahua Mountains and is probably within fifteen miles. This is an exhilarating feeling. It could be in any direction. If I think of a circle with a fifteen-mile radius around my location, Sombra is likely within the circle. It could be down in the foothills. It might be on the other side of the mountains. Or perhaps it is aware of my presence and watching me from a nearby hill just out of sight.

Sitting here reading, thinking, observing, and reading some more, I doze off. In the protection of this valley, it is quiet. After twenty minutes or so, I open my eyes and tilt my head up to look. Two Coues deer, a mother and yearling, run off. How they got so close without me hearing them is surprising. Clearly, I need to catch up on sleep.

My bivouac for tonight is beneath the outstretched branches of the colossal ponderosa pine. Its lower bark is covered with rich, burnt-orange scales outlined by black furrows. Bright and cheery colors are certainly attractive and catching, but subdued, rich, deep, earthy colors, like those in bark, appeal to my senses. The ponderosa pine's branches—those that are not fire-charred stumps—are seventy feet above. Beneath the tarp is a soft layer of pine needles. It is a perfect place to quietly observe nature, contemplate, and read.

Dinner is tuna and vegetables wrapped in a tortilla. Shaded from the rays of the western sun, my campsite is quickly enveloped by darkness. Turning on the flashlight, I continue reading, sitting in my sleeping bag. The air is chilling. Preparing for a cold night, I put on all my clothes.

Day Three

Upon awakening, my sense are engulfed. I am surrounded by towering pines. A couple of birds in upper branches are chirping. There is the chatter of a squirrel. Breathing in deeply, I smell pine needles, tree sap, and the earthy smell of forest duff. It is serene, quiet, and a pleasure waking up embraced by nature. Waiting for the morning chill to burn off, I finish reading my book while inside the sleeping bag. After a quick breakfast, it is time to go. I pack gear into the backpack, heft it onto my back, and trek toward the trailhead.

It has been a rare opportunity and privilege spending time in a forest with a jaguar. If our paths crossed, I was never aware of its presence. But who knows? Sombra may have been aware of me, watching and following but staying just out of sight. It is a glorious day, lit with bright sunshine and a blue sky. Following the trail back toward the trailhead, I stay vigilant, observing the rugged landscape for any motion or sign of Sombra. I pass through an area of burnt forest on the side of a hill. In my imagination, I see a large tawny-orange cat with black rosettes slinking up the hill, over the top, then disappearing from view.

Returning to the trailhead, I've come to absorb and appreciate this Sky Island wilderness, rising out of the desert—an oasis of nature. It is a beautiful and pristine area, one whose wilderness character is vividly enhanced knowing that a jaguar lives there. Sombra's existence makes the Chiricahua Wilderness more rugged, primeval, and compelling. Sombra is a wild echo from Earth's past. It is an echo that I hope reverberates far into the future.

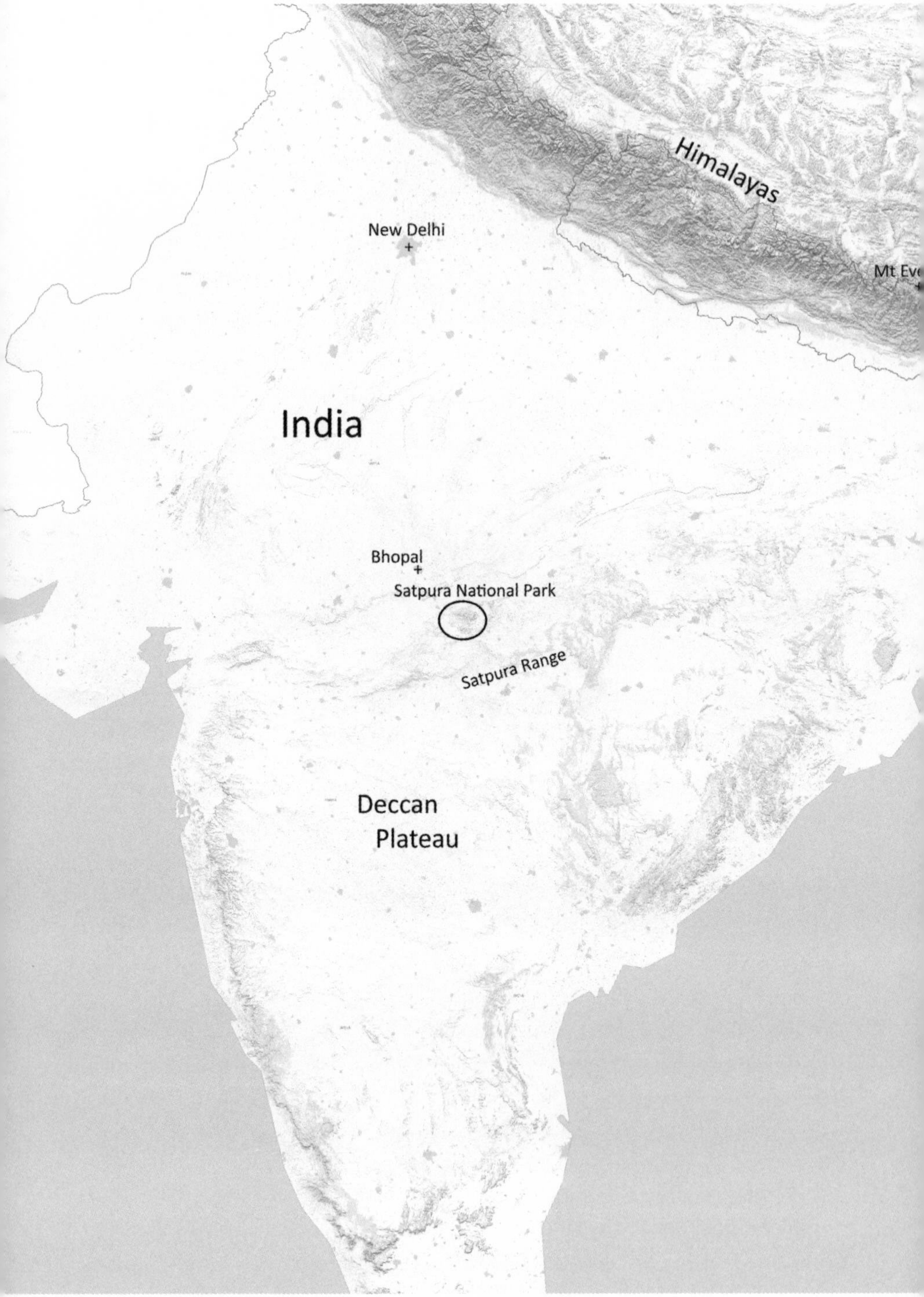

Himalayas
New Delhi
Mt Eve
India
Bhopal
Satpura National Park
Satpura Range
Deccan
Plateau

HUMBLED

"I have come face to face with wild tigers. I've come face
to face with jaguars, lions—all of them. Now, fear was
definitely a part of the menagerie of feelings that ran
through me. But I also felt flattered to be in the presence
of this unbelievable wildness that we don't feel during our
everyday lives."

—Dr. Alan Rabinowitz, "We Are All Wildlife," 2018

In ancient Greek mythology, Pan is the god of wild nature and Gaea is the primal mother of Earth. Three hundred million years ago, the supercontinents Gondwana and Euramerica (the latter also known as Laurussia) collided to form a single supercontinent called Pangaea: a C-shaped landmass that spanned from the Arctic, across the equator, and to the South Pole. It was surrounded by a single Earth-wide ocean—Panthalassa. As Earth's sole supercontinent, Pangaea was stable for 130 million years until fissures along its midsection split it apart. As the rifting progressed, Pangaea split into Laurasia (not to be confused with Laurussia) in the north and Gondwana to the south, with the Tethys Ocean between. The breakup completed about 170 million years ago. Laurasia was a collection of what today are North America, Europe, and Asia. Gondwana was a collection of what today are South America, Africa, Antarctica, Australia, and India.

Alfred Wegener, in 1912, first proposed the concept that in Earth's ancient past there existed a single giant continent he called *Urkontinent*, or "primal continent." Further, he proposed that Urkontinent broke apart into seven great continental pieces that drifted across Earth's surface until they reached the configuration that exists today. The theory of continental drift was met with skepticism and debated for fifty years. It wasn't until the 1960s that sufficient evidence had accumulated and a better understanding of Earth's crust and mantle made it clear that continental drift was correct and was included within the more complete theory of plate tectonics.

Within Earth's mantle, the convection forces that drive continents to fracture and drift are relentless. About 175 million years, Laurasia began to break apart, detaching North America from Eurasia and Africa, thus forming the North Atlantic. At the same time, Gondwana began to fracture as well. Between 150 and 100 million years ago, South America rifted from Africa, creating the South Atlantic. In a great convergence, the North Atlantic merged with the South Atlantic, creating the Atlantic Ocean that today spans from pole to pole. Not to be outdone, Africa broke away from Antarctica and drifted north while Australia fractured from Antarctica and drifted northeast.

During this period, India detached from Africa and Antarctica. For 70 million years, India was an island continent drifting northward in the Tethys Ocean. Eventually the tectonic plate conveying India closed the Tethys Ocean and collided with Eurasia—causing the uplift of the Himalayas. Even today the continental plates continue to collide, lifting the Himalayas at a rate of four inches per decade. The top of Mount Everest was once at the bottom of the Tethys Ocean. Limestone sedimentary layers from the bottom of the Tethys contain fossilized trilobites, crinoids, ostracod crustaceans, and microorganisms. These layers are now at Mount Everest's summit. However fascinating it would be to see marine fossils on top of Mount Everest, I am willing to accept the expertise of those who have climbed the mountain and identified them.

Sixty-five million years ago, before India collided with Eurasia, it drifted over one of Earth's hot spots under Reunion Island near Madagascar. As it drifted over the hot spot, super-volcanic eruptions and magma flows transformed the subcontinent, creating areas known as the Deccan Traps and the Deccan Plateau. While this was happening, on the opposite side of the Earth a seven-mile-wide extraterrestrial object impacted near the Yucatan Peninsula. The super-volcanic eruptions combined with the large meteorite impact spewed noxious fumes, soot, and dust into Earth's atmosphere, thus blocking sunlight and drastically changing the climate. It is no wonder that 75 percent of plant and animal species were extinguished. But life is resilient and has recovered, albeit slowly, evolving and filling newly vacated ecological niches. Today, the Indian subcontinent contains an astonishing diversity and quantity of flora and fauna.

Here, on the northern edge of the Deccan Plateau, the Satpura Range runs east-west for five hundred miles. The Satpura Range is in reality a series of rugged hills that supports a dry, deciduous forest of teak, sal, mahua, and several species of bamboo. Teak is a beautiful hardwood composed of golden yellows and dark browns with large ovoid leaves reaching fifteen inches in length. Sal is a hardwood that retains its leaves throughout the year in a wetter climate, but in the drier forest of the Satpura Range, they drop between February and April. The deciduous and evergreen mahua tree is prized by local villagers for seeds and flowers, using them for food, oils, and medicines and to make mahua liquor. Although the forests of the Satpura Range are dry for much of the year, the monsoon brings heavy rains from June through September.

My expedition partner and I ride in a jeep through a village outside of Satpura National Park, making our way along a sand-and-gravel road toward the Denwa River. Here is a broad, sandy river valley sporadically covered in low vegetation. In the distance, up on hills, are trees covered in green foliage. As we approach the Denwa, our guide parks the jeep and we disembark to cross on a floating bridge. On the other side, another jeep waits for our arrival. Today we are up for an afternoon and early evening exploration of Satpura. We climb into the back of the second jeep to sit on open-air bench seats that offer wide, all-around views. We travel a short distance up the hillside to where twenty spotted deer, also known as *chital*, come into focus near a large mango tree. Spotted deer are smaller than North American whitetail deer, but true to their name, they have white spots on their tawny coats throughout their lives. Beyond the deer are park buildings and a ranch-style entrance gate with a sign overhead that reads "Satpura Tiger Reserve, Madhai." Our guide stops the jeep at a park building momentarily to go over paperwork with a park administrator. With permit in order, we enter a broad, grassy savanna punctuated with trees and gray langur monkeys which sport black faces. Some of the langurs sit in groups in deep consultation with each other. Many of the females have infants clinging tightly to their undersides as they scurry about. We venture deeper into the park, bouncing around in the back of the jeep as the road becomes rough and rutted.

Low in the valley, to our left through the trees, we see a wetland and muddy pond; the water is clouded with various shades of algae. The area is interspersed with swamp vegetation and muddy islands. On shore, walking in mud is a woolly-necked stork. Its body is black, but its neck is white. The top of its head is black. The bill is gray but transitions to pink at the tip. Its long legs are pink. To the right of the stork on a vegetated island resting in mud is a marsh crocodile. Basking in the heat of the sun, its jaws are agape, releasing heat. The large protective scutes on its leathery skin vary in color from black and gray to light brown and green. Large yellow teeth protrude from upper and lower jaws, warning any animal which dares disturb it. Two parallel rows of scales jut upward along the top of the tail, forming a series of fins until they merge into a single row. Besides eating fish, marsh crocodiles often rest submerged in murky water, waiting for small reptiles, mammals, or a wading bird to venture nearby. The stork keeps its distance as it walks through mud, searching for insects or other small species to prey upon.

Moving past the lazing crocodile, our guide tells us that tiger paw prints, called *pugmarks*, were seen on the sand-and-gravel road that leads from our lodge. Upon hearing this, little did I realize that when walking between lodge buildings at night, I should be cognizant of encountering a tiger. Having been informed that tigers venture beyond the park, I ask if local villagers have conflicts with tigers. The guide indicates yes; old or injured tigers sometimes prey upon goats and cattle, but when this happens the government reimburses the owner. Following up, I ask if tigers attack villagers and prey upon them. The guide's answer is unclear as he vaguely says it doesn't really happen.

Although the guide's response is vague, tigers do attack and kill humans as they encroach on tiger reserves in the Himalayan foothills, when villagers collect firewood near tiger reserves in central India, or when they venture into the Sundarbans mangrove swamps to gather honey and crabs or net fish. Over a five-year period from 2014 through 2019, tigers killed 224 people in India according to the Ministry of Environment and Forest, but the number is likely higher.

Driving through the park, we encounter an abundance and variety of prey, including spotted deer, sambar deer, wild boar, nilgai, and gaur. Clearly this ecosystem supports a large biomass of prey species for tigers, leopards, and other predators. A male spotted deer may weigh 150 pounds. When a tiger or leopard is present, spotted deer give a short, shrieking alarm call. The sambar deer is larger, with males weighing up to 700 pounds. When alarmed, sambar give a short bark or what sounds like a quick blow of a horn. The wild boar, with its tusks and tough hide, is a formidable foe and can weigh up to 300 pounds, but tigers regularly prey upon them. Nalgai are a species of large Asian antelope, also called "blue bull" as adult males have a blue hue. Nalgai carry their heads high and resemble an elk, weighing up to 600 pounds.

A healthy adult gaur, due to its immense size, is unlikely to fall prey to most predators, but tigers will prey upon them, especially the young, those of extreme age, or those in poor health. The gaur is in the bovine family like the American bison but is generally larger. Unlike the bison with its shaggy fur for warmth, the short-furred gaur lives in a warmer climate. An adult male gaur averages around 1,800 pounds, with some reaching 3,000 pounds. An adult male bison may weigh around 1,600 pounds with some reaching 2,500 pounds.

Evening comes and we return to the lodge for the night. While walking in the dark to our cottage, my expedition partner and I discuss the abundance and variety of wildlife we have seen so far. It seems to us that Satpura supports a wider variety and number of animals than Yellowstone National Park.

Day Two

The last tiger census in Satpura was conducted in 2014. It counted fifty tigers. The count is determined by camera traps as well as volunteers who walk through the park looking for tiger sign such as pugmarks and scat. Being that stripes are as unique to individual tigers as fingerprints are to humans, photos captured by camera traps are effective in identifying tigers. I find it interesting that volunteers walk singly through the park as part of the census and without undue fear.

On this safari, we are exploring a buffer zone adjacent to Satpura. This is an area of semi-protected forest with less restrictions than Satpura that acts as a buffer between the park and nearby villages and agricultural fields cultivated by residents. On our way to the buffer zone, we drive through a village. There are various people sweeping front courtyards, collecting water from a well, and performing chores. Children, many of whom wave to us, play at the edge of the road. It is difficult to wrap my head around this setting. Villagers live out their day-to-day lives with tigers roaming nearby, with some occasionally coming into the village.

Leaving the village, we enter the forest and peer into the jungle as our jeep follows a curving and rutted trail. The trail straightens as we approach a watering hole. We slow and pull to a stop a short distance from the pool. The air is still, and all is quiet as we scan through the trunks of nearby trees to the far side of the pond. The shrill call of an Indian peafowl breaks the silence. Along the far shore are two peafowls, one male, one female. The peacock spreads its tail feathers in a resplendent display, but the peahen ignores the performance and struts away. Quietly, we wait to see what else may arise. To pass time, we pull out books and read, converse in low whispers, and occasionally swat at mosquitoes. At this time of year, the mosquitoes are not thick, but Satpura is near areas with high risk for malaria, so we are not taking chances. Our clothes are treated with permethrin, we have applied DEET to our skin, and we are taking an antimalaria drug daily.

With my eyes glued to the book, my partner elbows me. An animal with long black fur appears through the thick of the jungle. It slowly approaches the pond, and once out of the trees, it is apparent this is a sloth bear, named a sloth bear not because it is slow moving, but because it has long and highly visible claws like tree sloths from Central and South America. The sloth bear's long claws are used to dig into termite mounds. Our bear trundles down the muddy slope to the water's edge. Two small dark objects cling to its back—cubs. They disembark and crawl near the water's edge as the mother satiates her thirst. The cubs play in the mud for a few moments, but as soon as the mother makes a motion away from the water, the cubs quickly crawl over to her, grab her long, thick fur, and climb onto her back.

Besides termites, sloth bears eat fruit and plant matter including mahua flowers. With numerous mangos, mahua, and five-foot-high termite mounds spread throughout this area, they have plenty to eat. Although there is plenty to eat, sloth bears are aggressive. They instinctually defend themselves from tigers and leopards, but their aggressive nature also results in numerous attacks on humans.

The mother, with cubs firmly planted on her back, walks into the forest and disappears into the wild. With the sloth bear and cubs blending back into the forest, our guide decides it is time to check another watering hole. Although the sun is still hovering above the horizon this early evening, the forest canopy blankets everything with a subdued lighting. Our guide starts the jeep, turns it around, and we venture forward.

As we approach the next watering hole, the guide becomes excited and stops the jeep. Three Indian leopards are slinking away from the pond. The group is likely a mother with two subadults, or perhaps three older siblings that have not yet forged independent lives. As they walk away, one leopard looks back to see if we are following. Then in a few quick moments, they are gone as the last leopard blends into the forest with the white tip of its tail disappearing. Being that tigers dominate Satpura's core area, leopards often live in territory wedged between the park and villages and cultivated fields. Although there are no langur monkeys nearby, our guide explains that when a langur sees a tiger or leopard, they will give an alarm call that sounds like a cough or rough chirp to alert the troop. But if it's a leopard, the coughs are rapid and excited. This is because leopards climb trees to pursue them. With the leopards gone, we pause at the pool waiting for more wildlife before moving on.

After leaving the second water hole, we drive through the forest and into a clearing that opens up to the Denwa River Valley. The sky opens to a grand vista with the sun partially obscured and teetering above the horizon. The valley is bathed in gradations of pink, lavender, and mauve. Near the edge of the jeep trail, the ground is churned up.

The guide explains this was a wild boar rooting for tubers, roots, and bulbs. When in Satpura Park, we are not allowed to exit the jeep, but here in the buffer area I ask if we can get out. He indicates it is allowed, so I hop out of the jeep and walk over to the sandy shoreline to look for tiger tracks. Finding none, my gaze turns to the Denwa. A dozen eastern great egrets are peacefully wading in the shallows, feeding on frogs, invertebrates, crustaceans, and small fish. With such expansive views, it would be a serene experience to set up a tent here and spend a couple of days patiently scoping this area. Alas, it is not allowed. Nevertheless, I ask our guide if he has ever seen a tiger here, and his answer is "Yes, while in a canoe on the Denwa." Now that would be breathtaking: paddling the Denwa and seeing a tiger on shore. We hop back into the jeep to continue our trek. To our right, in a grassy area a hundred yards from the river, is a black ibis with a red cap and a white fleck on its wing. This is the Indian black ibis.

With only a sliver of sun above the horizon, dusk is at hand—closing time for the park's core area. But we are in a buffer zone, and regulations allow us to stay into the evening. As the jeep maneuvers forward, we enter a rugged and hilly area. The jeep creaks and moans as we navigate the trail up and down, left and right through thick forest. My expedition partner and I bounce vigorously in the back of the jeep. The rough terrain and thick forest seem like an excellent area for a tiger to ambush unsuspecting prey. Who knows what each twist and turn of the jeep will bring? Sure enough, we navigate a tight turn and the guide jerks the jeep to a stop. Perched in a tree twenty feet above is a crested serpent eagle. Despite our presence, it doesn't stir, giving us a perfect view. Its primary prey are snakes and lizards, although it feeds on other small animals. In the gloaming, our guide shines a spotlight on it which allows an excellent view. It has a gray, hooked beak and a distinctive yellow patch behind the beak, which leads to bright yellow eyes. Its breast is mottled light brown with wings and head dark gray. We move on in search of other predators, preferably the largest feline in the jungle: the Bengal tiger.

With the jeep's headlights turned on, we see into the darkness only as far as the lights allow. Within a few minutes of leaving the eagle, in the middle of the trail and reflecting the light of the headlights are two glowing eyes. An animal, low to the ground, moves from right to left and quickly creeps into brush at the edge of the trail. Our jeep crawls to a stop at the place it crossed the trail. Expecting to see it running deep into the forest, we are surprised to find it crouched behind a bush a few feet away. The guide shines a light on the bush. Its two amber eyes glow as they look back at us through vegetation. It doesn't move or twitch. This is a rusty-spotted cat. Not exactly a tiger, but it is a feline. Looking at it through the thick of the brush, we see its gray-and-tan fur, and indeed, it has subtle rusty spots. The rusty-spotted cat is one of the smallest cats in the world: an adult weighs two to four pounds—much smaller than a typical housecat. Such is fate. Here we are in the dark, in the forest, searching for one of the largest feline predators on Earth, and instead we find one of the smallest. The rusty-spotted cat is an efficient predator of small rodents, birds, lizards, frogs, and insects. Our guide tells us that few people who venture into Satpura come across this species.

It is now fully dark. We leave the rusty-spotted cat and follow the rocky trail illuminated by headlights. The forest canopy blocks all light coming from the moon or stars. Bouncing along, the jeep suddenly bottoms out, and it is hung up on a rock jutting up in the trail. "No problem," the guide says. He shifts the jeep into reverse. The engine stalls. He turns the ignition key and the engine moans as it turns over but doesn't start.

My partner and I look at each other with slight smiles on our faces. *What if we are stuck here for the night?* We discuss in low whispers as the guide fiddles with the ignition. What would we do? What are our options? My partner recommends we leave the jeep and walk six miles, sticking together through the gloomy forest, and follow the trail out of the park and back to the lodge. I express reluctance to be walking at night where the Bengal tiger is an apex predator. My inclination is to stay in the jeep, which although it is open air, is a raised platform with sidewalls that have a semblance of protection. Yes, we should spend the night sleeping in the jeep, with one person on guard. My partner again disagrees. He insists we have better odds walking to the lodge in the dark. He says we should walk together as a group, following the guide who knows the route.

The discussion becomes irrelevant as the engine starts, the guide rocks the jeep back and forth, and we are now free of the rock and moving forward. As the driver guides the jeep along the dark trail, we sit in silence, contemplating our individual thoughts. Upon our return to the lodge, dinner is traditional Indian cuisine. After dinner, we walk through darkness to our cottage for the night. Sleep comes quickly.

Day Three

After an early morning safari, my partner and I eat lunch at the lodge then catch up on rest. Our guide finds us relaxing in the main building and greets us. We have secured a permit for this evening's safari as well as a permit for a safari tomorrow morning. Our guide explains that we could combine them. This would allow us to stay overnight in the Churna region inside the park's core area. It would be a rare opportunity that is generally not available. The lodging will not be luxurious—a simple forest rest house with four walls, a roof, and a mattress—but the opportunity would allow us to spend more time in the park's core area and enhance our chances of seeing tigers. My partner and I agree we should not pass on this and inform him of our enthusiasm for the plan.

When Satpura National Park was created in 1981, there were many people living in small villages sprinkled within its boundaries. The Churna region of Satpura is named after the Churna village of about seventy families and four hundred people that occupied the area. They lived a basic lifestyle of cultivating mung and chana beans and had livestock that grazed in the forest. With the creation of the park, the people were relocated to areas outside the park. Now the villagers have access to electricity, drinking water, schools, markets, and healthcare.

The lodge we are staying at is a short distance from a nearby village. In the village and nearby fields, people go about their lives, working the fields, cultivating crops, and tending livestock, oftentimes before sunrise or after sunset. When not in school, children run and play freely, sometimes well into darkness. All this human activity with tigers and leopards living in close proximity. When we ask the lodge staff about this, we are told that many people that work for the lodge or the park not only grew up in this area, but have seen tigers many times.

My expedition partner and I gather our personal items for our overnight safari. After meeting our guide at the lodge entrance, we hop into the back of the jeep and are off. Driving forward, our path veers away from well-traveled routes as we follow rutted trails. After traveling for an hour, our driver stops the jeep. The guide points out large dark animals crawling in the tree canopy. These are giant squirrels that Satpura is well known for. They are a dark, rusty color with creamy-white underbellies. They have a body length of a foot or so with a tail up to two feet long. They prefer forests where the canopy is continuous so that they can leap from tree to tree, as they rarely venture to the forest floor. Birds of prey feed on the giant squirrels, and occasionally a leopard will climb a tree and attempt to capture one.

Leaving the giant squirrels, our next stop is an ancient Hindu temple constructed six hundred years ago built out of colossal stones, each weighing several tons. Large stone columns, some of which have tilted away from vertical, hold up layers of stacked stone, giving the temple a semi-pyramidal shape. Inside the temple, it is dark and cool with a dirt floor. We are told that leopards and tigers rest in the coolness of the temple or seek shelter from inclement weather here. Walking back to the jeep, our guide reaches down, picks up a couple mahua fruits, and suggests we try them.

Driving on, we scan the forest. We follow the trail as it curves sharply to the right. On the left is a ravine that winds back behind us. The guide lets out a quiet whistle. This signals the driver to stop the jeep. Looking back into the ravine we spot a black shape. A sloth bear. It does not run off, but instead holds its ground and is not disturbed as it continues to eat mahua flowers and fruit. The guide tells us that after eating large quantities of mahua fruit, sloth bears become drunk and lethargic. Perhaps that is why it is not alarmed and ignores us. Even so, they are often aggressive toward humans if they feel threatened. Being that sloth bears encounter large ferocious animals such as tigers, leopards, Indian rhinoceros, and Asian elephants, maybe they evolved an aggressive nature as a defense mechanism. We stay in the jeep.

Driving on, we continue our exploration. The driver stops the jeep every so often and we listen. The air is calm. Birds chirp. We listen for alarm calls of the langur monkey, spotted deer, or sambar deer. Hearing none at the moment, we move on, but shortly the driver stops the jeep again. The guide leans over the edge of the jeep to examine the dusty trail. Imprinted in the sand are large prints. Tiger paw prints. Slowly moving the jeep forward, we follow the pugmarks, and the driver stops the jeep again. On the edge of the trail are elongated tubes of brown fur. Tiger scat embedded with sambar fur. We know we are in the vicinity of a tiger, but we don't know where it is.

The driver shifts gears from low to high as we move forward on the trail, ever deeper into Satpura. Although we have seen and noted a variety of bird, animal, and tree species, we have not seen a tiger. Pugmarks—yes. Scat—yes. Tiger prey—yes. Tiger—no. We have traveled halfway around the world to explore India, in particular Satpura National Park. If there were no tigers in Satpura, we would not be here. Seeing a flock of Malabar pied hornbills—beautiful and interesting as they are—that is not the ultimate goal. We hope to get a glimpse of a tiger, face-to-face, in the wild. To be in the vicinity of one of Earth's largest predatory cats. To be in its habitat, on its terms, with no barrier between it and us. Befriending people, learning local customs and culture, observing exotic wildlife: these are all bonuses. They add richness and texture to our adventure. But the tiger is the goal. It is here in Satpura where some of the world's last tigers live. In 2016, it was estimated that there were 3,890 tigers on the planet. One of Earth's rarest and most beautiful lifeforms.

We drive on, but without warning, the driver stops the jeep. Ahead are three rusty-colored animals trotting this way, about the size and shape of a North American coyote but with short golden-orange fur. Their tails have long black fur, but their underbellies and the inside of their legs are creamy white. Ignoring us and the jeep, they casually trot by. Our guide tells us they are dholes, Asiatic wild dogs. They are extremely rare, with only 2,500 left on Earth. Often persecuted and treated as pests by villagers, dholes are adaptable and live in packs. They prey on small mammals such as mice. Dholes also use the power of the pack to take down some surprisingly large mammals such as sambar and nilgai. As the dholes recede out of sight into the thick of the forest, our driver moves the jeep forward. The light is dimming, and the sun is setting. Visibility is hindered by lack of good light.

With twilight encroaching, the deep groan of the engine and vibrations of the jeep put us into a trance as we travel in silence toward the rest house. Feeling tired, we should call it a night.

Abruptly the jeep slams to a stop with our upper torsos lurching forward. The ranger whispers excitedly, "Tiger, tiger, tiger!" Looking around, my partner and I see nothing but a murky forest. Speaking Hindi, the guide whispers loudly telling the driver to back up. The jeep shifts into reverse and backs up. The guide is looking to the right. Following his gaze, we look to the right. With its lower body hidden in thick grass, a tiger is crouched, staring at us. Being not more than fifty feet away, we see its head, back, and upper body above the top of the grass. Snarling and grimacing, it is agitated and not pleased with our presence. Each time it opens its mouth, long strings of drool drip down. But I am mistaken, that is not drool. Those are white fangs jutting from its upper jaw, glinting off low light. Anxiety pervades the air. We are face-to-face with an agitated tiger. We are in an open-air jeep with no barrier between it and us. My gut is telling me loudly we should back away. I want to express that feeling to our guide but can't speak. We humans are not in control. We have crossed a line and come too close to a large, wild, unpredictable, and dangerous predator. A predator with free will. It has the capacity to take action in its own interests. Before I open my mouth to tell the driver to back away, it is too late. It happens too quickly. The tiger lunges at us in a flash that will forever be seared into my psyche. Charging half the distance to the jeep in an instant, it emits a deep-seated roar while its front paws flail the air. Someone gives out a pathetic yelp. Instinctively we hunch over and lower our heads in preparation for the onslaught. One person puts a curled arm in their face with elbow pointing outward. Someone else lets out a muffled shriek. We are petrified with horror. Logical thinking of the prefrontal cortex has ceased. Our reactions are instinctual–emerging from the primeval cores of our brains. We are at the mercy of a charging tiger.

In another moment the tiger stops, landing on its paws just feet away. It turns and walks away. It does not look back, for it has nothing to fear. We will not challenge its dominance and the tiger knows it. We also know it and are humbled. None of us has anything as formidable as the tiger's claws and teeth, power, or strength. The park ranger does not carry a gun. Now I know how members of species *Homo sapiens* react in the face of a charging tiger. We cower in fear. All of us in the jeep are shaking with a combination of fear and excitement. Some more with fear, some more with excitement. This is the single most exciting moment of my life. With great relief, we watch the tiger slowly walk into the gloom of the forest and disappear. But it is not far away. It may be watching us from a distance, laying in grass among scattered forest detritus.

We spend several minutes recovering—trying to grasp what occurred. It is dark now, and best we move on. The driver starts the jeep and we rattle forward, winding through black forest with the jeep's headlights leading the way. With senses alert, I peer intently into darkness, hoping to catch a glimpse of another tiger. After forty minutes following the rutted and twisty trail, we arrive at the Churna rest house. It is a four-acre site enclosed by a rudimentary fence that would not keep anything out but merely demarks the boundary. With evening, the sky is black and feels especially gloomy—knowing a tiger lurks in the nearby darkness. Inside the fenced courtyard is a single light on a pole that shines onto a couple of gazebos and tables. There are three small buildings, one of which contains our sleeping room. Attached to the sleeping quarters is a bathroom with Western-style toilet and running water. This is a much-appreciated luxury as it is an upgrade to the bush toilets we used while on safari, which are nothing more than four thatched walls. We are told that tiger prints were found on the road outside the fence last night. This is good to know, in case we go traipsing around in the dark. After dinner, we retire to our bare room, which has a stack of shelves against one wall and a couple of mattresses on the floor.

Day Four

This morning we are treated to a traditional Indian bush breakfast, which includes chapati flatbread. During our drive back to the lodge, we encounter one of my favorite species—the nilgai. Nilgai numbers are expanding in India, to the point they are considered pests by farmers because they raid and trample crops. The proliferation of nilgai is due in part to a decrease in the population of the Indian wolf, with the current estimate at about three thousand. The Indian wolf is smaller than the North American wolf, with shorter fur, gray, but often reddish and gold. Indian wolves occasionally prey upon humans. The most vulnerable are small children unattended at the edge of a village or near a field while a parent is working. Called child-lifting, a wolf will approach in the evening, grab an unattended child, and run off into the bush. In contrast, there are very few instances of wolves attacking or preying on humans in North America.

Continuing our drive, we encounter several species we have already seen, including langur monkeys, a crested serpent eagle, wild boar, and a group of massive gaur. Our guide tells us that he grew up near Kanha, a tiger reserve close to Satpura. As a young child, he often saw tigers. My encounters with wildlife as a youth were sightings of a woodchuck, a red-headed woodpecker, garter snakes, frogs, and tiger salamanders.

Upon our return to the lodge, staff greet us graciously with wet towels to wipe dust off our hands and faces, and cool, refreshing lemon water to drink. They ask about our safari, so we describe our encounter with the tiger. Some of the staff have lived their entire lives here and have seen tigers many times. By the expressions on their faces and nodding of heads, they indicate understanding. They then anoint our foreheads with the tilaka, a sign of welcome and honor. We are deeply grateful to be here and are forever humble.

AFTERWORD

"Life is good to those who know how to live. I do not ever
hope to accumulate great funds of worldly wealth, but I
shall accumulate something far more valuable, a store of
wonderful memories. When I reach the twilight of life
I shall look back and say I'm glad I lived as I did,
life has been good to me."

—Sigurd Olson

For the rest of my days alive on this majestic Earth, I will never forget experiencing wild nature in all of its moods: relentless and violent storms, drenching rain that lasts for hours, thunderous booms of lightning making me jump out of my skin, night so cold that I am grateful to be alive in the morning, desiccating and faint-inducing heat, the gentle calmness of falling snow in moonlight, and the trance-inducing patter of a drizzle. Has a person lived and experienced life on Earth unless they have experienced these things? Perhaps not. Forever, I will cherish memories of seeing predators in the wild, knowing that we are kindred spirits, equally experiencing and dealing with the elements, breathing the same air, drinking the same water—all part of the grandeur of life on Earth, embedded within the Cosmos, so vast, so intricate, so incomprehensible, yet so beautiful. I will keep these memories in my heart until my last breath.

When in wilderness, unhurried and away from civilization's clamor, we ponder the night sky. It is during these moments that we begin to grasp things outside of ourselves, the greater Cosmos, and Earth's infinitesimal place. Full of wonder, we comprehend but a tiny fraction of the vastness of the Universe. But that doesn't matter—as we are enthralled by the mystery of the Universe's majesty.

It is estimated there are between 100 and 400 billion stars in the Milky Way. A recent paper estimates there are two trillion galaxies in the observable Universe. Combining these produces a truly astronomical and unfathomable number of stars and possible planetary systems (on the order of 10^{22} or 10^{23}). Likely, the vast majority of planets, their satellites, or other objects in the Universe are barren of life. We know that for almost three billion years, or about 80 percent of the time that life existed on Earth, it was limited to microorganisms. It wasn't until the Cambrian explosion that life started to develop complex forms. Keeping this in mind, for the miniscule number of objects in the Universe that perhaps do harbor life, it may be that nothing beyond simple microbes have developed. If one considers the uniqueness of complex life on Earth, it is arguably a vanishingly rare phenomenon in the greater Cosmos, possibly on the order of one in a billion or one in ten billion. Considering the odds, we might be inclined to have gratitude that we are here, living on a unique and precious rocky object, cradled by liquid water oceans, enveloped by a life-sustaining atmosphere.

Many of my excursions have had an objective of observing predators in nature. Many however, were simply journeys to get away from the hustle and bustle of life and its many demands; to find peace and become immersed in Earth's natural beauty and solitude. Most of the adventures described in this book are highlights where predators were encountered. There have been many occasions where I have come away partially disappointed because the electrifying presence of a predator was not observed. With time, I have come to enjoy just being in nature, appreciating its beauty, and I have lowered my expectations. Whether or not I observed a predator on any given exploration, my life has been enriched in unforeseen ways. Having a goal has taken me to wild places that I otherwise would not have visited. It has also given me the opportunity and motivation to learn about the natural world, and an appreciation for wildlife's struggle to survive. Spending time immersed in the solitude of nature has been a soothing influence on my soul. May it be for you as well, whether you are living at the time of this book's publication or far into the future.

The next time you venture into wilderness, I hope you enjoy safe travels and return unscathed. Do not be disheartened if you do not see one of Earth's magnificent predators. For they were aware of you and may have meandered out of sight. It is a privilege and a thrill knowing they exist and are nearby, hidden in the shadows of trees, around a bend in the trail, concealed among mountainside boulders, or obscured behind brush.

"In the end we will conserve only what we love. We love only what we understand. We will understand only what we are taught."

—Baba Dioum

ACKNOWLEDGMENTS

We are all shaped and influenced by the people around us. This is also true with this manuscript. Thank you to the multitude of people, family, friends, and associates that have contributed either directly or indirectly or have supported this endeavor. No person lives in complete isolation, and so it is with this publication, which has been influenced by a multitude of other works and authors.

I am very grateful for my family. They have put up with my lifelong obsession with wilderness travel and my never-ending quest to observe predators in the wilderness. They have also gently suggested that I be prudent and cautious at times when my judgment was lacking. Without them I would not be here. I am thankful they decided to send a rescue boat when I was off track, overdue, low on food, and losing weight while kayaking in Katmai National Park. In particular, I am thankful for my wise daughter's foresight when she suggested I take an extra paddle while kayaking in Katmai. I am thankful for my resourceful, patient, and unflappable son, who has unfailingly participated in many adventures that I have concocted and has never had a critical word despite the difficult conditions we experienced together. Without him, some of these adventures would not have been possible.

Reviewers

- Dr. Lee Frelich, director for the University of Minnesota Forest Ecology Center, reviewed the entire manuscript from a forest ecology and terrestrial viewpoint.

- Dr. Layne Adams, Alaskan large-mammal researcher for USGS, reviewed the entire manuscript and provided comments and corrections throughout.

- Dr. David Mech, senior research scientist and wolf researcher for USGS, fact-checked and reviewed sections on the history of wolves in Yellowstone Park.

- Dr. Peter Sorensen, Department of Fisheries, Wildlife and Conservation Biology at the University of Minnesota, reviewed the aquatic science.

- Dr. Yadvendradev Jhala, of the Wildlife Institute of India, reviewed the chapter on wildlife and tigers in Satpura Tiger Reserve in India.

- Kevin Proescholdt, wilderness advocate and coauthor of *Troubled Waters: The Fight for the Boundary Waters Canoe Area Wilderness.*

- K.J. Metcalf, the first Admiralty Island Wilderness and National Monument Ranger and founding member of the Friends of Admiralty Island.

- Nancy Gibson, naturalist and cofounder of the International Wolf Center in northern Minnesota, reviewed chapters on wolves.

Influencers and Supporters

- Laurie Herrmann and Judith Brenner at Beaver's Pond Press for their dedication to this project and their patience in working with me while putting this manuscript to print. This book would not be what it is today without their expertise.

- Sven Bellanger—scientific illustrator for his wonderful artwork.

- Lyle Bradley, Anoka Senior High School biology teacher. Lyle introduced me to the Teton Wilderness and the wilds of the American West. His leadership exposed dozens of high school students to the outdoors doing things that, without him, we could only dream about. Among them: rafting the Snake River, rock climbing the Black Hills, backpacking the Tetons, gaining confidence and experience on survival excursions, sleeping in a winter bivouac at a temperature of -20°F, and searching for and excavating fossils in Wyoming. Lyle Bradley's western biology field trips prepared many of us to go on to further challenges, not only in the outdoors but in life.

- Dick Brown, for your tireless and lifelong effort to protect wildlife and all of nature.

- John Hickman, for the initial edit and polishing the prose.

- Leroy Pomraning, a good friend who ignited in my spirit a love for winter trekking in the Boundary Waters Canoe Area Wilderness of northern Minnesota. During our first winter trip into the Boundary Waters, temperatures plummeted to -40°F. His experience and steady manner demonstrated that extreme winter conditions can be successfully navigated and enjoyed.

- Darby and Gerri Nelson, lifelong teachers and conservationists. For encouragement and believing that these experiences and observations while in nature were worth sharing with others.

- Collette Adkins, carnivore conservation director for the Center for Biological Diversity.

- Fred Swanson, author. For encouragement and advice.

- Kevin Proescholdt, for lifelong advocacy and passion for protecting the Boundary Waters Wilderness in Minnesota and all wilderness areas around the country.

- Swanand Deshpande, wilderness guide and naturalist in Satpura National Park. Swanand went out of his way to bring us to interesting areas of Satpura. His knowledge of Satpura's flora and fauna was crucial in providing background information and in our understanding of what we were seeing.

- Please note that although I have consulted with many people, any remaining errors, misrepresentations, or inaccuracies are unintentional by the author. I am thankful to all for providing guidance, corrections, and suggestions, as well as for believing in this project.

APPENDIX 1:
CAUTIONS WHEN TRAVELING IN
WILDERNESS

When in brown bear country, I almost always carry pepper spray. I have never used it. A few times it has been at the ready. Air travel with pepper spray is problematic. Airlines and the Transportation Security Administration are very strict; they don't allow it even in checked baggage. Pepper spray is expensive. It is wasteful and costly to fly, buy pepper spray, carry it for the duration of the trip, then leave it at the destination. Recently, when I have taken a float plane or a water taxi into the wilderness, the outfitter has lent pepper spray. At the end of the trip, it is returned to the outfitter. Yellowstone Park and some outfitters rent bear spray. Denali National Park has spare canisters of pepper spray that rangers lend out to backcountry users. At one Alaskan outfitter, I met a group of people that were pack-rafting and brought handguns for protection. Some groups bring an electric fence. I have never brought either of those. When traveling by float plane, pepper spray and fuel for the camp stove can be stored in one of the floats during the flight.

When in bear country, always hang your food or bring bear-proof canisters, which can be purchased or checked out at the park service visitor center. Store food at least one hundred yards from camp. When with a group, we have sometimes used two or three bear-proof canisters. I have never traveled in a group larger than five. Some groups bring a sealable barrel for food and scented items. When kayaking and space is limited, we store food in a sealed dry bag and hang it twelve feet above the ground. Never bring food into a tent in brown bear country. When hiking, make noise and talk to each other. When a bear is nearby, gather near each other to make the group look intimidating. Face the bear, talk steadily, clap your hands. Make yourself look large by putting your hands over your head or holding a paddle. Once a grizzly gnawed into our duffle bags on the beach while we slept in the tent. Woken by the noise, I exited the tent and raised a canoe paddle overhead. But the bear ignored me. When a second companion joined, the bear wandered away. Bears have walked by the front door of my tent, not more than five feet away. Once in the Boundary Waters Canoe Area Wilderness, a black bear poked its nose into the screen mesh of my tent door, nudging my back while I was trying to fall asleep, then nonchalantly walked away. Be careful, but try to keep in mind that bears are not necessarily out to get you.

Wilderness impels us to plan and be prepared, whether the adventure is weeks long or a simple day hike. Longer and more remote outings require more preparation and experience. But even a simple day hike can result in difficult circumstances if one is not prepared. Being unprepared for cold, wet weather is a common threat for backcountry hikers and can result in hypothermia. Day hiking in Denali along the Savage River once left me miserably cold and soaked after a rainstorm. Being the eternal optimist, I had failed to bring rain gear. Another threat is crossing cold-water streams or rivers. The force of the current pushing against one's legs can be surprisingly strong. Crossing is made more difficult while maintaining balance hauling a heavy pack and stepping on slippery irregular rocks. Another common hazard is hiking on rough terrain and falling, thus resulting in many injuries and deaths. Paddling through cold-water rapids or during inclement weather on a cold-water lake is hazardous. Dehydration is a threat, as there have been a few hiking trips where I have traveled twelve-plus miles at altitude with a heavy pack in hot weather. Failing to stay hydrated resulted in lethargy and an inability to clearly think and observe. In one instance, I missed a fork in the trail, which caused confusion and several miles of backtracking. Solo wilderness travel is another hazard and is not recommended. Although I have done much solo hiking and paddling over the years, being solo, one must be exceptionally cautious. When traveling alone in the wilderness, it is especially prudent to carry a satellite-based emergency beacon.

APPENDIX 2: WILDERNESS DAY HIKE SAFETY ITEMS

These items are lightweight, compact, and easily transported in a small pack. Having them can make the difference between a safe and comfortable wilderness hike and returning to civilization unscathed, or becoming disorientated, wet, cold, or having to stay overnight.

1) Map

2) Compass

3) Water

4) Snacks

5) Lighter

6) Flashlight

7) Rain jacket

8) Hat and gloves

9) Bear pepper spray when in grizzly territory

10) Satellite communications device

NOTES

Wilderness

1. As wilderness and predators have diminished and become rare . . .
   Stephen R. Kellert, Matthew Black, Colleen Reid Rush, and Alistair J. Bath,
   "Human Culture and Large Carnivore Conservation in North America,"
   Conservation Biology 10 (1996): 977–90. https://doi.org/10.1046/j.1523-
   1739.1996.10040977.x. See also: Karen Jones, "From Big Bad Wolf
   to Ecological Hero: *Canis Lupus* and the Culture(s) of Nature in the
   American–Canadian West," *American Review of Canadian Studies* 40, no.
   3 (2010): 338–50. https://doi.org/10.1080/02722011.2010.496902.

2. Many are keystone species whose effects are felt directly and indirectly . . .
   William Ripple and Robert Beschta, "Trophic Cascades in Yellowstone:
   The First 15 Years After Wolf Reintroduction," *Biological Conservation*
   145 (2012): 205–13. doi: 10.1016/j.biocon.2011.11.005. See also:
   Christopher Wilmers, Robert Crabtree, Douglas Smith, Kerry Murphy,
   and Wayne Getz, "Trophic Facilitation by Introduced Top Predators:
   Grey Wolf Subsidies to Scavengers in Yellowstone National Park," *Journal
   of Animal Ecology* 72 (2003): 909–16. https://doi.org/10.1046/j.1365-
   2656.2003.00766.x.

Circle of Life

1. The Shoshone led by Chief Washakie traded with migrants . . .
   Grace R. Hebard, *Washakie: Chief of the Shoshones* (Winnipeg, Canada:
   Bison Books, 1995).

Panic

1. The fossilized remains of ancient sea-life can be found on many slopes . . .
   Charles D. Walcott, "Cambrian Geology and Paleontology No. 3. Middle
   Cambrian Holothurians and Medus/e," *Smithsonian Miscellaneous
   Collections* 56, no. 3 (1911). See also: Stephen Jay Gould, *Wonderful Life:*

The Burgess Shale and the Nature of History (New York: W. W. Norton, 1989). See also: Timothy Topper, Luke Strotz, Lars Holmer, and Jean-Bernard Caron, "Survival on a Soft Seafloor: Life Strategies of Brachiopods from the Cambrian Burgess Shale," *Earth-Science Reviews* 151 (2015). https://doi.org/10.1016/j.earscirev.2015.10.015.

2. There have been twenty or so periods of interglacial warmth . . .
   Homo sapiens have significantly altered Earth's landscape and have changed the composition of the atmosphere through the industrial emission of carbon dioxide and methane. Thus, Earth's current period of interglacial warmth will last longer and be warmer than what would have occurred without the changes wrought by humans.

3. Since the last glacial maximum . . .
   Chris Wood and Dan Smith, "Dendroglaciological Evidence for a Neoglacial Advance of the Saskatchewan Glacier, Banff National Park, Canadian Rocky Mountains," *Tree-Ring Research,* no. 60 (2004): 59–65, doi: 10.3959/1536-1098-60.1.59. See also: Brian Luckman, "The Little Ice Age in the Canadian Rockies," *Geomorphology,* no. 32 (2000): 357–84. https://doi.org/10.1016/S0169-555X(99)00104-X. See also: Dan Smith, *Dendroglaciological Investigations at Saskatchewan Glacier* (1999). www.geog.uvic.ca/dept/uvtrl/2000-02.pdf.

4. My disorientation is sufficient . . .
   A compass can go bad. Storing it next to a magnet or having an electronic device near the compass for a period can destroy or reverse the north-south polarity of the needle.

5. By the time you read this, Earth's magnetic North Pole may have shifted . . .
   Lawrence Newitt, Arnaud Chulliat, and Jean-Jacques Orgeval, "Location of the North Magnetic Pole in April 2007," *Earth, Planets and Space,* no. 61 (2009): 703–10. https://doi.org/10.1186/BF03353178.

Erratic

1. For the past two million years the hotspot has been . . .
   Kenneth L. Pierce, Don G. Despain, Lisa A. Morgan, and John M. Good, "The Yellowstone Hotspot, Greater Yellowstone Ecosystem, and Human Geography," Professional Paper 1717 (2007): 1–38. https://pubs.usgs.gov/pp/1717/downloads/pdf/p1717A.pdf.

2. As pressure builds and the outer crust weakens . . .
   Colin Wilson, "How Long Does a Big Yellowstone Explosive Eruption Last?" *Yellowstone Caldera Chronicles* (November 9, 2020), www.usgs.gov/center-news/how-long-does-a-big-yellowstone-explosive-eruption-last.

3. It burst through Earth's surface with a Volcanic Explosivity Index (VEI) of 8 . . .
   Naomi E. Matthews, Jorge A Vázquez, and Andrew T. Calvert, "Age of the Lava Creek Super-Eruption and Magma Chamber Assembly at Yellowstone Based On 40Ar/39Ar And U–Pb Dating of Sanidine and Zircon Crystals," *Geochemistry, Geophysics, Geosystems* 16, no. 8 (2015): 2508–28.

4. As Doug Smith, Rolf Peterson, and Douglas Houston wrote, "The reintroduction of gray wolves to Yellowstone National Park . . .
   Douglas W. Smith, Rolf O. Peterson, and Douglas B. Houston, "Yellowstone after Wolves," *BioScience* 53, no. 4 (2003): 330–40. https://doi.org/10.1641/0006-3568(2003)053[0330:YAW]2.0.CO;2.

5. Rainfall averages about ten to twenty inches annually . . .
   Yellowstone's Northern Range (Yellowstone National Park, 1997). https://archive.org/details/yellowstonesnort00mamm/page/n9/mode/2up.

Druids

1. Whatever the species, it very naturally could . . .
   Maybe Stanley Kubrick was right. Perhaps the femur of a large animal was the first tool ever used by ancient hominids, as depicted in the classic scene in *2001: A Space Odyssey*.

2. It has been proposed that extinct species of cheetah-like cats . . .
   Xiaoming Wang and Larry Martin, "Late Pleistocene, Paleoecology and Large Mammal Taphonomy, Natural Trap Cave, Wyoming," *National Geographic Research & Exploration*, no. 9 (1993): 422–35. See also for a discussion of cheetahs at La Brea Tar Pits and Natural Trap Cave: Rachel Dunn, Candice Cooper, Joshua Lemert, Natalie Mironov, and Julie A Meachen et al., "Locomotor Correlates of the Scapholunar of Living and Extinct Carnivorans." *Journal of Morphology* 280 (2019): 1197–1206. https://doi.org/10.1002/jmor.21024.

3. One study shows that during summer, elk avoid wolves . . .
   Julie S. Mao, Mark S. Boyce, Douglas W. Smith, Francis J. Singer, David J. Vales, John M. Vore and Evelyn H. Merrill, "Habitat Selection by Elk Before and After Wolf Reintroduction in Yellowstone National Park," *The Journal of Wildlife Management* 69 (2005): 1691–1707. https://doi.org/10.2193/0022-541X(2005)69[1691:HSBEBA]2.0.CO;2.

4. Another study indicates that Yellowstone's "Landscape of Fear" . . .
   John Laundre, Lucina Hernández, and Kelly Altendorf, "Wolves, Elk, and Bison: Reestablishing the 'Landscape of Fear' in Yellowstone National Park, USA." *Canadian Journal of Zoology/Revue Canadienne De Zoologie* 79 (2001): 1401–09. https://doi.org/10.1139/cjz-79-8-1401. See also: Lucina

Hernández and John Laundre, "Foraging in the 'Landscape of Fear' and Its Implications for Habitat Use and Diet Quality of Elk Cervus Elaphus and Bison Bison Bison," *Wildlife Society Bulletin* 113 (2005): 215–20, 10.2981/0909-6396(2005)11[215:FITLOF]2.0.CO;2. See also: Joshua S. Halofsky and William J. Ripple, "Fine-Scale Predation Risk on Elk after Wolf Reintroduction in Yellowstone National Park, USA," *Oecologia* 155 (2008): 869–77. https://doi.org/10.1007/s00442-007-0956-z.

5. Growth of willow, aspen, and alder in open areas . . .
    W. J. Ripple, R. L. Beschta, and L.E Painter, "Trophic Cascades from Wolves to Alders in Yellowstone," *Forest Ecology and Management* 354, no. 15 (2015): 254–60. See also: T. K. Ruth, P.C. Buotte, MG Hornocker, *Yellowstone Cougars: Ecology Before and During Wolf Reestablishment* (Boulder: University Press of Colorado, 2014).

6. During winter, elk carrion supplies a large portion . . .
    R. L. Crabtree and J. W. Sheldon, "The Ecological Role of Coyotes on Yellowstone's Northern Range," *Yellowstone Science* 7, no. 2: (1999):15–23.

7. In Yellowstone, cougars prey on elk and mule deer . . .
    L. Mark Elbroch, Patrick E. Lendrum, Jesse Newby, Howard Quigley, Derek Craighead et al., "Seasonal Foraging Ecology of Non-Migratory Cougars in a System with Migrating Prey," *PLoS One* 8, no. 12 (2012). See also: Douglas W. Smith, Rolf O. Peterson, and Douglas B. Houston, "Yellowstone after Wolves," *BioScience* 53, no. 4 (April 2003): 330–40. https://doi.org/10.1641/0006-3568(2003)053[0330:YAW]2.0.CO;2.

8. With the restoration of wolves to the Yellowstone ecosystem . . .
    Aldo Leopold, *A Sand County Almanac, and Sketches Here and There* (New York: Oxford University Press, 1949), 224–25.

9. In 1995, the northern range elk herd was near a high point . . .
    Francis J. Singer, Albert L. Harting, Kate K. Symonds, and Michael B. Coughenour, "Density Dependence, Compensation, and Environmental Effects on Elk Calf Mortality in Yellowstone National Park," *Journal of Wildlife Management* 61, no. 1 (January 1997): 12–25.

10. During the severe winter of 1997, hunting success . . .
    L. Mech, Douglas Smith, Kerry Murphy, and Daniel Macnulty, "Winter Severity and Wolf Predation on a Formerly Wolf-Free Elk Herd," *Journal of Wildlife Management* 65 (2001): 998. https://doi.org/10.2307/3803048.

11. Except of course, when a predator chases . . .
    I have come across many carcasses and skeletons in the wild, which are not tranquil to view. It is a reminder that life is short and all creatures are mortal. I have witnessed a snake swallow a frog, a spider capture a fly in its web, bald eagles and osprey pluck fish out of water, pelicans dive for fish, and bears capture and eat salmon. Observing these instances of

predators capturing and eating prey has not been disturbing. Many online videos, however, have dramatic scenes of predators chasing, capturing, and devouring prey. Some of these are gut-wrenching to view, especially if the prey is a mammal and calling for its mother or others of its kind. For however much people enjoy being immersed in nature's beauty and serenity, that predators kill and devour prey affirms that the natural world is not always tranquil and at times consists of harsh, brutal reality.

Toklat

1. Two archeological sites in Denali National Park . . .
   Samuel C. Coffman, "Archaeology at Teklanika West (HEA-001): An Upland Archaeological Site, Central Alaska" (master's thesis: University of Alaska, Fairbanks, 2011).

2. Other archeological sites within the park are the . . .
   Brian T. Wygalaster, "Prehistoric Upland Tool Production in the Central Alaska Range," *Alaska Journal of Anthropology* 8, no.1 (2010).

3. During Denali's short summer season . . .
   Carol L. McIntyre, "Birds, Bird Studies, and Bird Conservation in Denali National Park and Preserve," *Arctic Research of the United States* 16 (2002): 22.

4. One wonders what evolutionary forces . . .
   Carsten Egevang, Iain J. Stenhouse, Richard A. Phillips, and Janet R. D. Silk et al., "Tracking of Arctic Tern Reveals Longest Animal Migration," *Proceedings of the National Academy of Science of the United States of America* 107 (2010): 2078–83.

5. One group inhabited Alaska's St. Paul Island . . .
   S. Vartanyan, K. Arslanov, T. Tertychnaya, and S. Chernov, "Radiocarbon Dating Evidence for Mammoths on Wrangel Island, Arctic Ocean, Until 2000 BC," *Radiocarbon* 37, no.1 (1995): 1–6. https://doi.org/10.1017/S0033822200014703.

6. Occasionally found frozen in arctic permafrost are . . .
   Gennady G. Boeskorov, Olga R. Potapova, Eugeny N. Mashenko, Albert V. Protopopov, Tatyana V. Kuznetsova, Larry Agenbroad, Alexey N. Tikhonov et al., "Preliminary Analyses of the Frozen Mummies of Mammoth (*Mammuthus primigenius*), Bison (*Bison priscus*) and Horse (*Equus* sp.) from the Yana-Indigirka Lowland, Yakutia, Russia," *Integrative Zoology* 9 (2014): 471–80. https://doi.org/10.1111/1749-4877.12079.

7. Maybe a Canada lynx?
   There are no bobcats or mountain lions in interior Alaska.

8. It is digging up and eating the roots . . .
    The seeds of this plant can be toxic when eaten in large quantities. They may have contributed to the death of Christopher McCandless, subject of Jon Krakauer's bestseller *Into the Wild,* just outside the northern border of Denali National Park.

9. After decades of work, the drug Pemetrexed was isolated and approved . . .
    Edward C. Taylor, "From the Wings of Butterflies, the Discovery and Synthesis of Alimta," *Chemistry International* 33, no. 5 (September-October 2011). http://publications.iupac.org/ci/2011/3305/1_taylor.html.

10. Today in the high mountains of the American West . . .
    Donald R. Currey "An Ancient Bristlecone Pine Stand in Eastern Nevada," *Ecology* 46, no. 4 (1965): 564–66.

11. A golden eagle flies overhead . . .
    Denali National Park contains one of the highest densities of nesting Golden Eagles in North America . . .
    Michael N. Kochert, Karen Steenhof, Carol L. McIntyre, and Erica Craig, "Golden Eagle (Aquila Chrysaetos)," in *The Birds of North America,* eds. A. Poole and F. Gill (2002).

12. Before the 1900s, coyote range . . .
    James Hody and Roland Kays, "Mapping the Expansion of Coyotes (*Canis latrans*) across North and Central America," *ZooKeys* 759 (2018): 81–97. https://doi.org/10.3897/zookeys.759.15149.

13. It was here long before us and will continue to be the Monarch of the North . . .
    D. L. Egholm, M. F. Knudsen, and M. Sandiford, "Lifespan of Mountain Ranges Scaled by Feedbacks Between Landsliding and Erosion by Rivers," *Nature* 498, no. 7455 (June 2013): 475–58. https://doi.org/10.1038/nature12218. PMID: 23803847.

Vigil

1. Head-Smashed-In Buffalo Jump, in southern Alberta . . .
    B. O. K. Reeves, "Head-Smashed-In: 5500 Years of Bison Jumping in the Alberta Plains," *Plains Anthropologist Memoir Series* 14 (1978): 151–74.

2. At low elevations with less snow . . .
    P. J. White, Kelly Proffitt, L. David Mech, Shaney B. Evans, Julie A. Cunningham, and Kenneth L. Hamlin et al., "Migration of Northern Yellowstone Elk: Implications of Spatial Structuring," *Journal of Mammalogy* 91, no. 4 (August 2010): 827–37. https://doi.org/10.1644/08-MAMM-A-252.1. See also: P. J. White, Troy L. Davis, Kerey K. Barnowe-Meyer, Robert L. Crabtree, and Robert A. Garrott, "Partial Migration

and Philopatry of Yellowstone Pronghorn," *Biological Conservation* 135 (2007): 502–10. https://doi.org/10.1016/j.biocon.2006.10.041. See also: E. Glenn Plumb, P. J. White, Michael B. Coughenour, and Rick L. Wallen, "Carrying Capacity, Migration, and Dispersal in Yellowstone Bison," *Biological Conservation* 142, no. 11 (2009): 2377–87. See also: John J. Craighead, Gerry Atwell, and Bart W. O'Gara "Elk Migrations in and near Yellowstone National Park" *Wildlife Monographs*, no. 29 (August 1972): 3–48. See also: Joel Berger, "The Last Mile: How to Sustain Long-Distance Migration in Mammals," *Conservation Biology* 18 (2004): 320–31. https://doi.org/10.1111/j.1523-1739.2004.00548.x.

3. While traversing mountain passes . . .
    Matthew J. Kauffman, Douglas E. McWhirter, John G. Cook, Rachel C. Cook, Abigail A. Nelson, Michael D. Jimenez, and Robert W. Klaver et al., "Animal Migration Amid Shifting Patterns of Phenology and Predation: Lessons from a Yellowstone Elk Herd," *Journal of Ecology* (2013). https://doi.org/10.1890/11-2298.1. See also: Arthur D. Middleton, Thomas A Morrison, Jennifer Kay Fortin, Charles T. Robbins, Kelly Proffitt, Philip J. White, Douglas E McWhirter, Todd M Koel, Douglas G. Brimeyer, W. Sue Fairbanks and Matthew J Kauffman et al., "Grizzly Bear Predation Links the Loss of Native Trout to the Demography of Migratory Elk in Yellowstone," *Proceedings of the Royal Society B: Biological Sciences* 280 (2013): n. page.

4. One study analyzed the composition of bone and hair . . .
    The skulls and mounts of the Tsavo man-eaters are on display at the Field Museum of Natural History in Chicago, Illinois.

5. Along with their natural diet . . .
    Justin D. Yeakel, Bruce D. Patterson, Kena Fox-Dobbs, Mercedes M. Okumura, Thure E. Cerling, Jonathan W. Moore, Paul L. Koch, and Nathaniel J. Dominy, "Cooperation and Individuality among Man-Eating Lions," *Proceedings of the National Academy of Sciences of the United States of America* 106, no. 45 (November 2009) 19040–43. https://doi.org/10.1073/pnas.0905309106.

Winter Solitude

1. A billion years ago, the area underneath Lake Superior . . .
    W. R.Van Schmus and W. J. Hinze, "The Midcontinent Rift System," *Annual Review of Earth and Planetary Sciences* 13, no. 1 (1985): 345–83.

2. As the continental ice sheet melted, the giant scoured depressions . . .
    Randall Schaetzl Grahame, "Origin and Evolution of the Great Lakes," *Journal of Great Lakes Research* 27, no. 4 (2001): 518–46. https://doi.org/10.1016/S0380-1330(01)70665-X.

3. Humans have lived in the Quetico and Boundary Waters areas for nine thousand years . . .
Evan Larson, Kurt Kipfmueller, and Lane Johnson, "People, Fire, and Pine: Linking Human Agency and Landscape in the Boundary Waters Canoe Area Wilderness and Beyond," *Annals of the American Association of Geographers* (2020): 1–25. https://doi.org/10.1080/24694452.2020.1768042 . See also: Susan C. Mulholland, Stephen L. Mulholland, Gordon R. Peters, James K. Huber, and Howard D. Mooers, "Paleo-Indian Occupations in Northeastern Minnesota: How Early?" *North American Archaeologist* 18, no. 4 (1998): 371–400. https://doi.org/10.2190/PDHK-9FAK-E8QW-FQ4J.

4. Before the melting of North America's continental glacier, caribou roamed . . .
Charles S. Churcher, Paul Woodburn Parmalee, Gordon L. Bell, and James P. Lamb, "Caribou from the Late Pleistocene of Northwestern Alabama," *Canadian Journal of Zoology* 67, no. 5 (1898): 1210–16. https://doi. org/10.1139/z89-175. See also: Robert A. Martin and Joel M. Sneed, "Late Pleistocene Records of Caribou and Elk from Georgia and Alabama," *Georgia Journal of Science* 47 (1989): 117–22. https://eurekamag.com/ research/019/298/019298919.php. See also: C.L. Cooper, "The Pleistocene Fauna of Kentucky," *in The Paleontology of Kentucky: Kentucky Geological Survey,* ed. W. R. Jillson, 36 (1931): 435–61. See also: Thomas P. Myers and Richard G. Corner, "Possible Evidence for a Pre-Clovis Bone-Tool Industry from the Central Plains," *Transactions of the Nebraska Academy of Sciences and Affiliated Societies* 14 (1986): 41–5. See also: Richard G. Corner, "A Late Pleistocene-Holocene Vertebrate Fauna from Red Willow County, Nebraska," *Transactions of the Nebraska Academy of Sciences* 4 (1977): 77–93. See also: John E. Guilday, Harold W Hamilton, and P. W. Parmalee, "Caribou (*Rangifer tarandus L.*) from the Pleistocene of Tennessee," *Journal of Tennessee Academy of Sciences* 50 (1975): 109–12. See also: Donald R. Whitehead, Stephen T. Jackson, Mark C. Sheehan and Barbara W. Leyden "Late-Glacial Vegetation Associated with Caribou and Mastodon in Central Indiana," *Quaternary Research* 17, no. 2 (1982): 241–57. https://doi.org/10.1016/0033-5894(82)90061-8. See also: John E. Guilday, "Rangifer Antler from an Ohio Bog," *Journal of Mammalogy* 47, no. 2 (1966): 325–26. https://doi.org/10.2307/1378131. See also: Richard L. Josephs, "A Late Pleistocene Ceiling Collapse in Bogus Cave, Jones County, Iowa: A Potential Relationship to Coeval Accelerated Mass Wasting Events Across the Central Midwest," *Journal of Cave and Karst Studies* 64 (2002): 175–79. See also: Reimers Eigil, "The Return of Caribou to Ungava," *Rangifer* 28 (2008). https://doi.org/10.7557/2.28.1.153.

5. A tea made from a conifer . . .
Don J. Durzan, "Arginine, Scurvy and Cartier's 'Tree of Life,'" *Journal of*

Ethnobiol Ethnomed 5, no. 5 (2009). https://doi.org/10.1186/1746-4269-5-5.

6. Extracts from white cedar . . .
Sushil Dubey and A. Batra, "Role of Phenolics in Anti-Atherosclerotic Property of *Thuja Occidentalis* Linn.," *Ethnobotanical Leaflets* 13 (2009). See also: Raktim Biswas, Sushil Kumar Mandal, Suman Dutta, Soumya Sundar Bhattacharyya, Naoual Boujedaini, and Anisur Rahman Khuda-Bukhsh, "Thujone-Rich Fraction of *thuja occidentalis* Demonstrates Major Anti-Cancer Potentials: Evidences from In Vitro Studies on A375 Cells," *Evidence-Based Complementary and Alternative Medicine* (2011). https://doi.org/10.1093/ecam/neq042. See also: B. K. Ojeswi, M. Khoobchandani, D. K. Hazra, and M. M. Srivastava, "Protective Effect of *thuja occidentalis* Against DMBA-Induced Breast Cancer with Reference to Oxidative Stress," *Human and Experimental Toxicology* 29, no. 5 (2010): 369–75. https://doi.org/10.1177/0960327110364150. See also: S. K. Dubey and A. Batra, "Role of Phenolic Compound Rich Ethanol Fraction of *Thuja Occidentalis Linn.* in Protective Mechanism," *Journal of Pharmacy Research* 2, no. 2 (2009): 217–25.

7. Extracts from this orange lichen . . .
Hasan Turkez, Elanur Aydin, and Ali Aslan, "Xanthoria Elegans (Link) (Lichen) Extract Counteracts DNA Damage and Oxidative Stress of Mitomycin C in Human Lymphocytes," *Cytotechnology* 64, no. 6 (2012): 679–86. https://doi.org/10.1007/s10616-012-9447-0.

8. Although many lichens are leafy . . .
D. J. Hill, "The Nature of the Symbiotic Relationship in Lichens," *Endeavour* 18 (1994): 96–103.

Frustrated

1. The oldest evidence of Paleo-Arctic people living in the Katmai area . . .
Don E. Dumond, *A Naknek Chronicle: Ten Thousand Years in a Land of Lakes and Rivers and Mountains of Fire,* National Park Service (December 9, 2005).

2. Their artifacts have been found along with . . .
Don E. Dumond, "The Arctic Small Tool Tradition in Southern Alaska," *Alaska Journal of Anthropology* 3, no. 2 (2005): 67–78.

3. One mind-expanding sentence from the book stands out . . .
Evolution: A Scientific American Reader (Chicago: University of Chicago Press, 2006): 63.

4. The Milky Way, Andromeda, and Triangulum are the major galaxies . . .
J. Richard Bond, Lev Kofman, and Dmitry Pogosyan, "How Filaments Of

Galaxies Are Woven into the Cosmic Web," *Nature* 380 (1996): 603–6. https://doi.org/10.1038/380603a0. See also: Marius Cautun, Rien van de Weygaert, Bernard J. T. Jones, and Carlos S. Frenk, "Evolution of the Cosmic Web," *Monthly Notices of the Royal Astronomical Society* 441, no. 4 (2014): 2923–73. https://doi.org/10.1093/mnras/stu768.

5. Or, within the human mind's fragile and limited ability to comprehend . . . Rien van de Weygaert, "The Cosmic Foam: Stochastic Geometry and Spatial Clustering across the Universe," in *Statistical Challenges in Astronomy*, ed. Eic D. Feigelson and G. Jogesh Basbu (New York: Springer, 2003): 175–96. See also: Pekka Teerikorpi, M. J. Valtonen, Kirsi Lehto, Harry Lehto, Gene Byrd, and Arthur Chernin et al., "Large-Scale Structure of the Universe," in *The Evolving Universe and the Origin of Life* (New York: Springer, 2019). See also: Delia Perlov and Alex Vilenkin, "Structure Formation," in *Cosmology for the Curious* (New York: Springer, 2017): 175–85. See also: X. Xu, Jessi Cisewski, Sheridan Green, and Daisuke Nagai, "Finding Cosmic Voids and Filament Loops Using Topological Data Analysis," *Astronomy and Computing* 27 (2019) 34–52. https://doi.org/10.1016/j.ascom.2019.02.003. See also: Nicola Malavasi, Nabila Aghanim, Hideki Tanimura, Victor Bonjean, and Marian Douspis, "Like a Spider in Its Web: A Study of fhe Large-Scale Structure around the Coma Cluster," *Astronomy & Astrophysics* (2019): 634. https://doi.org/10.1051/0004-6361/201936629.

6. In 1966, Graham Cairns-Smith theorized it may have started . . . A. G. Cairns-Smith, "The Origin of Life and the Nature of the Primitive Gene," *Journal of Theoretical Biology* 10, no. 1 (1966): 53–88.

7. An alternative proposal by Jack Corliss . . . J. B. Corliss and Ja Baross Se Hoffman, "An Hypothesis Concerning the Relationships Between Submarine Hot Springs and the Origin of Life on Earth," *Oceanologica Acta* (1981). https://archimer.ifremer.fr/doc/00245/35661/. See also: John B. Corliss, J.G. Dymond, Louis I. Gordon, John M. Edmond, Richard P. von Herzen, Robert D. Ballard, Kenneth Green, D. L. Williams, Arnold Bainbridge, Kathy Crane, and Tj. H. van Andel "Submarine Thermal Springs on the Galapagos Rift," *Science* 203 (1979): 1073–83. https://doi.org/10.1126/science.203.4385.1073. See also: J. B. Corliss and Ja Baross Hoffman Se, "An Hypothesis Concerning the Relationships Between Submarine Hot Springs and the Origin of Life on Earth," *Oceanologica Acta* (1981). https://archimer.ifremer.fr/doc/00245/35661/.

8. In 2016, Jack Szostak wrote . . . J.W. Szostak, "On the Origin of Life/*Sobre el Origen De la Vida*," *Medicina* 6, no. 4 (2016): 199–203.

9. Once primitive proto-cells formed . . .
Jason P Schrum, Ting F Zhu, and Jack W Szostak, "The Origins of Cellular Life," *Cold Spring Harbor Perspectives in Biology* 2, no. 9 (2010). https://doi.org/10.1101/cshperspect.a002212. See also: Pier Luigi Luisi, Peter Walde, and Thomas Oberholzer, "Lipid Vesicles as Possible Intermediates in the Origin of Life: Current Opinion in Colloid and Interface," *Science* 4 (1999): 33–39.

10. Earth life is categorized into three groups . . .
Carl R. Woese and George E. Fox, "Phylogenetic Structure of the Prokaryotic Domain: The Primary Kingdoms," *Proceedings of the National Academy of Sciences of the United States of America* 74, no. 11 (1977): 5088–90. https://doi.org/10.1073/pnas.74.11.5088. See also: Carl R. Woese, Otto Kandler, and Mark L. Wheelis, "Towards a Natural System of Organisms: Proposal for the Domains Archaea, Bacteria, and Eucarya," *Proceedings of the National Academy of Sciences of the United States of America* 87, no. 12 (June 1990): 4576–79.

11. Another archaean, but at the other end of the thermal spectrum, is *Methanogenium frigidum* . . .
Peter D. Franzmann, Yitai Liu, David L. Balkwill, Henry C. Aldrich, Everly Conway De Macario, and David R. Boone, "Methanogenium Frigidum Sp. Nov., A Psychrophilic, H2-Using Methanogen from Ace Lake, Antarctica," *International Journal of Systematic Bacteriology* 47, no. 4 (1997): 1068–72.

12. For the first three billion years, life consisted . . .
John Tyler Bonner, "The Origins of Multicellularity," *Integrative Biology* 1 (1998): 27–36. See also: Abderrazak El Albani, Stefan Bengtson, Donald E. Canfield, Andrey Bekker, Roberto Macchiarelli, Arnaud Mazurier, Emma U. Hammarlund, Philippe Boulvais, Jean-Jacques Dupuy, Claude Fontaine, Franz T. Fürsich, François Gauthier-Lafaye, Philippe Janvier, Emmanuelle Javaux, Frantz Ossa Ossa, Anne-Catherine Pierson-Wickmann, Armelle Riboulleau, Paul Sardini, Daniel Vachard, Martin Whitehouse and Alain Meunier, "Large Colonial Organisms with Coordinated Growth in Oxygenated Environments," *Nature* 466 (2010): 100–104. https://doi.org/10.1038/nature09166. See also: S. Blair Hedges, Jaime E. Blair, Maria L. Venturi and Jason L. Shoe, "A Molecular Timescale of Eukaryote Evolution and the Rise of Complex Multicellular Life," *BMC Evolutionary Biology* 4, no. 2 (2004). https://doi.org/10.1186/1471-2148-4-2. See also: Stefan Bengtson, Therese Sallstedt, Veneta Belivanova, and Martin Whitehouse, "Three-dimensional Preservation of Cellular and Subcellular Structures Suggests 1.6 Billion-Year-Old Crown-Group Red Algae," *PLoS Biology* 15, no. 3 (2017). https://doi.org/10.1371/journal.pbio.2000735. See also: Stefan Bengtson, Birger Rasmussen, Magnus Ivarsson, and Janet Muhling, "Fungus-Like Mycelial Fossils in 2.4-Billion-Year-Old Vesicular Basalt," *Nature Ecology and Evolution* 1, no. 0141 (2017). https://doi.org/10.1038/

s41559-017-0141. See also: Corentin C. Loron, Camille François, Robert H. Rainbird, Elizabeth C. Turner, Stephan Borensztajn and Emmanuelle J. Javaux, "Early Fungi from the Proterozoic Era in Arctic Canada," *Nature* 570 (2019): 232–35. https://doi.org/10.1038/s41586-019-1217-0.

13. As already mentioned, evidence for the Cambrian Explosion can be found . . .
Simon Conway-Morris, "Burgess Shale Faunas and the Cambrian Explosion," *Science* 246, (1989): 339–46.

14. It is during the "explosion" that multicellular animal life evolved . . .
Andrey Zhuravlev and Robert Riding, *The Ecology of the Cambrian Radiation* (New York: Columbia University Press, 2000).

15. One animal, pikaia, was a flat worm . . .
Simon Conway Morris and Jean-Bernard Caron, "Pikaia Gracilens Walcott, a Stem-Group Chordate from the Middle Cambrian of British Columbia," *Biological Reviews* 87 (2012): 480–512.

16. Anomalocaris grew to three feet in length and had two frontal appendages . . .
Harry Blackmore, Briggs Whittington, and Derek Ernest Gilmour, "The Largest Cambrian Animal Anomalocaris, Burgess Shale, British Columbia," *Philosophical Transactions of the Royal Society of London* (1985).

17. During the Cambrian Explosion, animals with eyes . . .
Michael S. Y. Lee, James B. Jago, Diego C. García-Bellido, Gregory D. Edgecombe, James G. Gehling and John R. Paterson, "Modern Optics in Exceptionally Preserved Eyes of Early Cambrian Arthropods from Australia," *Nature* 474 (2011) 631–34.

18. Trilobites were one of the first animals to evolve complex eyes . . .
Euan Clarkson, Riccardo Levi-Setti, and Gabor Horváth, "The Eyes of Trilobites: The Oldest Preserved Visual System," *Arthropod Structure and Development* 35, no. 4 (2006): 247–59.

19. Thus, eyesight may have initiated a visual acuity competition . . .
Andrew Parker, *In the Blink of an Eye: How Vision Sparked the Big Bang of Evolution* (New York: Basic Books, 2004).

20. People of the North Pacific extracted the deadly toxin . . .
Robert F. Heizer, "Aconite Arrow Poison in the Old and New World," *Journal of the Washington Academy of Sciences* 28, no. 8 (1938): 358–64. www.jstor.org/stable/24530304.

Kootznoowoo

1. Despite DNA evidence of their ancestry, the bears of the ABC Islands . . .
    James A. Cahill, Richard E. Green, Tara L. Fulton, Mathias Stiller, Flora
    Jay, Nikita Ovsyanikov, Rauf Salamzade, John St. John, Ian Stirling,
    Montgomery Slatkin, and Beth Shapiro, "Genomic Evidence for Island
    Population Conversion Resolves Conflicting Theories of Polar Bear
    Evolution," *PLOS Genetics* 9, no. 3 (March 2013). https://doi.org/10.1371/
    journal.pgen.1003345.

2. Its bark contains the compound Paclitaxel . . .
    Jonathan D. Adams, Karl P. Flora, Barry R. Goldspiel, James W. Wilson,
    Susan G. Arbuck, and Rebecca Finley, "Taxol: A History of Pharmaceutical
    Development and Current Pharmaceutical Concerns," *Journal of National
    Cancer Institute Monographs* (1993): 141–47.

3. Although it is painful to touch the spines . . .
    Taichi Inui, Yuehong Wang, Shixin Deng, David C. Smith, Scott G.
    Franzblau, and Guido F. Pauli, "Counter-Current Chromatography Based
    Analysis of Synergy in an Anti-Tuberculosis Ethnobotanical," *Journal of
    Chromatography A.* 1151, no. 1–2 (Jun 2000): 211–15. See also: Colin M
    McGill, Estefania J Alba-Rodriguez, Shuo Li, Charles J Benson, Regina
    M Ondrasik, Lindsey N Fisher, David F Claxton, and Brian M Barth,
    "Extracts of Devil's Club (*Oplopanax horridus*) Exert Therapeutic Efficacy
    in Experimental Models of Acute Myeloid Leukemia," *Phytotherapy
    Research* 28, no. 9 (2014): 1308–14.

4. Several compounds in old man's beard . . .
    Moumita Dandapat and Santanu Paul, "Secondary Metabolites
    from Lichen *Usnea longissima* and Its Pharmacological Relevance,"
    Pharmacognosy Research 11, no. 2 (2019): 103.
    Ana Zugic, Ivica Jeremic, Aleksandra Isakovic, Ivana Arsic, Snezana Savic,
    and Vanja Tadic,"Evaluation of Anticancer and Antioxidant Activity of
    a Commercially Available CO_2 Supercritical Extract of Old Man's Beard
    (*Usnea barbata*)," *PLoS ONE* 11, no. 1 (2016). https://doi.org/10.1371/
    journal.pone.0146342.
    Xuelong Yu, Qiang Guo, Guozhu Su, Ailin Yang, Zhongdong Hu, Changhai
    Qu, Zhe Wan, Ruoyu Li, Pengfei Tu, and Xingyun Chai, "Usnic Acid
    Derivatives with Cytotoxic and Antifungal Activities from the Lichen
    Usnea longissimi," *Journal of Natural Products* 79, no. 5 (2016): 1373–80.
    https://doi.org/10.1021/acs.jnatprod.6b00109.

5. Away from the southern coast . . .
    Frederick C. Dean, "Brown Bear Density, Denali National Park,
    Alaska, and Sighting Efficiency Adjustment," *Bears: Their Biology and
    Management* 7 (1987): 37–43. https://doi.org/10.2307/3872605. See
    also: Jeff Keay, "Grizzly Bear Population Ecology and Monitoring Denali

National Park and Preserve," *Alaska US Geological Survey* (Anchorage: Alaska Biological Center, 2001). See also: www.nps.gov/articles/denali-animal-count.htm.

6. In Alaska's far north, on the arctic coastal plain and in the mountains of the Arctic National Wildlife Refuge . . .
   Gerald W. Garner, Mark Masteller, Gary E. Muehlenhardt, Michael K. Phillips, Harry V. Reynolds, "Ecology of Brown Bears Inhabitating the Coastal Plain and Adjacent Foothills and Mountains of the Northeastern Portion of the Arctic National Wildlife Refuge," *ANWR Progress Report Number FY 18-11*, Alaska Department of Fish and Game.

7. In comparison, brown bear density in Glacier National Park in Montana . . .
   Katherine C. Kendall, Jeffrey Stetz, David A. Roon, Lisette P. Waits, John Boulanger, and David Paetkau, "Grizzly Bear Density in Glacier National Park, Montana," *Journal of Wildlife Management* 72, no. 8 (2008): 1693–1705. https://doi.org/10.2193/2008-007.

8. Since then, the number of Yellowstone Ecosystem grizzlies has risen . . .
   Frank T. van Manen, Mark A. Haroldson, and Suzanna C. Soileau, eds., *Yellowstone Grizzly Bear Investigation 2014—Report of the Interagency Bear Study Team.*

9. Inside the 2.2 million acres within Yellowstone Park, there are an estimated . . .
   Yellowstone National Park grizzly link: www.nps.gov/yell/learn/nature/grizzlybear.htm.

10. Bullwhip and other species of kelp contain extracts . . .
    Yvonne Yuan and Natalie Walsh, "Antioxidant and Antiproliferative Activities of Extracts from a Variety of Edible Seaweeds, Food and Chemical Toxicology," *An International Journal Published for the British Industrial Biological Research Association* 44 (2006): 1144–50. https://doi.org/10.1016/j.fct.2006.02.002.

11. The predators of blue mussels are Dungeness crabs, green sea urchins . . .
    Cecile S. Briscoe and Kenneth P. Sebens, "Omnivory in *Strongylocentrotus droebachiensis* (Müller) (Echinodermata: Echinoidea): predation on subtidal mussels," *Journal of Experimental Marine Biology and Ecology* 115, no. 1 (1988): 1–24.

12. Proteins found in sea urchins have been found to kill cancer cells . . .
    Tammy Yau, Xiuli Dan, Charlene Cheuk Wing Ng, and Tzi Bun Ng , "Lectins with Potential for Anti-Cancer Therapy," *Molecules* 20, no. 3 (2015): 3791–810, doi:10.3390/molecules20033791. See also: Maria Di Bernardo and Marta Carlo, *The Sea Urchin Embryo: A Model for Studying Molecular Mechanisms Involved in Human Diseases and for Testing*

Bioactive Compounds (2017). https://doi.org/10.5772/intechopen.70301. See also: Mariavaleria Pellicanò, Pasquale Picone, Vincenzo Cavalieri, Rita Carrotta, Giovanni Spinelli, and Marta Di Carlo, et al., "The Sea Urchin Embryo: A Model to Study Alzheimer's Beta Amyloid Induced Toxicity," *Archives of Biochemistry and Biophysics* 483, no. 1 (2009): 120–26. See also: Gennady A. Buznikov, Lyudmila A. Nikitina, Vladimir V. Bezuglov, Ivan Milosević, Lidija Lazarević, Ljubica Rogac, Sabera Ruzdijić, Theodore A. Slotkin, and Ljubisa M Rakić et al. (2008). "Sea Urchin Embryonic Development Provides a Model for Evaluating Therapies Against Beta-Amyloid Toxicity," *Brain Research Bulletin* 75 (2008): 94–100. https://doi.org/10.1016/j.brainresbull.2007.07.026.

13. When predator numbers are low, urchin populations explode . . . Robert S. Steneck, Michael H. Graham, Bruce J. Bourque, Debbie Corbett, Jon M. Erlandson, James A. Estes, and Mia J. Tegner et al., "Kelp Forest Ecosystems: Biodiversity, Stability, Resilience and Future," *Environmental Conservation* 29 (2002): 436–59. https://doi.org/10.1017/S0376892902000322.

14. The predators limited herbivores, which alleviated stress on Yellowstone's grasses . . . Rolf O. Peterson, John A. Vucetich, Joseph M. Bump, and Douglas W. Smith, "Trophic Cascades in a Multicausal World: Isle Royale and Yellowstone," *Annual Review of Ecology, Evolution, and Systematics* 45, no. 1 (2014): 325–45. See also: L. Mech, "Is Science in Danger of Sanctifying the Wolf Biol," *Biological Conservation* 150 (2012): 143–49. https://doi.org/10.1016/j.biocon.2012.03.003.

Death Gulch

1. Becoming increasingly rare in the modern world, large intact ecosystems . . . David Tilman and John A. Downing, "Biodiversity and Stability in Grasslands," *Nature* 367 (1994): 363–65. https://doi.org/10.1038/367363a0. See also: Shahid Naeem and Shibin Li, "Biodiversity Enhances Ecosystem Reliability," *Nature* 390 (1997): 507–9. https://doi.org/10.1038/37348. See also: David Tilman, "Biodiversity: Population Versus Ecosystem Stability," *Ecology* 77 (1996): 350–63. https://doi.org/10.2307/2265614. See also: Robert S. Steneck, Michael H. Graham, Bruce J. Bourque, Debbie Corbett, Jon M. Erlandson, James A. Estes, and Mia J. Tegner, "Kelp Forest Ecosystems: Biodiversity, Stability, Resilience and Future," *Environmental Conservation* 29 (2002): 436–59. https://doi.org/10.1017/S0376892902000322. See also: Theodore A. Kennedy, Shahid Naeem, Katherine M. Howe, Johannes M. H. Knops, David Tilman, and Peter Reich, "Biodiversity as a Barrier to Ecological Invasion," *Nature* 417 (2002):

636–38. https://doi.org/10.1038/nature00776. See also: David U. Hooper, F. Stuart Chapin III, J.J. Ewel, Andy Hector, Pablo Inchausti, Sandra Lavorel, J.H. Lawton, David M. Lodge, Michel Loreau, Shahid Naeem, Bernhard Schmid, Heikki Setälä, Amy J. Symstad, Vandermeer J.J., and David Wardle, "Effects of Biodiversity on Ecosystem Functioning: A Consensus of Current Knowledge," *Ecological Monographs* 75 (2005): 3–35. https://doi. org/10.1890/04-0922. See also: Yann Hautier, David Tilman, Forest Isbell, Eric W. Seabloom, Elizabeth T. Borer, and Peter B. Reich, "Plant Ecology: Anthropogenic Environmental Changes Affect Ecosystem Stability via Biodiversity," *Science* 348, no. 6232 (2015): 336–40. doi:10.1126/science. aaa1788. See also: Michel Loreau and Claire de Mazancourt, "Biodiversity and Ecosystem Stability: A Synthesis of Underlying Mechanisms," *Ecology Letters* 16, no. 1 (2013): 106–115. https://doi.org/10.1111/ele.12073.

2. Multiple layers reveal a long history and multiple types of projectile points . . .
    Arthur H. Harris, "The Mummy Cave Tetrapods in *The Mummy Cave Project* in Northwestern Wyoming Buffalo Bill Historical Center," *Cody* 160 (1978): 146–50.

3. Standing in solemn silence, one can still hear their spirits . . .
    Waldo R. Wedel, Wilfred M. Husted, and John H. Moss, "Mummy Cave: Prehistoric Record from Rocky Mountains of Wyoming," *Science* 160 (1968): 184–86. See also: Wilfred M. Husted and Robert Edgar, "Archeology of Mummy Cave Wyoming: An Introduction to Shoshonean Prehistory," National Park Service, Midwest Archeological Center and Southeast Archeological Center, Special Report No. 4, Technical Reports Series No. 9 (1967). https://doi.org/10.6067/XCV8PC30RQ.

4. They often followed the seasonal migrations of bighorn sheep . . .
    Ryan Yonk, Jeffrey Mosley, and Peter Husby, "Human Influences on the Northern Yellowstone Range," *Rangelands* 40 (2018). https://doi. org/10.1016/j.rala.2018.10.004. See also: Anne Marie Mistretta, "The Mountain Shoshone—A History of the Sheep Eater Indians in the Big Sky Area," *Montana Outlaw Magazine* (2012).

5. To the east is the Laurentide Ice Sheet, stretching for thousands of miles . . .
    Arthur Dyke, "An Outline of North American Deglaciation with Emphasis on Central and Northern Canada," *Developments in Quaternary Sciences* 2 (2004). https://doi.org/10.1016/S1571-0866(04)80209-4.

6. As fascinating as this scenario is, early peoples likely lived in North America . . .
    Mikkel W. Pedersen, Anthony Ruter, Charles Schweger, Harvey Friebe, Richard A. Staff, Kristian K. Kjeldsen, Marie L. Z. Mendoza, Alwynne B. Beaudoin, Cynthia Zutter, Nicolaj K. Larsen, Ben A. Potter, Rasmus Nielsen, Rebecca A. Rainville, Ludovic Orlando, David J. Meltzer, Kurt

H. Kjær, and Eske Willerslev, "Postglacial Viability and Colonization in North America's Ice-Free Corridor," *Nature* 537 (2016): 45–49. https://doi.org/10.1038/nature19085.
See also: Lionel Jackson and Michael Wilson, "The Ice-Free Corridor Revisted," *Geotimes* 49, no. 2 (2004): 16–19.

7. An alternative route follows the Pacific coast using watercraft . . .
Phillip Endicott, *The First Americans: The Pleistocene Colonization of the New World,* ed. Nina G. Jablonski (Berkeley: University of California Press, 2002).

8. Discovered by Thomas Brock, one bacterium named *Thermus aquaticus* thrives in hot water up to 175°F . . .
Thomas D. Brock and Hudson Freeze, "Thermus Aquaticus Gen. N. and Sp. N., A Nonsporulating Extreme Thermophile," *Journal of Bacteriology* 98, no. 1 (1969): 289–97. https://doi.org/10.1128/JB.98.1.289-297.1969.

9. Harvard geologist Thomas Jaggar explored this hot spring in 1897. He found eight dead bears . . .
T. A. Jaggar, "Death Gulch, A Natural Bear-Trap," *Popular Science Monthly* 54 (1899).

10. In that case, one person was killed by a wolf . . .
"Ontario Man Killed in Wolf Attack, Coroner's Jury Finds," www.cbc.ca/news/canada/saskatchewan/ontario-man-killed-in-wolf-attack-coroner-s-jury-finds-1.690056.

11. A person near Chignik Lake, Alaska, was killed . . .
Lem Butler, Bruce Dale, Kimberlee Beckmen, and Sean Farley, "Findings Related to the March 2010 Fatal Wolf Attack Near Chignik Lake, Alaska," *Wildlife Special Publication* (2011).

Sombra

1. The peregrine falcon can dive over 200 miles per hour, while the hefty golden eagle can dive at 150 miles per hour . . .
F. Darling, "Speed of a Golden Eagle's Flight," *Nature* 134 (1934): 325–26. https://doi.org/10.1038/134325c0. See also: https://animaldiversity.org/accounts/Aquila_chrysaetos/. See also: https://rockies.audubon.org/blog/bird-of-the-week/golden-eagle.

2. A golden eagle can live twenty years and migrate 2,500 miles . . .
Carol L. McIntyre, David C. Douglas, Michael W. Collopy, "Movements of Golden Eagles (*Aquila chrysaetos*) from Interior Alaska During Their First Year of Independence," *The Auk* 125, no. 1 (2008): 214–24. https://doi.org/10.1525/auk.2008.125.1.214.

3. Evidence for a cooler, wetter past in low elevation areas is provided by fossilized pack rat middens and soil cores . . .
Owen K. Davis and David S. Shafer, "A Holocene Climatic Record for the Sonoran Desert from Pollen Analysis of Montezuma Well, Arizona, USA," *Palaeogeography, Palaeoclimatology, Palaeoecology* 92, no. 1–2 (1992): 107–119 (discusses grass and oak). See also: Richard Hevly and Paul S. Martin, "Geogchronology of Pluvial Lake Cochise, Southern Arizona. I. Pollen Analysis of Shore Depoistis, and II. Pollen Analysis of A 42-Meter Core," *Ecology* 44, no. 3 (1963): 436–44, www.jstor.org/stable/1932522. See also: Thomas R. Betancourt, Van Devender, and Paul S. Martin, *Packrat Middens. The Last 40,000 Years of Biotic Change (Tucson: University of Arizona Press, 1990): 104–33. See also:* Thomas Devender, "Holocene Woodlands in the Southwestern Deserts," *Science* 198, no. 4313 (1977): 189–92. https://doi.org/10.1126/science.198.4313.189.

4. The Naco site contained a Columbian mammoth and eight Clovis projectile points . . .
Donald Grayson and David Meltzer, "Clovis Hunting and Large Mammal Extinction: A Critical Review of the Evidence,"*Journal of World Prehistory* (December 2002): 313–59. *See also:* E. Haury, E. Sayles, and W. Wasley, "The Lehner Mammoth Site, Southeastern Arizona," *American Antiquity* 25, no. 1 (1959): 2–30. https://doi.org/10.2307/276674. *See also:* Emil. W. Haury, "Artifacts with Mammoth Remains, Naco, Arizona: Discovery of the Naco Mammoth and Associated Projectile Points," *American Antiquity* 19 (1953): 1–14. *See also:* C. Vance Haynes and Bruce B. Huckell, *Murray Springs: A Clovis Site with Multiple Activity Areas in the San Pedro Valley, Arizona* (Tucson: University of Arizona Press, 2007).

5. It expelled 120 cubic miles of magma and ash, generated massive pyroclastic flows, and shaped 1,200 square miles of landscape . . .
Edward. A. du Bray and John. S. Pallister, "An Ash-Flow Caldera in Cross Section: Ongoing Field and Geochemical Studies of the Mid-Tertiary Turkey Creek Caldera," *Journal of Geophysical Research* 96, no. B8 (1991): 13,435–13,457.

6. They also prey on green sea turtles, caimans, tapirs, and anacondas . . .
M. Weckel, W. Giuliano, and S. Silver, "Cockscomb Revisited: Jaguar Diet in the Cockscomb Basin Wildlife Sanctuary, Belize," *Biotropica* 38 (2006): 687–90. https://doi.org/10.1111/j.1744-7429.2006.00190.x. *See also:* Ronis Da Silveira, Emiliano E. Ramalho, John B. Thorbjarnarson, and William E. Magnusson, "Depredation by Jaguars on Caimans and Importance of Reptiles in the Diet of Jaguar," *Journal of Herpetology* 44, no. 3 (2010): 418–24. https://doi.org/10.1670/08-340.1. *See also:* Mark. Weckel, W. Giuliano, and Scott C. Silver, "Jaguar (*Panthera onca*) Feeding Ecology: Distribution of Predator and Prey Through Time and Space," *Journal of Zoology* 270 (2006): 25–30. https://doi.org/10.1111/j.1469-7998.2006.00106.x. *See also:*

Rodrigo Núñez, Brian Miller and Fred Lindzey, "Food Habits of Jaguars and Pumas in Jalisco, Mexico," *Journal of Zoology* 252, no. 3 (2000): 373–79. https://doi.org/10.1111/j.1469-7998.2000.tb00632.x. *See also:* Louise H. Emmons, "Jaguar Predation on Chelonians," *Journal of Herpetology* 23, no. 3 (1989): 311–14. https://doi.org/10.2307/1564460. *See also:* Sandra M. C. Cavalcanti and Eric M. Gese, "Kill Rates and Predation Patterns of Jaguars (*Panthera Onca*) in the Southern Pantanal, Brazil," *Journal of Mammalogy* 91, no. 3 (2010): 722–36. https://doi.org/10.1644/09-MAMM-A-171.1.

Humbled

1. Further, he proposed that Urkontinent broke apart into seven great continental pieces that drifted . . .
   Alfred Wegener, "The Origin of Continents and Oceans / *Die Herausbildung der Grossformen der Erdrinde (Kontinente und Ozeane), auf geophysikalischer Grundlage*," English edition 1924, German edition 1912, *Petermanns Geographische Mitteilungen* 63: 185–195, 253–256, 305–309.

2. It wasn't until the 1960s that sufficient evidence had accumulated and a better understanding of Earth's crust . . .
   Geoffrey F. Davies, "Whole-Mantle Convection and Plate Tectonics," *Geophysical Journal International* 49, no. 2 (May 1977): 459–86. https://doi.org/10.1111/j.1365-246X.1977.tb03717.x.

3. For 70 million years, India was an island continent drifting northward in the Tethys Ocean . . .
   Masaki Yoshida and M. Santosh, "Voyage of the Indian Subcontinent Since Pangea Breakup and Driving Force of Supercontinent Cycles: Insights on Dynamics from Numerical Modeling," (July 2017), www.sciencedirect.com/science/article/pii/S1674987117301536.

4. These layers are now at Mount Everest's summit . . .
   Harutaka Sakai, Minoru Sawada, Yutaka Takigami, Yuji Orihashi, Tohru Danhara, Hideki Iwano, Yoshihiro Kuwahara, Qi Dong, Huawei Cai, and Jianguo Li, "Geology of the Summit Limestone of Mount Qomolangma (Everest) and Cooling History of the Yellow Band Under the Qomolangma Detachment," *Island Arc* 14 (2005): 297–310. https://doi.org/10.1111/j.1440-1738.2005.00499.x.

5. While this was happening, on the opposite side of the Earth, a seven-mile-wide extraterrestrial object impacted near the Yucatan Peninsula . . .
   Hector Javier Durand-Manterola and Guadalupe Cordero-Tercero, "Assessments of the Energy, Mass and Size of the Chicxulub Impactor," *arXiv* (Cornell University, 2014). https://doi.org/arXiv:1403.6391.

6. Although the guide's response is vague, tigers do attack and kill . . .
Sujeet Kumar Singh, Vipin Sharma, Sudhanshu Mishra, Puneet Pandey,
Ved P Kumar, and Surendra Goyal, "Understanding Human-Tiger
Conflict around Corbett Tiger Reserve India: A Case Study Using Forensic
Genetics," *Wildlife Biology in Practice* (2015). See also: Harshawardhan
S. Dhanwatey, Joanne C. Crawford, Leandro Abade, Poonam Dhanwatey,
Clayton K. Nielsen, and Claudio Sillero, "Large Carnivore Attacks on
Humans in Central India: A Case Study from the Tadoba-Andhari Tiger
Reserve," *Oryx* 47 (2013). https://doi.org/10.1017/S0030605311001803.
See also: Arabinda N. Chowdhury, Arabinda Brahma, Ranajit Mondal, and
Mrinal K. Biswas, "Stigma of Tiger Attack: Study of Tiger-Widows from
Sundarban Delta, India," *Indian Journal of Psychiatry* 58, no. 1 (2016):
12–19. https://doi.org/10.4103/0019-5545.174355. See also: Chandan
Surabhi Das, "Pattern and Characterisation of Human Casualties in
Sundarban by Tiger Attacks, India," *Sustainable Forestry* 1 (2018). https://
doi.org/10.24294/sf.v1i2.873.

7. Over a five-year period from 2014 through 2019, tigers killed . . .
OrissaPost (June 28, 2019). https://www.orissapost.com/human-animal-
conflict-has-claimed-over-2500-lives-in-last-5-years-environment-
ministry/.

8. An adult male bison may weigh around . . .
In general, the gaur is larger and weighs more than American bison,
African Cape buffalo, Himalayan yak, or the Asian water buffalo, but all
can reach weights over two thousand pounds.

9. The last tiger census in Satpura was conducted in 2014 . . .
Yadvendradev Jhala, Qamar Qureshi, and Rajesh Gopal, "Can the
Abundance of Tigers Be Assessed from Their Signs?" *Journal of
Applied Ecology* 48 (2011): 14–24. https://doi.org/10.1111/j.1365-
2664.2010.01901.x.

10. Dholes also use the power of the pack to take down some surprisingly large
mammals such as sambar and nilgai . . .
James A Cohen, Michael W. Fox, A. J. T. Johnsingh, and Bruce D. Barnett,
"Food Habits of the Dhole in South India," *Journal of Wildlife Management*
42, no. 4 (1978): 933–36. https://doi.org/10.2307/3800791. See also: K. M.
Selvan, G. G. Veeraswami, and S. A. Hussain, "Dietary Preference of the
Asiatic Wild Dog (*Cuon Alpinus*)," *Mammalian Biology* 78 (2013): 486–89.
https://doi.org/10.1016/j.mambio.2013.08.007.

Afterword

1. A recent paper estimates there are two trillion galaxies in the . . .
Christopher Conselice, Aaron Wilkinson, and Alice Mortlock, "The

Evolution of Galaxy Number Density at z < 8 and its Implications," *The Astrophysical Journal* 830 (2016). https://doi.org/10.3847/0004-637X/830/2/83.

2. We know that for almost 3 billion years . . .
   Jack T. Trevors, "Why on Earth: Self-assembly of the first bacterial cell to abundantand diverse bacterial species," *World Journal of Microbiology and Biotechnology* 15 (1999): 297–304. https://doi.org/10.1023/A:1008962900542.

3. If one considers the uniqueness of complex life on Earth, it is arguably a vanishingly rare phenomenon in the greater Cosmos . . .
   Peter Ward, Donald Brownlee, and Lawrence Krauss, "Rare Earth: Why Complex Life Is Uncommon in the Universe," *Physics Today* 53 (2000). https://doi.org/10.1063/1.1325239.

BIBLIOGRAPHY

Alaska River Guide: Kayaking and Rafting in the Last Frontier, Karen Jettmar, Menasha Ridge Press, 2008

Alone in the Fortress of the Bears, Bruce "Buck" Nelson, 2015

American Serengeti: The Last Big Game Animals of the Great Plains, Dan Flores, University Press of Kansas, 2016

Assembling Life: How Can Life Begin on Earth and Other Habitable Planets? David Deamer, Oxford University Press, 2019

Atlas of Yellowstone, W. Andrew Marcus, James Meacham, Ann Rodman, Alethea Steingisser, University of California Press, 2012

Bear Aware, Bill Schneider, Falcon Guides, 2004

Bear Attacks: Their Causes and Avoidance, Stephen Herrero, Lyons Press, 2018

Black Holes & Time Warps: Einstein's Outrageous Legacy, Kip S. Thorne, W. W. Norton, 1994

Borderland Jaguars, David Brown and Carlos Gonzales, University of Utah Press, 2001

A Brave New World, Aldous Huxley, Harper Perennial, 2006

A Brief History of Earth, Andrew Knoll, HarperCollins, 2021

Calculating the Cosmos: How Mathematics Unveils the Universe, Ian Stewart, Basic Books, 2016

Canoeing the Congo: The First Source to Sea Descent of the Congo River, Phil Harwood, Summersdale, 2014

The Complete Tracker: Tracks, Signs, and Habits of North American Wildlife, Len McDougall, Lyons Press, 2012

Darwin's Fossils, Adrian Lister, Smithsonian Books, 2018

81 Days Below Zero: The Incredible Survival Story of a World War II Pilot in Alaska's Frozen Wilderness, Brian Murphey, Da Capo Press, 2016

Death in Yellowstone: Accidents and Foolhardiness in the First National Park, Lee Whittlesey,

Roberts Rinehart Publishers, 2014

Death on the Barrens, George Grinnell, North Atlantic Books, 2010

Denali Guidebook to Hiking, Photography, and Camping in Denali National Park, Alaska, Ike Waits, Wild Rose Guidebooks, 2001

The Diversity of Life, Edward O. Wilson, W. W. Norton, 1999

End of the Megafauna: The Fate of the World's Hugest, Fiercest, and Strangest Animals, Ross MacPhee, W. W. Norton, 2019

Evolution—A Scientific American Reader, University of Chicago Press, 2006

Evolution: What the Fossils Say and Why it Matters, Donald Prothero, Columbia University Press 2017

Expedition Canoeing, Cliff Jacobson, Globe Pequot Press, 2001

Exploring the American West: 1803—1879, Richard Bartlett and William Goetzmann, National Park Handbook, 1982

The Future of Life, Edward O. Wilson, Vintage Books 2003

Glaciers, Michael Hambrey and Jurg Alean, Cambridge University Press, 1992

The God Particle, Leon Lederman and Dick Teresi, Mariner Books, 2006

The Grizzly: Our Greatest Wild Animal, Enos A. Mills, Comstock Editions, [1919] 1947

Ice Age Mammals of the San Pedro River Valley—Southeastern Arizona, Arizona Geological Survey

In the Blink of an Eye: How Vision Sparked the Big Bang of Evolution, Andrew Parker, Basic Books, 2004

Into the Wild, Jon Krakauer, Anchor Books, 1997

Into Africa: The Epic Adventure of Stanley and Livingstone, Martin Dugard, Broadway Books, 2004

The Invention of Nature: Alexander Von Humboldt's New World, Andrea Wulf, Vintage, 2016

Jim Bridger: Mountain Man, Stanley Vestal, Bison Books, 1970

John Colter: His Years in the Rockies, Harris Burton, Bison Books, 1993

The Jim Corbett Omnibus ("Man-eaters of Kumaon," "Man-eating Leopard of Rudraprayag," and "Temple Tiger and More Man-eaters of Kumaon"), Jim Corbett, Oxford University Press India, 1991

Katmai National Park and Preserve, Alaska, Jean Bodeau, Alaska Natural History Association and Greatland Graphics, 1996

Life Ascending: The Ten Great Inventions of Evolution, Nick Lane, W. W. Norton, 2010

Life on Earth: A Natural History, David Attenborough, Little, Brown and Company, 1979

Life in the Valley of Death: The Fight to Save Tigers in a Land of Guns, Gold, and Greed, Alan Rabinowitz, Shearwater Press, 2010

Life on a Young Planet: The First Three Billion Years of Evolution on Earth, Andrew Knoll, Princeton University Press, 2003

Lord Grizzly, Frederick Manfred, Bison Books, 2011

Lost in the Wild: Danger and Survival in the North Woods, Carey Griffith, Borealis Books, 2007

The Journals of Lewis and Clark, edited by John Bakeless, New American Library, 1964

The Life and Adventures of John Muir, James Mitchell Clarke, The Word Shop, 1979

The Man-Eaters of Tsavo, Lt. Colonel John Henry Patterson, St. Martin's Press, 1986

Mammals of North America, Ronald Kays and Doxn Wilson, Princeton University Press, 2002

The Meaning of Human Existence, Edward O. Wilson, Liveright Publishing, 2014

Mother of God: An Extraordinary Journey into the Uncharted Tributaries of the Western Amazon, Paul Rosolie, Harper, 2014

Naturalist, Edward O. Wilson, Warner Books, 1994

A New History of Life, Peter Ward, Joe Kirschvink, Bloomsbury Press, 2016

On the Origin of Species, Charles Darwin, Penguin Random House, [1859] 2009

Origins: The Scientific Story of Creation, Jim Baggott, Oxford University Press, 2015

Outdoor Safety and Survival, Mike Nash, Rocky Mountain Books, 2012

Photographic Field Guide: Wildlife of Central India, David Raju and Surya Ramachandran, Norton Press, 2016

The Return of the Wolf to Yellowstone, Thomas McNamee, Henry Holt and Company, 1997

Rare Earth: Why Complex Life is Uncommon in the Universe, Peter D. Ward and Donald Brownlee, Springer Science Business & Media, 2003

Ruthless River: Love and Survival by Raft on the Amazon's Relentless Madre de Dios, Holly Fitzgerald, Vintage, 2017

Safe Travel in Bear Country, Gary Brown, Lyons Press, 1996

A Sand County Almanac, Aldo Leopold, Ballantine Books, 1986

Savage Harvest, Carl Hoffman, William Morrow, 2014

A Short History of Nearly Everything, Bill Bryson, Broadway Books, 2004

The Singing Wilderness, Sigurd
Olson, University of Minnesota
Press, 1997

*Sustaining Life: How Human Health
Depends on Biodiversity*, edited
by Eric Chivian and Aaron
Bernstein, Oxford University
Press, 2008

*Thread of Life: The Smithsonian
Looks at Evolution*, Roger Lewin,
Smithsonian Books, 1982

The Tigers of Kanha, Dr. Sanjay
Kumar Shukla, Kanha Workers
Co-opertive Society, 2018

*The Twenty-Ninth Day: Surviving a
Grizzly Attack on the Canadian
Tundra*, Alex Messenger, Black-
stone Publishing, 2019

*The Vital Question: Energy, Evolu-
tion, and the Origins of Complex
Life*, Nick Lane, W. W. Norton,
2015

The Voyage of the Beagle, Charles
Darwin, edited by Leonard
Engel, Doubleday, [1839] 1962

Washakie: Chief of the Shoshone,
Grace Raymond Hebard, Bison
Books, 1995

Wild Hunters: Predators in Peril,
Monte Hummel and Sherry
Pettigrew, Key Porter Books
Limited, 1991

*Wilderness First Aid: Emergency Care
for Remote Locations*, Howard
Backer, Warren Bowman, Bruce
Paton, Peter Steele, and Alton

Thygerson, Jones and Bartlett
Publishers, 1998

*Winter Camping: Wilderness Travel
and Adventure in the Cold
Weather Months*, Stephen Gor-
man, Appalachian Mountain
Club Books, 1991

The Wolves of Denali, L. David Mech,
Layne Adams, Thomas Meier,
John Burch, and Bruce Dale,
University of Minnesota Press,
1998

The Wolves of Yellowstone, Michael
Phillips and Douglas Smith,
Voyageur Press, 1996

Yellowstone Wolves in the Wild,
James Halfpenny, Riverbend
Publishing, 2003

INDEX

ABOUT THE AUTHOR

John Rust has spent a lifetime exploring and living in Earth's most wild places, pristine and primeval areas where both predator and prey are still found in abundance. He has visited Yellowstone National Park's backcountry and Minnesota's Boundary Waters Canoe Area Wilderness a multitude of times. He has explored, hiked, and paddled the wilds of Alaska over two dozen times, including backpacking Denali National Park, kayaking near tidewater glaciers in Kenai Fjords National Park, exploring Katmai's desolate Valley of Ten Thousand Smokes, paddling Katmai's backcountry and Admiralty Island's "Fortress of the Bears," and hiking Wrangell-St. Elias National Park. John has kayaked rivers alongside porpoises, paddled freshwater springs with manatees, and canoed estuaries with basking alligators. He has paddled Costa Rica's Gulf of Nicoya with Portuguese man-of-war tentacles clinging to his arms while crocodiles and stingrays swam nearby. John has been charged by brown bears in Alaska and Bengal tigers in India. He has been confronted by growling wolves at night in Yellowstone and has spent lazy afternoons laying hidden in snow while large wolf packs napped nearby. He has trekked the Boundary Waters' maze of frozen lakes during winter and hiked the Superior Hiking Trail while being confronted by wolves at night. All with a keen eye toward observing wildlife and documenting adventures in a journal.

John has bachelors of science degrees in mathematics and computer science. His day job is in IT, quantifying geospatial risks for the insurance industry. He is the father of two children whom he has taken on many adventures. With his grandchildren, John plans to continue to explore nature anew through their eyes. John has organized many public events describing the beauty and wonder of nature and written articles for the Izaak Walton League of America describing nature, ecology, and the value of ecosystems. He is the current president of the Minnesota Division of the Izaak Walton League.